The Byronic Hero
and the Rhetoric of Masculinity
in the 19th Century British Novel

The Byronic Hero and the Rhetoric of Masculinity in the 19th Century British Novel

D. Michael Jones

McFarland & Company, Inc., Publishers
Jefferson, North Carolina

LIBRARY OF CONGRESS CATALOGUING-IN-PUBLICATION DATA

Names: Jones, D. Michael, 1976–
Title: The Byronic hero and the rhetoric of masculinity in the 19th century British novel / D. Michael Jones.
Description: Jefferson, N.C. : McFarland & Company, Inc., Publishers, 2017. | Includes bibliographical references and index.
Identifiers: LCCN 2016056881 | ISBN 9781476662282 (softcover : acid free paper) ∞
Subjects: LCSH: English fiction—19th century—History and criticism. | Men in literature. | Masculinity in literature. | Heroes in litrerature. | Men—Identity.
Classification: LCC PR868.M45 J66 2017 | DDC 823/.80935211—dc23
LC record available at https://lccn.loc.gov/2016056881

BRITISH LIBRARY CATALOGUING DATA ARE AVAILABLE

ISBN (print) 978-1-4766-6228-2
ISBN (ebook) 978-1-4766-2745-8

© 2017 D. Michael Jones. All rights reserved

No part of this book may be reproduced or transmitted in any form or by any means, electronic or mechanical, including photocopying or recording, or by any information storage and retrieval system, without permission in writing from the publisher.

Front cover illustration of scene from *Treasure Island* © 2017 iStock

Printed in the United States of America

McFarland & Company, Inc., Publishers
Box 611, Jefferson, North Carolina 28640
www.mcfarlandpub.com

For my beloved mother

Table of Contents

Preface 1

Introduction 5

Part I. The Byronic Hero in the Domestic Novel

One. A Home at Sea: Piracy in Lord Byron's *The Corsair* and Jane Austen's *Persuasion* 17

Two. A House Fit for a Lady: Lord Byron's *Manfred* and Emily Brontë's *Wuthering Heights* 32

Three. Bad Romancers: Domestic Enclosures in George Eliot's *Middlemarch* and H. Rider Haggard's *She* 53

Part II. The Rhetoric of Romance Masculinity

Four. A Secret History: The Byronic Hero in Charles Dickens's *David Copperfield* 71

Five. "Hey you, there!" Transforming Dickens's Domestic Masculinity into Romance Masculinity in Stevenson's *Treasure Island* 88

Six. Being Home: The Schizophrenic Enclosure as Dr. Jekyll and Dorian Gray 101

Seven. Writing the Rebel into Shape: Schizophrenia as Form in Sir Arthur Conan Doyle's *Sign of Four* and E.W. Hornung's *Raffles* Stories 115

Eight. The Double Agent: Romance Masculinity in Rudyard Kipling's *Kim*, Baden-Powell, and the Boy Scouts 134

*Conclusion: Romance Masculinity
   and Contemporary Masculinity* 159

Chapter Notes 163

Works Cited 173

Index 179

Preface

The question of what a man was and how a man was supposed to act was a practical problem for me. My parents divorced young and my father died not long after. I was raised by a single mother.

Real men were scary and distant. I chose instead to build my concept of masculinity around TV and movies. These figures were drawn exclusively from action and adventure narratives—*Indiana Jones, Star Wars,* and my favorite, *James Bond*. As I learned during the writing of this book, my identification with what I would come to call the romance hero and his ethic of romance masculinity was hundreds of years in the making. Romance masculinity is defined by powerful mastery—especially over other men—anti-domesticity, and a freedom to seek individual meaning through violence. It is an alluring commodity that can be delivered in almost every economic and cultural context.

Growing up in the rural, working-class South, the ideal of romance masculinity dovetailed nicely into the rigid heteronormativity of competitive sports and casual violence that defined the boundaries of our shared identity. Over time, however, this ideal began to turn on me. I could never come close to inhabiting the silence and the mastery of the alpha-male, romance hero, and my emotional needs rubbed painfully against the fantasy of myself. I tried instead to inhabit its opposite: the sensitive, domesticated male. I failed at that too.

I see now that working on the genealogy of the masculine romance hero, the omnipresent hero of countless detective and spy novels, summer blockbusters, and TV shows was a way to understand the historical and cultural roots of my gendered fantasy life. Over time, I began to see that fantasy life as a commodity itself, or, as Marx puts it in the *Grundrisse*, "consumption reproduces the need" (229).

I began my research on the genealogy of romance masculinity during my graduate work in English at the University of Connecticut, nearly ten years ago. First with Charles Mahoney and then with Sarah Winter, I traced the revolutionary impulses of Second Generation Romanticism into the novels of Victorian domestic literature and then further into the works of the adventure fiction of the 1880s romance revival. At the center, I found Lord Byron and the afterlife of his Byronic hero.

This study tangibly traces a key element in the commodification of contemporary masculine fantasy by chronicling the journey of the Byronic hero from its birth in the Regency to its domestication in the Victorian novel and ultimately to its repackaging as a romance masculinity in the works of the 1880s romance revival. More than a literary genealogy, however, this study of the Byronic hero and its heir, romance masculinity, outlines the radical changes nineteenth- and early twentieth-century masculinity undergoes during the rise of the middle-class, the massive upheavals of industrialization, the demands of global competition, and finally the price of empire. From political and sexual revolutionary in the Regency, to ideal Victorian husband, to weaponized servant of the state in the years running up to World War I, the Byronic hero and its afterlife as a romance masculinity are still with us in more ways than just action heroes like James Bond. This masculine commodity, developed over the long nineteenth century, still helps create men's potential and limitations. As a young man growing up in rural East Tennessee, it did for me.

This study is broken into two parts: "The Byronic Hero in the Domestic Novel" and the "Rhetoric of Romance Masculinity." The first part traces the Byronic hero beginning with the reimagining of masculinity after nearly fifty years of national violence that started with the Seven Years War (1754–63), continued through the American Revolution (1775–83), and reached its culmination in the first global conflict, the Napoleonic Wars (1803–15). The journey of the violent hero's return to domestic control in Byron's *Corsair* and Jane Austen's *Persuasion* (1816) set the stage for the domestic fiction of the Victorian period. Emily Brontë's *Wuthering Heights* (1847) rewrote the Byronic hero and heroine, Heathcliff and Catherine the first, as emblems of sublimely transgressive love that became a fantasy foundation for the Victorian domestic doxa and its competitive economic unit, the Victorian family. In these first two chapters, we see how masculine competitive violence and sexual transgression were reimagined to create a hegemonic masculine ideal that was both competitively market-driven and domestic. Two very different works, George Eliot's *Middlemarch* (1871–72) and H. Rider Haggard's *She* (1886–87), both elucidate how heretical forms of masculine thinking were totalized back into a domestic hierarchy that excluded masculine romance rhetoric and subject potential.

In the second part of the study, "The Rhetoric of Romance Masculinity," I show how the tension between market-driven competition and female domestication of masculinity breaks down. I begin with the great Victorian bildungsroman, Dickens's *David Copperfield* (1849–50). David's childhood idol, J. Steerforth, is transformed from a stock Victorian villain to early anti-hero because he is a repressed Byronic hero and he absolutely confounds David, the classic formulation of Victorian masculinity. This model of romance masculinity, derived from the Byronic hero and reimagined by Dickens, returned with the publication of Robert Louis Stevenson's *Treasure Island* (1883). The intense global economic and political competition brought on by the Long Depression and the Second Industrial Revolution gave Stevenson's slim adventure story a different context and afterlife. "In its afterlife," to quote Benjamin, the Byronic hero, "the original undergoes a change" (73) and becomes something new: a romance masculinity. In Stevenson's *Strange Case of Jekyll and Hyde* (1886) and Oscar Wilde's *Picture of Dorian Gray* (1890), texts of schizophrenic liberation and tragic enclosure, domestic values are set against romance desire. In the penultimate chapter, which examines Sir Arthur Conan Doyle's Sherlock Holmes stories (1887–1927), I argue that the Holmes Watson narrative structure worked to sell romance violence and domestic surveillance back to the Victorian middle class as an answer to the fin de siècle crisis of masculinity. Conan Doyle's brother-in-law, E.W. Hornung, did give a brief image of masculinity as comradeship, and even love, in the Raffles Stories, in which Raffles, a criminalized version of Holmes, explores the underworld of London with another version of Watson, Bunny. That comradeship ends with both of them joining the fight against the Boers, prefiguring the Pals Movement that would carry off so many friends, arm in arm, to the Western Front in first years of World War I. In the final chapter, I concentrate on how romance masculinity has been incorporated into the British ideal, and how texts like Rudyard Kipling's *Kim* (1900–01) and Baden-Powell's *Scouting for Boys* (1908) worked to redefine hegemonic masculinity in the years between the disastrous Second Boer War (1899–1902) and the start of World War I.

More than a literary or commodity history, this is a study of the roots of Western masculine value and the loneliness and violence at its center. Romance masculinity taught me. This book was an attempt to take myself back.

Introduction

In June of 1938, Byron's remains were disentombed from his resting place beneath the family vault at Bucknall Tokard. Rumors had persisted for years that his body had been stolen. When the small party, led by the vicar, entered the dark and damp vault, they found it had been vandalized and robbed. The shifting walls had loosened old bones, and they had fallen across the dirt floor. Byron's tomb was still intact, but the lid was ajar. By midnight, they were looking at the body of Byron. It had not aged (MacCarthy 571–74). According to the vicar, "the body of Byron [was] in as perfect a condition as when it was placed in the coffin" (qtd. in MacCarthy 573). The surveyor added that he was still very handsome. This account, however true, elucidates something essential about Byron and the Byronic hero: they have a long afterlife. In fact, they have had such an impact on the popular imagination far beyond nineteenth-century Great Britain that his name has become an adjective, the Byronic.

From the publication of the first Canto of *Childe Harold* in 1812, Byron and the Byronic hero was a publishing phenomenon, which culminated in 1830 with Thomas Moore's biography, *Letters and Journals of Lord Byron with Notices of His Life*. The biography, often sold as part of multivolume collected works, did even more to tie the poet to his hero. The popularity of Byron's poetry and the deep interest in his life only tells part of the account, however. There is something else that turns the popular poet "Byron" into a way of being—into the "Byronic." Tom Mole, for example, sees Byron and his hero as a space where the "crucial changes that produced modern celebrity culture occurred" (4) and argues that the "cultural apparatus—individual, the industry, and the audience" intersect over Byron's biography and literary production (3). For Andrew Elfenbein, Byron's celebrity is a self-reproducing commodity based on "the marketing of Byron's subjectivity, because his fame depended on making it accessible to a wide audience, including many who never read him. Byron the celebrity was ... what fame meant in a capitalist literary system" (47). Drawing on Marx's concept of the commodity fetish—the exchange of things mystifying the human exchange of labor and class—Elfenbein argues that Byron "the celebrity was a peculiar commodity because the 'thing' that gave value to his products was his subjectivity" (48). There is no doubt that the Byronic hero is a literary commodity, and he now belongs, in Mole's words, to "an *audience*—massive, anonymous, socially diverse, geographically distributed—[that] consumes and interprets" (3) his commodification. Byron and, by extension, the Byronic hero have become a commodity in "the capitalist literary system" (Elfenbein 47) and, by extension, the larger economic and ideological reality of nineteenth-century Great Britain and beyond.

As Elfenbein's reading of Marx's classic formulation of the commodity fetish underscores, it is difficult to theorize Byron's commodification. Elfenbein sees mystification and alienation at the heart of literary production itself: mystification and alienation between Byron, the historical person, and Byron, the hero of his work, between his readers who think they are hearing a confession but consuming a product, down to the most basic structural labor alienation: the mobilization of labor and capital in the production of books, reviews, and mementos for mass consumption. But how the Byronic commodity functions as a fetish is less clear. According to Elfenbein, "Byron the celebrity replaced person-to-person contact between producer and consumer with a person-to-'personality' contact between consumer and fetishized subjectivity" (49).

While Elfenbein is not arguing that prior to the advent of Byron and the Byronic there was an idyllic, unalienated relationship between "producer and consumer" in the literary marketplace, he does demonstrate that the commodification of the Byronic introduced an innovation into that market. I would add that the Byronic innovation was subjective *reproducibility* as value. For Marx in *Capital*, what ultimately defines a commodity, "what converts every product into a social hieroglyphic," is value (322). For "the secret of our social products ... the object of utility as value, is just as much a social product as language" (322). The innovation of the Byronic commodity is, however, "a social product *as* language" itself, a form of value that is readily reproducible inside a sign system materialized in a literary and cultural marketplace from 1812 up to today. It is thus a product of a language and a product of material history that can be reproduced over and over again in different contexts. As it moves across the nineteenth century, the Byronic commodity becomes a reproducing rhetoric, one very much with us today. I call it the rhetoric of romance masculinity. This is a study of that rhetoric's history through the long nineteenth century and how that rhetoric relates to the developing ideology of masculinity in the first industrialized nation and the first industrialized empire

"A peculiar commodity"

The rhetoric of romance masculinity is thus, in both Raul Ricoeur and Louis Althusser's sense, a *toujours déjà*: an always already.[1] Ricoeur, with his concentration on narration, gives a broad structure for understanding how Byronic language is commodified and repackaged back to the amorphous audience. Drawing on the work of structural anthropologists, Ricoeur argues that if "human action can be narrated, it is because it is always already symbolically mediated" (57). For Ricoeur, this mediation occurs on the three levels of mimesis, or imitation: the mimesis, the narrative organization of reality, mimesis$_2$ the organization of reality into a symbolic, textual act, and mimesis$_3$ the consumption through reading or through watching of the sign system.[2] What, then, is the commodified subject? The commodification of a subjectivity, Byron's in this case, is a reproduction of the potential for mimesis or imitation, a prepackaged way of mediating reality through an always already commodified subject. It is a way of thinking, and potentially a way of being. In the case of Byron this kind of commodification is monetized. If you want it, you have to pay for it.

That only begs another question: how is the commodified subjectivity consumed, how does the "person-personality" exchange, to use Elfenbein's language, function as a fetish? Again, Ricouer gives us a hint. In mimesis$_3$ "through the hearer or reader" the sign system "reaches its fulfillment" (71). Or, in Marx's language of consumption, "only by decomposing the product does consumption give the product the finishing touch; for the product is production not as objectified activity, but rather as object for the active subject" (*Grundrisse* 229). The active subject, the consumer, gives it the "finishing touch" and "fulfillment" by decomposing the body of language through imitation of its rhetoric, adhering to his "persuasion," as Aristotle calls it. And "persuasion," Aristotle goes on to argue in his *Thesis of Rhetoric*, "is affected through the *medium of the hearer*, when they shall have been brought to the state of excitement under the influence of the speech; for we do not, when influenced by pain or joy, or partiality or dislike, award our decisions in the same way" (12).

The Byronic commodity is a reproduced rhetoric, a mimesis of thinking made real through the "*medium of the hearer*" (Aristotle 12) by "decomposing the product" (*Grundrisse* 229). It mystifies the "the capitalist literary system" (Elfenbein 47) itself by the fetish of its mimetic potential because the final phase of consumption, according to Marx in the *Grundrisse*, "creates the need for *new* production, that is it creates the ideal, internally impelling cause for production" (228). It alienates in order to create more mimetic alienation—what Ricouer calls the "vicious circle" of mimesis (71). To conclude with Marx, mimetic consumption "*ideally posits* the object of production as an internal image, a need, as a drive and as purpose" (228). If we apply this formulation to Byron, the Byronic commodity "ideally posits" an "internal image" of masculinity, as object of desire or object to be desired.

The Byronic hero, the productive legacy of Byron's self-commodification, is always transforming as it moves across the long nineteenth century. Like any other commodity in any other market, its rises and falls and its multiple transformations elucidate the darker realms of the economic, political, and cultural constitution of Great Britain as it was emerging as the first modern industrial economy and first superpower. We should follow it. Commodities can tell us things. If one were to have followed a bale of cotton, for example, from the hot soil of Mississippi or Louisiana and the slave labor that produced it, over wagon roads, railroads, barges to the great port city of New Orleans for the almost 5000-mile journey across the Atlantic to the industrial capitols of Birmingham and Manchester where the raw material is transformed into a yards of muslin, divided and sold to wholesalers, who in turn divide it again and sell it to retailers, who perhaps sell back to the Southern gentry whose slaves produced the raw material in the first place—we start to see something of the violent, interwoven reality of nineteenth century capitalism.

The Byronic commodity presents us with different problems and possibilities; because it is a social product of language, it, therefore, tells us much more about the symbolic, ideological history of the nineteenth century. The Byronic hero as a language commodity never stays the same because it is, by definition, an afterlife. In fact, Walter Benjamin defines afterlife as transformation and change. As he puts it in "The Task of the Translator," "in its [the original's] afterlife—which could not be called that if it were not a transformation and a renewal of something living—the original undergoes a change" (73). The Byronic heroes' journey through nineteenth-century fiction is a living history, a genealogy that grows and changes through new commodifications of Byronic rhetoric. We can see the Byronic commodity change with the times, reproduced in the form of Heathcliff in *Wuthering Heights* (1847), or Steerforth in *David Copperfield* (1850), only to be transformed yet again in the work of Robert Louis Stevenson and Sir Arthur Conan Doyle, writers of the romance revival. The Byronic commodity's afterlife in the nineteenth century narrative fiction has two distinct and interconnected phases: its journey through the domestic novel of the high Victorian period, and its reemergence as a hero in adventure, spy, and detective fiction as part of the romance revival's creation of a male literary marketplace. Inside this male fantasy marketplace is a distinct and recognizable rhetoric of being a man. Born of the Byronic hero's afterlife in Victorian domestic fiction, it will become something genuinely new: romance masculinity.

Key Elements of the Byronic Hero

The Byronic hero hit the English reading public fully born. The first Cantos of *Childe Harold's Pilgrimage* (1812) outline what will define the Byronic hero and the romance masculinity that it will become. Though in its first incarnation, the Byronic hero stays close to eighteenth century tropes of libertinism:

> Whilome in Albion's isle there dwelt a youth,
> Who ne in virtue's ways did take delight;
> But spent his days in riot most uncouth,
> And vex'd with mirth the drowsy ear of Night [II:14].

Beyond his lust for the sensual pleasures, Childe Harold, like its author with whom he would be immediately connected, is an aristocrat of "linage long" (3). There is an definitive difference, however, between Childe Harold and the infamous Lord Rochester or hardy Tom Jones— the Byronic hero is defined by his rejection of libertinism:

> And now Childe Harold was sore sick at heart,
> And from his fellow bacchanals would flee;
> 'Tis said, at times the sullen tear would start,
> But pride congeal'd the drop within his ee:
> Apart he stalked in joyless reverie [VI:47–50].

This rejection of sexual and sensual license is a rebellion against aristocratic class privilege, and one that no doubt endeared him to middle class readers, but it also marks the Byronic hero as a wanderer outside of his own class: "And from his fellow bacchanals [he] would flee" because of heart sickness and "joyless reverie." Harold's renunciation of sensual pleasure, so dear to Christian moralists, does not lead, however, to moral and spiritual rejuvenation because "pride," the first and most deadly sin as well as the most aristocratic, "congealed the drop within his ee." He exists, therefore, beyond the pleasures of aristocratic libertinism and middle class moral regeneration. This class crisis between aristocratic hauteur and middle class sensibilities is not only left unresolved, it is constitutive of the Byronic hero and the romance masculinity that will follow it.

The Byronic hero is thus defined by an internal classlessness that is deepened by his exile from any recognizable domestic life. But like his class status, which is both haughtily aristocratic and sentimentally middle class, his relationship to domesticity is constructed through internal contradiction. For "though he loved but one,"

> And that loved one, alas! could ne'er be his.
> Ah, happy she! to 'scape from him whose kiss
> Had been pollution unto aught so chaste;
> Who soon had left her charms for vulgar bliss,
> And spoiled her goodly lands to gild his waste,
> Nor calm domestic peace had ever deigned to taste [V:40-45].

The Byronic hero's inability to find wholeness and redemption in domesticity—in what will become by midcentury the ideal for men—leaves him to roam, forever outside of stable class and domestic constructions. The image, in fact, is one of the destruction of property itself, for he would have "spoiled her goodly lands to gild his waste," and was incapable of cultivating "calm domestic peace" because he never "deigned to taste" its fruit. This separation from aristocratic libertinism and middle class domesticity places the Byronic hero outside of easy nineteenth century identification. Indeed, in all of its guises—spiritual pilgrim Childe Harold, or Conrad the pirate, or Manfred the sorcerer—the Byronic hero remains outside the fulfilling promise of a lasting and transformative domesticity, as well as the cynical libertinism of his own class.

The Byronic hero to follow is thus always on a search for a wholeness denied him, he is defined by always being *in search of*. Like Childe Harold, who

> from his native land resolved to go,
> And visit scorching climes beyond the sea;
> With pleasure drugg'd, he almost long'd for woe,
> And e'en for change of scene would seek the shades below [VI:51-54].

A search for wholeness outside of recognizable nineteenth century models of masculinity is connected from the beginning with "woe" and even "the shades below"—with death itself. This internal volatility drives the search for wholeness, the romance. This internal romance with its class confusion and anti-domesticity, is driven by gender fantasy—the fantasy of masculine wholeness. J.A. Morgan calls this "manliness." For "manliness," Morgan writes, "symbolized an attempt at a metaphysical comprehension of the universe. It represented an effort to achieve a 'Weltanschauung'—a totalizing world view" (1). What this Weltanshamang will look like across the nineteenth century will tell us a great deal about the social and economic forces that were shaping and reshaping masculinity during this time. As it developed across the nineteenth century, the Byronic commodity, what I call romance masculinity, at its center promised just this masculine wholeness. This would become something very different from Byron's vision of masculine wholeness, which as we will see, meant on some level the erasure of gender itself. Yet the Byronic hero and the figure of the romance masculinity, which would evolve out of it, share these constituting elements: confuses class identification; anti-domestic; always on the search for masculine wholeness; has the capacity to subordinate others.

It is this final element of Byronic/romance masculinity that will help us define amorphous terms such as "masculinity" and "wholeness." The ability to subordinate others, to command, will connect the Byronic hero to romance masculinity as it develops across the nineteen century and as it reaches out from our own TVs and computers and to our own lives.

"About Men"

In one of the foundational texts of Masculinity studies, R.W. Connell's *Masculinities* (1993), there is a definition of masculinity that can help us nest these contradictory masculine possibilities engendered by the Byronic. In fact, the most basic, commonsense definition of masculinity will help us unpack how the Byronic hero and its derivative, romance masculinity, create a commodity that promises masculine wholeness. Connell, tellingly, defines masculinity through what it is not. An nonmasculine person would be "peaceable rather than violent, conciliatory rather than dominating, hardly able to kick a football, uninterested in sexual conquest, and so forth" (67). In contrast, of course, a masculine person would be violent, dominating, good a physical sports, and heterosexually virile. This familiar definition of masculinity, as Connell points out, is a "conception [that] accompanied the bourgeoisie ideology of 'separate spheres' in the nineteenth century" (68) and "is a fairly recent historical product, a few hundred years old and most" (68). One might argue that the image of masculine violence and mastery define Greek, Biblical Hebrew, and Roman definitions of masculinity from Achilles to King David to Caesar. Yet the divine or almost divine status of these men suggest, on the other hand, this concept of masculinity was reserved for a very elite few. This ideal of masculinity was for the rarefied class, for Odysseus, Alexander the Great, Alcibiades, Aeneas and Scipio Africanus; for the great masses of the ancient and the medieval world, subordination and subservience were at the heart of men's lives.

As we will see throughout my study, the Byronic hero reflects the drastic changes in normative masculinity across the nineteenth century and thus helps us understand the economic and social roots of our own everyday definition of masculinity. In fact, the internal class contradictions of the Byronic hero help us understand, superficially at this point in our study, the social and economic roots of the transformation of masculinity. That is to say, the Byronic hero is a democratization and thus a commercialization of the image of masculine prowess. That is at the root of the commodities power.

As we have seen, the Byronic hero, even when he is an aristocrat like Childe Harold or Manfred, eschews the power and value derived from his social position and instead embraces an intrinsic privilege of his "manliness," and the possibility of achieving J.A. Morgan's "totalizing world view" (1). Particularly in Byron's *Corsair* (1814), the fact that Conrad the pirate, a self-made man, dominates everything in his world through the vigor of his mind, his martial prowess, and his courage suggests the kind of democratization of masculinity that will give us characters as different as Emily Brontë's Heathcliff and Rudyard Kipling's Kim. But this celebration of masculine prowess and violence is deeply complicated by the ideology of domesticity.

We see this conflict in the history of the Byronic hero itself. At the start of *The Corsair*, Conrad is the totally dedicated husband to an adoring wife, Medora, as well as a violent pirate chief. Of course, the Byronic hero's journey ends, as always, outside of any kind of static domesticity—yet the anomaly of a pirate and loving husband in the wildly successful *Corsair* should give us pause. There are two stories going on here at once: the development of an ideal of masculinity as assertive, violent and competitive and an ideal of masculinity that is dedicated to the developing domestic Victorian virtues. In the Byronic hero there are oppositional impulses operating from the first: the fantasy of romance freedom along side the fantasy domestic love. But those contradictory fantasy structures are only part of our study. The real focus is the larger ideological structures that the Byronic commodity, like our bale of cotton, elucidates with its circulation through the nineteenth century. How the Byronic hero is transformed tells us how bourgeois capitalism genders men.

Defining a Hegemonic Masculinity

Nineteenth century British masculinity was a contradiction slowly turning into a tragedy. As we will see, the repression or reassertion of the rhetoric of the Byronic hero and romance masculinity across the nineteenth century is deeply related to what Nancy Armstrong identifies in *How Novels Think* (2005) as a fundamental discontinuity in representations of nineteenth-century British masculinity. This contradiction again is defined, on one hand, by violent, market-driven self-assertion, and, on the other, by passive, domestic partnership. It "not only shaped the scientific and literary discourse of the period but also proved virtually impossible to resolve: Victorian culture was of one mind in maintaining both the continuity and incompatibility of the two aspects of British masculinity" (81). This contradiction between violent competition and domestic passivity reflects the ideological ordering of the state and the private life. According to Althusser's reading of Antonio Gramsci's concept of hedgemogony, the reign of bourgeois society structures itself on "a distinction between the public and the private" in its legal statutes and in the "subordinate domains in which bourgeois law exercises its authority" (137), through punishment and cultural surveillance. Armstrong develops Gramsci's and Althusser's insights into a reading of Victorian middle-class ideology, in which an outside (public) / inside (private) dichotomy worked to balance marketplace aggression (outside) and a soothing, pacific domesticity (inside).

Even more, this inside / outside dichotomy was, in fact, central to the construction of gender identity and the self-imposed surveillance of the bourgeois subject within bourgeois ideology. In fact, it was the ideology of the domestic that instituted this kind of surveillance. The superstructural mechanics of Victorian values were created through writing, from the domestic or realist fiction that dominated three quarters of the nineteenth century and still has currency to this day. As Armstrong argues:

> A home espoused by various subgroups aspiring for the status of "respectability," a home overseen by a woman, actually preceded the formation of other social insti-

tutions by at least fifty years. There is little to suggest this household took root in practice much before the beginning of the nineteenth century.... From writing, it can be argued, the new family passed into the realm of common sense, where it came to justify the distribution of national wealth through wages paid to men ["Some Call it Fiction" 1424–25].

"The home overseen by woman" was the dominant middle-class ideological mechanism for subject control, and the enormous superstructure for moral and social hygiene set in motion during the nineteenth century was, in part, the product of domestic fiction's reconstruction of the subject in light of heteronormative domesticity, the ever-ubiquitous code of respectability.

This leads us back to Masculinity studies, and how this scholarship can help us understand the historical gendering of men. Like Armstrong, Connell's conception of competitive, market-driven masculinity is informed by Gramsci's concept of hegemony. For Connell, the concept of hegemonic masculinity helps explain how multiple masculinities—heterosexual, homosexual, introverted, extroverted, working class, middle class, artistic, athletic—can all serve one limited, hegemonic masculinity based on competition and aggression. For Connell, hegemonic masculinity is the "configuration of gender practices which embodies the currently accepted answer to the problems of the legitimacy of patriarchy" (77). We are going to use the Byronic hero's commodification and recommodification as romance masculinity across the nineteenth century in order to show how hegemonic masculinity changed and to detail how "patriarchy," which is nothing more than a justification for "the distribution of national wealth through wages paid to men" (Armstrong "Some Call It Fiction" 1424–25) created masculine value. That is to say, the Byronic commodity will allow us to interrogate the internal ideology of industrial capitalism through the way it genders its boys and men, both in the nineteenth century and today as it is still producing "men and women fit to occupy the institutions of an industrialized society" (Armstrong *Desire* 164).

There is another element to the Byronic that makes it a unique literary commodity: its rebellion. As Peter Thorslev argues, the Byronic hero is "most intimately related to ... the tradition of 'metaphysical' or 'total' rebellion. It is total rebellion not only on a political level, but also on the philosophical and religious level—and sometimes, in nihilistic extremes, against life itself" (197). It is this social and philosophical rebellion that marks the Byronic commodity at its most Byronic. These rebellions, as we will see again and again, upsets the easy representation of hegemonic masculinity through symbolic acts of sexual and political deviance that question the very reality of masculinity itself and the economic patriarchy underpinning it.

Why Byronic Afterlife?

Because of the ubiquitous presence of Anglophone media, the afterlife of the Byronic reaches well beyond the narrow, elite bourgeois world in which it was first articulated. As it moved from Byronic commodity to the rhetoric of romance masculinity during the romance revival, this way of being a man became part of a seemingly endless serial reproduction that starts with Sherlock Holmes and spirals ever outward, helping to inform the commodification of James Bond, Indiana Jones, and Batman, to name only a few. Today, as the tentacles of global capitalism extend into every possible marketplace, they bring with them the historical afterlife of the Byronic commodity, romance masculinity—its social rebellion, masculine power, sexual promise, and commodity alienation. Nor is it only a "masculine" form of commodification anymore, as demonstrated by the recent success of women as romance heroes in *Buffy the Vampire Slayer* (1997–2003), *Alias* (2001–06), *Kill Bill I* and *II* (2003; 2004), and the *Hunger Games* franchise (2012–2015). Nor is this structure simply heterosexual any longer. As our gender binaries break down, the commodification of romance subjectivity simply finds new markets. As an always already, in Althusser's sense, romance masculinity is interpellated into the endless reproducibility of ideology itself. The Byronic commodity's afterlife, the rhetoric of romance masculinity and the symbolic gaps it filled and the fantasies it promised elucidate men's relationship to larger systems of power—economic, national, and transnational. Tracing that journey can help us start the process of seeing how our own creations and commodities mystify our experiences of ourselves.

Part I. The Byronic Hero in the Domestic Novel

CHAPTER ONE

A Home at Sea
Piracy in Lord Byron's *The Corsair* and Jane Austen's *Persuasion*

> *That policy which, originating with "great statesmen now no more," has survived the dead to become a curse on the living, unto the third and fourth generation!*
> —Lord Byron, Speech to the House of Lords

Louisa Musgrove's fall from the Cobb at Lyme Regis, the turning point of Jane Austen's last novel, *Persuasion* (1817), interrupts a quotation from and discussion of Lord Byron: "Anne found Captain Benwick again drawing near her. Lord Byron's 'dark blue seas' could not fail of being brought forward by their present view, and she gladly gave him all her attention as long as attention was possible. It was soon drawn per force another way" (73). Austen's reference comes from the first line of *The Corsair* (1814), the song of the pirates. In the floating music of Byron's heroic couplets, it is a wild hymn to freedom, danger, and violence—a romance space beyond the limits of nations and their societal boundaries. It is a celebration of piracy:

> O'er the glad waters of the dark blue sea,
> Our thoughts as boundless and our souls as free,
> Far as the breeze can bear, the billows foam,
> Survey our empire and behold our home!
> These are our realms, no limits to their sway—
> Our flag the sceptre all who meet obey.
> Ours the wild life in tumult still to range
> From toil to rest, and joy in every change.
> Oh, who can tell? not thou, luxurious slave! [1.1–9].[1]

In *Persuasion*, the pleasures and dangers of piracy, Byron's "dark blue sea," are transformed by domestic tragedy and returned to the world of women and families.

The entire plot of *Persuasion* turns on Louisa's fall, and her fall interrupts Benwick's discussion of Lord Byron. In fact, there is in Louisa's fall this haunting literary figure who almost seems to be walking with Anne Elliot and the emotionally poetic Captain Benwick, "getting near her.... Their conversation, the preceding evening, did not disincline him to seek her again ... talking as before of Mr. Scott and Lord Byron, and still as unable as before, and as unable as any other two readers, to think exactly alike of the merits of either" (72). Everyone is reading Byron and everyone is talking about him. It makes sense that one of Byron's most popular works "could not fail of being brought forward."[2] According to John Murray, *The Corsair* had sales that were "unprecedented"; it was read and discussed consistently (Murray 72). For Anne Elliot and Captain Benwick, Byron is literally in the air.

The allusion to Byron is more than one of Austen's jokes at the expense of the effeminate, "romantic" Captain Benwick (the wanna-be romantic hero) and his affected pose.[3] For Anne Elliot and Captain Benwick's "present view," the "dark blue sea," is interrupted "per force another way." They are drawn to Louisa Musgrove's fall, her screams for help, and the ghastly scene of her unconscious body. The irony of Byronic reverie being broken by a tragic, yet prosaic, accident suggests a deeper historical and textual relationship between Austen's *Persuasion* and Byron's *The Corsair*. Austen's pirating of Byronic reverie in order to reverse its effect, to turn it into a painful irony, elucidates a textual genealogy between *The Corsair* and *Persuasion* which speaks not only to the generic conflicts between the poetry of second-generation Romanticism (particularly Byron's narrative poetry) and the burgeoning domestic novel, but also how gender discourses are shaped by Britain's total war against Napoleon (1803–15). It is a moment of deep ideological destabilization and retrenchment. *The Corsair* and *Persuasion* use piracy to reimagine what men and women might be during this time of political and social ferment.[4] The freedom, the capitol of the pirate, can only be accrued through theft and violence. The texts, with their different generic structures and narrative trajectories, write the freedom of piracy toward very different ends. In reimagining masculinity at the end of the Napoleonic Wars, Jane Austen is as much the pirate as Lord Byron.

Persuasion is rife with the sexual and political liberation second-generation Romantics espoused: the aggressive masculine posture of the Byronic hero and the dangers posed by its poetry.[5] In Austen's final novel, the gender anxiety created by the Byronic hero's representation of masculinity manifests itself as an anxiety about genre. Concerning these generic dangers, Austen is not shy; in fact, Anne's conversation with Benwick is a rare moment of didacticism. When Anne Elliot is speaking to the Byronic straw man, Captain Benwick, Austen makes clear the dangers of poetry, particularly narrative Romantic poetry:

> Having talked of poetry, the richness of the present age, and gone through a brief comparison of opinion as to the first-rate poets, trying to ascertain whether *Marmion* or *The Lady of the Lake* were to be preferred, and how ranked the *Giaour* and the *Bride of Abydos*; and moreover, how the *Giaour* was to be pronounced, he shewed himself so intimately acquainted with all the tenderest songs of the one poet [Sir Walter Scott], and all the impassioned descriptions of hopeless agony of the other; he repeated, with such tremulous feeling, the various lines which imaged a broken heart.... She ventured to hope he did not always read only poetry; and to say, that she thought it was the misfortune of poetry, to be seldom safely enjoyed by those who enjoyed it completely [67–68].

"The other" poet, with his "impassioned descriptions of hopeless agony," is, of course, Lord Byron. The interconnection between Lord Byron and the male heroes of his wildly successful Eastern Tales was central to the myth developing around their poet. As Austen makes clear, "poetry" can "be seldom safely enjoyed." The "impassioned" Byron and his Byronic hero are already dangerous.[6] Though Byron is ironic about the connection between himself and his heroes in later works like *Don Juan* (1819–1824), in the early years of his career he went out of his way to connect himself with them. Thomas Phillips's famous *Portrait of a Nobleman in the Dress of an Albanian* (1813) certainly portrays all the dangerous allure of the exotic, violent pirate. As Andrew Elfenbein puts it, "while Jane Austen's leading men rarely live up to the vividness of her heroines[,] Byron rescued masculinity for literature by transforming the masculine character, which elsewhere was a clue to moral worth, into an enigma" ("Byron" 60). The explosion of the Byronic hero onto the literary landscape of the Regency was so dramatic that Austen's *Persuasion* had already begun the process of rewriting the Byronic hero for a more domestic consumption. That is to say, Captain Wentworth, Anne Elliot's love interest in *Persuasion*, was the first domesticated Byronic hero, a proto Heathcliff or Rochester.[7] Austen's domestication of the Byronic hero in *Persuasion* is connected to the politics of gender in the Regency because Wentworth, as a naval captain recently returned from combat, is a character of romance and therefore far different from the cheerful clergymen or the dour gentlemen of property that "rarely live up to the vividness of her heroines" (Elfenbein 60). As Susan Allan Ford writes of *Persuasion*, "like the male characters valorized in *Persuasion*, the heroes of Scott and Byron are men of action—knights, pirates, sympathetic outlaws. They are not defined in terms of inheritance of land or power; instead they act in problematic relationships—covertly loyal or in open revolt—to those who do hold power" (78).[8] In both *The Corsair* and *Persuasion* what is at stake is the role of women in the violent and aggressive world of seafaring and piracy. Jane Austen's quasi-Byronic hero, Captain Wentworth, sees no place for women at sea, no space for women to romance. In *Persuasion*, rewriting the Byronic hero begins by teaching this new, enigmatic model of masculinity the power of domesticity at home and abroad.

To teach the value of women to these "knights, pirates, sympathetic outlaws" (Ford 78), the heroines of *Persuasion* and *The Corsair* usurp male power. Thus the story of Anne and Gulnare is one of transformation of resources from the masculine accumulator to the female administrator. It is a kind of liberation. At the beginning of *Persuasion*, Anne Elliot is controlled by her father and her mother-figure, Lady Russell; in *The Corsair* Gulnare is a slave to the pasha, Seyd. Yet both Anne and Gulnare move from these modes of subjection—fantastical harem slave and old maid-in-waiting—to those of genuine agency. Indeed, the acts of textual piracy in Austen's *Persuasion*—allusion, reference, and this Byronic masculine representation—point to a deeper rewriting of Byron's romance, *The Corsair*, and the place of women in not only the generic sphere of romance, but in how women wield power in domestic spaces, on land and even at sea.

Like Gulnare's transformation from the damsel in distress to Conrad's savior, Anne's transformation from the overlooked, old maid to romance heroine is directly related to the fortunes of war. For the young Anne Elliot had wanted to marry the then ambitious, but penurious, young naval officer, Fredrick Wentworth. She was, however, persuaded by her title-vain father, Sir Walter, and mother figure, Lady Russell, to break the tie. The result is a physical and emotional lethargy that touches Anne's very physiognomy—she "had been a very pretty girl, but her bloom had vanished early" (5). Her bloom, however, revives with Wentworth's return from the Napoleonic wars. The resurrection of Anne's physical and spiritual life is directly related to the democratic potential unleashed by the Napoleonic Wars, particularly by the English Navy.[9] Anne's escape is still tied to marriage, but it is a very different kind.

The model for the "good marriage" in *Persuasion* is that of Admiral and Mrs. Croft. Mrs. Croft, the sister of Captain Wentworth, makes very clear what that means:

> "[N]othing can exceed the accommodations of a man of war; I speak, you know of the higher rates. When you come to a frigate, of course, you are more confined—

though any reasonable woman may be perfectly happy in one of them; and I can safely say, that the happiest part of my life has been spent on board a ship. While we were together, you know, there was nothing to be feared. Thank God! I have always been blessed with excellent health ... as long as we could be together, nothing ever ailed me, and I never met with the smallest inconvenience" [47–48].

The fundamental power of the British Empire, the Royal Navy, is domesticated. In the description of the Crofts' ideal marriage, the enormous state organization behind the British war against Napoleon is reimagined as domestic bliss—"the happiest part of my life has been spent on board a ship. While we were together, you know, there was nothing to be feared. Thank God!" That is exactly what happens: the total war against Napoleon creates the structural changes in the British economy that results in the reign of the bourgeoisie and their domestic ideology.

During the buildup and the war years, the navy went from 15,000 sailors to 135,000 sailors, and doubled the size of its fleet. Given the state of industrial development and state centralization in the first decades of the nineteenth century, the national mobilization amounted to total warfare. "British manufactures," Roger Knight writes, "ship-builders, canon-founders, gunsmiths and City financiers expanded production and distribution far beyond the capacity of the state's dockyards, victualing yards, and munitions and gunpowder factories" (Knight 463). The ship owners fared very well too because they "chartered their vessels to government" for transport and logistic support. Agriculture also "achieved ever-increasing production" in order to feed the navy and army (Knight 463). The debt (£778,000,000) was 237 percent the GDP in 1816.[10] The total war amounted to an enormous transfer of national wealth to the financial and manufacturing classes—the British bourgeoisie. Lord Byron lays the blame for the violence of the Luddite Revolt (1811–13) on English total war policy in his maiden speech to the House of Lords in 1812, arguing "that it is the bitter policy, the destructive warfare, of the last eighteen years which has destroyed their comfort [frame breakers], your comfort, all men's comfort;—that policy ... has survived the dead to become a curse on the living" (Moore 1:154–55). The affects of the mobilization would reach far beyond the Regency. The transfer of wealth and the growth of economic output during the war years culminate later in the century with the First Reform Bill (1832), the Bank Charter Act of 1844, which institutes the gold standard, and the repeal of the Corn Laws (1846) that guarantees free trade.

Thus Claudia L. Johnson is right in describing the real politics of *Persuasion* as a disagreement between Captain Wentworth and his sister on the "right" of women to be present on combat vessels such as privateers, frigates, and "m[e]n of war" because the real politics of *Persuasion* is about domesticating this new wealth created by the Napoleonic Wars. The ideal marriage in *Persuasion* is tied to the sea and the battle for prize money, which for a captain in Austen's time would have been "one-third" (Lewis 134) of the total worth of the vessel and cargo, which could raise someone in a short time from a pauper to a gentleman of means.[11] That is the grounds for Wentworth's initial proposal to a lady of the landed class. As Austen writes, "he was confident that he should soon be rich ... he knew that he should soon have a ship, and soon be on a station that would lead to every thing he wanted" (19). It is not surprising that Austen is so matter-of-fact about how Wentworth grew "rich"; in fact, government-sanctioned piracy in the form of "prize-money" often dominated the tactics of maritime warfare. As Michael Lewis points out, "chasing after enemy merchantmen was, or might be, so very profitable ... that captains, and good ones too, might sometimes be tempted to make this their primary occupation" (330–31). The literal sea change in what makes a sufficient match for a daughter of the gentry in *Persuasion* suggests that class skepticism about the accumulation of wealth in the Regency was moving decidedly away from inheritance of lands and titles to more democratic methods of raw capitalism, which would epitomize the Victorian period. The actual structure of naval service: the distribution of prize-money, impressment, and the continual deaths and injuries that resulted in resisting the press gang, or the fitting of privateers for the express purpose of legally sanctioned piracy creates the possibility of this new domestic accumulation.

The Napoleonic wars, as Susan Morgan argues, opened new "possibilities and limitations of men and women ... at the beginning of the nineteenth century" (89). They open up the possibility of a home at sea, a life of shared accumulation—a kind of capitalist romance. But the acceptance of women's place at the center of this new infusion of capital will be earned the same way the money is earned, through violence. What Gulnare and Anne pirate is nothing less than the representation masculine mastery,[12] and that usurpation recreates the male heroes, Wentworth and Conrad—*les corsairs*,[13] the pirates—into men in light of female authority.[14]

When Louisa Musgrove fell from the Cobb at Lyme Regis "her eyes were closed, she breathed not, her face was like death.—The horror of that moment to all who stood around!" (74). That is what the assembled company of ladies and heroic naval officers do: stand around. Mary and Henrietta swoon. Captain Benwick gapes, and Wentworth goes to his knees: "'Is there no one to help me?' were the first words which burst from Captain Wentworth, in a tone of despair, and as if all his own strength were gone" (74). Captain Wentworth's literal collapse in the face of a violent upheaval, the drastic turn of events, places him in the symbolic position of the classic fainting female. He instantly goes from the flirting, controlled, handsome naval officer to an image of complete helplessness. "The first words which burst from Captain Wentworth" define his new place: "Is there no one to help me?" he asks, with a "tone of despair." It is his physical immobility more than his plea for help that inaugurates his feminization and Anne's pirating of masculine prowess during a moment of violence. For Wentworth is on his knees clutching the unconscious Louisa, while Anne assumes his place of command. Before Louisa's fall from the Cobb, Wentworth's masculine value is formed around an ability to cope with violence and to manage disaster in a romance economy where the only currency is violence. This value structure ends when he falls to his knees in complete despair; he is literally useless.

The exchange of positions, Anne's pirating of the symbolic space of male power, is punctuated by Wentworth's absolute loss of that power. In a crowd of heroes, Anne is the only one capable of command. She takes hold of Louisa and orders the still gaping Benwick to "go to him [Wentworth], go to him ... for heaven's sake go to him. I can support her myself. Leave me, and go to him," while at the same time telling the women to "rub her [Louisa's] hands, rub her temples, here are salts—take them, take them" (74). It is a remarkable moment in the Austen canon. Anne Elliot steals the language of command from men of action during a moment of violent danger. In fact, almost every sentence is a command: "Go to him.... Leave me.... Rub her." There is even a curse ("for heaven's sake"), which punctuates Anne's performance of levelheaded effectiveness in spite of the bumbling men around her. At the moment where violence disrupts the movement of events, he is left "staggering" (74), unable to support himself, while Anne captains the other men. The exasperated Anne usurps their position of masculine mastery and they snap to. For "Captain Benwick obeyed, and Charles at the same moment" (74). As Anne's new crew works to help Louisa, making sure that "everything [is] done that Anne had prompted" (74), Wentworth is completely absent from the effort; in fact, he is lost in hysterics. "Staggering against the wall for his support," he "exclaimed in the bitterest agony, 'Oh, God! her father and mother!'" (74). With this outburst, the exchange of symbolic gender value is completed.

This moment quickly becomes a moment of domestic education for Wentworth. On the carriage journey to Uppercross to inform the Musgroves about Louisa, Wentworth moans with regret over giving in to her "at the fatal moment" because she was "so eager and so resolute" (78). As he stews, Anne "wonder[s]" if he will learn from it: "whether it ever occurred to him now, to question the justness of his own previous opinion as to the universal felicity and advantage of firmness of character" (78). She goes on to muse, with a little brutality, if "it might not strike him" (78) that a balanced mind is preferable and concludes that "it could scarcely escape him to feel that a persuadable temper might sometimes be as much in favour of happiness" (79). As Anne reasons through the unavoidable education Wentworth must have received, it becomes clear that there is another, more subtle violence taking place on the carriage ride back to Uppercross. Anne, the "persuadable temper," is taking the affections of Wentworth from Louisa, the "resolute character." The irony of "resolute character" lying unconscious and near death while "persuadable temper" rides with the *objet d'amour* suggests both the price and the reward of romance interruptions.

At the same time, the replacement of the romantic ideal of the "resolute character" by the "persuadable temper" also suggests the limits of a romance economy after the sailors and soldiers have returned home. Success inside the domestic enclosure that Wentworth wants to enter hinges on the ability to be persuaded by your own social and class obligation whatever its manifestation: religious, moral, aesthetic, or political. We can see at this early stage of its development how "domestic fiction," as Armstrong writes, "transformed this fantasy of self-production into the procedures designed to produce men and women fit to occupy the institutions of an industrialized society" (*Desire* 164). It is making them persuadable.

Domestic education through violence is at the center of Byron's *Corsair* as well. For Conrad, the Byronic hero of the Eastern Tale, is on one hand the ultimate figure of aggressive male mastery, and on the other the fully domesticated husband. He controls his wild band of pirates through "the power of Thought—the magic of the Mind! / Link'd with success, assumed and kept with skill" (1.182–83). He is also the "unchangeable—unchanged" loving husband to Medora—Conrad being the first and one of the only married pirates (1.287). Medora, the ideal wife, is placed on "the summit of his tower-crown'd hill" to play soft lays while either begging for Conrad to stay or waiting for him to return (1.342).

Medora, pirate wife that she is, is still a romance image of perfect domesticity. She does not share in Conrad's accumulation but begs Conrad to "be silent, Conrad!—dearest! come and share / The feast these hands delighted to prepare" (1.420–21). She only exists to reflect his masculine supremacy and prowess. This is the classic romance economy, where the violent male hero exists perfectly in the eyes of the passive and waiting refection of that heroism. The story of *The Corsair* is the story of the unraveling of just such an economy. Byron idealizes the passive Medora in order to transform Conrad into a waiting Medora, the startled beneficiary of female piracy.

Fittingly, the reversal of Conrad's masculine position begins with the shedding of a disguise. Coming as a spy, dressed in the religious robes of a dervish, to the palace of his sworn enemy, Seyd, Conrad reveals himself as his men start burning Seyd's ships:

> Up rose the Dervise with that burst of light,
> Nor less his change of form appall'd the sight:
> Up rose that Dervise—not in saintly garb,
> But like a warrior bounding on his barb [2.142–45].

Conrad and his men have burned the ships and are moving on to the city. They seem on the verge of victory when Conrad hears "on his ear the cry / Of women struck, and like a deadly knell / Knock'd at that heart unmoved by battle's yell" (2.199–201). And it is a "deadly knell" because Conrad orders his men to remember that "*we* have wives" (2.203). The pirates obey and place the members of Seyd's harem safely inside the mosque at the expense of their own momentum, which ends in either their retreat or capture. In the act of saving the harem queen, Gulnare, Conrad is taken captive. Ironically, his initial downfall comes through his chivalry toward women, and his "saving" of a woman ultimately places Conrad in the position of a woman.

Susan Wolfson argues compellingly from the formal use of "feminine" and "masculine" rhyme that Byron's "hero's progressive feminization ... is also a position that refigures Medora's patient arrest in the tower that becomes her actual tomb. These alignments of Conrad's powerlessness with an orthodox feminine position are amplified by Gulnare's evolution into a figure of masculine potency in female guise" (158). There is no doubt that Wolfson is correct that the narrative and formal trajectory of the Byronic hero in *The Corsair* is toward "progressive feminization." The disintegration of masculine power and prowess does not "leave its hero incompletely resorted" (162), but is instead an education toward a different kind of masculine representation—one that is free from the need of the worshipful woman, the Medora. The ideal romance reflection of masculine prowess ends because Conrad takes her position. He becomes Medora "in the high chamber of his [Seyd's] highest tower sate Conrad," (2.366) the waiting female. He waits for Gulnare, while for the first time questioning his love for Medora:

> "Oh! she [Medora] is all that still to earth can bind—
> And this will break a heart so more than kind,
> And blight a form—till thine appear'd, Gulnare!
> Mine eye ne're ask'd if others were as fair" [2.487–90].

The initial violence corrects the fantasy of male mastery of violence that is so much a part of masculine representation, particularly for the captains of fighting ships, replacing it with weakness and need. It is the exact same symbolic mechanics as *Persuasion*: Gulnare replaces Medora and Anne replaces Louisa—who shows herself a Medora. There is, however, a serious departure between these two cardinal texts of the Regency. In the domestic novel *Persuasion*, Wentworth discovers his need to be valued by Anne, whereas Byron's romance explores the possibility of a masculine value without women at all.

The ultimate trajectory of *The Corsair* is concerned with untying masculine value from the female gaze, the phallus from female recognition to use Judith Butler's phraseology. But it is a process. In Canto III, Conrad is still trying to reconceive of himself via woman. Conrad turns to Gulnare to vouchsafe his masculinity. Empty of rage, captive, he is given new life through a new female mirror:

> That fair she!
> Whate'er her sins, to him a guardian saint,
> And beauteous still as hermit's hope can paint [3.273–75].

For all of Byron's talk of Conrad's sin and crime, it is a strange reversal to have Gulnare as the Byronic paradox—the sinful guardian—and Conrad as the waiting hermit, the Medora figure. Though he had breathlessly waited for Gulnare four days, he still tries to maintain the aggressive pose he struck before the feminizing capture took place: "'Lady! I look to none—my lips proclaim / What last proclaim'd they—Conrad still the same'" (3.282–83). His claim to be "Conrad still the same," a unified, aggressive, male representation, is rendered hollow by the repetition of "proclaim" and "proclaim'd." Lacking the ability to act against his enemy, Seyd, or save himself from imprisonment, he is reduced to relying on "my lips," to empty proclaiming.

Gulnare, on the other hand, is in command. Like Anne at the time of Louisa's fall, her worth is connected to action, not her ability to return an ideal image, to acknowledge male power and thus actualize it. Again like Anne, she is making herself a part of the currency of violence at the heart of the romance genre. Gulnare claims to be a genuine partner in Conrad's piracy: "'Were I thine own—thou wert not lonely here: / An outlaw's spouse—and leave her lord to roam!'" (3.301-03). Gulnare's claim on Conrad rests on her ability to strike, to act on his behalf. She even challenges him: "'If thou hast courage still, and wouldst be free, / Receive this poniard—rise—and follow me!'" (3.306-07). But he begs her not to kill Seyd with the "'secret knife'" (3.364) or make him part of it, because that act alone belongs to men. She is, however, clear: "'I'll try the firmness of a female hand'" (3.381).

Manacled, her captive, Conrad follows Gulnare through a dark, winding passage, losing her and, despite what she has said, imagining she is innocent. When she finds him, all is changed for Conrad. He sees "a spot" of blood:

> They meet—upon her brow—unknown, forgot—
> Her hurrying hand had left—'twas but a spot—
> Its hue was all he saw, and scarce withstood—
> Oh! slight but certain pledge of crime—'tis blood! [3.414-17].

This spot of blood is more destructive to "Conrad the same" (3.283) than anything Seyd could inflict.

Gulnare's killing of Seyd destroys the dichotomy between male aggression and female passivity which maintains the early formulation of the Byronic hero in *The Corsair*: "That spot of blood, that light but guilty streak, / Had banish'd all the beauty from her cheek!" (3.426-27). The "spot of blood" is suggestive the violence that marked the domestic enclosure in Shakespeare's *Macbeth*. Lady Macbeth cannot wash the blood from her hands, "Yet here's a spot!" (5.1.23), and Conrad cannot escape Gulnare's murder. This "guilty streak" completes his domestic education: women are not a reflection of male desire. It reveals both gender positions, male and female, as a form of enclosure, as the "guilty streak" itself, an emptiness, where collapsing semantic structures reappear and repeat themselves in different moments for different subjects.[15] Femaleness migrates from Gulnare (the harem slave) to Conrad (the prisoner), back to Gulnare (the "spot of blood"), and back to Conrad.[16] In their parting, they are still helplessly confused. For when Conrad goes to embrace "Gulnare, the homicide" (3.463) in a gesture of understanding, it is with a hand that "lost its firmness" (3.539).[17] Because by "trying the firmness of a female hand" (3.381) in killing Seyd, Gulnare explodes the binary of male aggression and female passivity that underpins the potential for desire in a traditional romance economy.

The confusion of gender roles structures the final metaphor of the penultimate section (XXIII) of the poem. After it, Conrad disappears. All that is left of him is a broken mooring and a missing boat. In the penultimate section, however, Byron employs a final extended metaphor that is both an elegy and envoi for Conrad. In the first line, Byron gives us the tension that maintains his hero: "his heart was form'd for softness—warp'd to wrong" (3.663). He is "softness" that has "harden'd" (3.665). This hardening left "one flower [to grow] beneath its rugged brow,"

> Though dark the shade—it shelter'd, saved till now.
> The thunder came—that bolt hath blasted both,
> The Granite's firmness, and the Lily's growth:
> The gentle plant hath left no leaf to tell
> Its tale, but shrunk and wither'd where it fell;
> And of its cold protector, blacken round
> But shiver'd fragments on the barren ground! [3.671-77].

In this final metaphor, Byron performs the representational death of his hero. For what creates the Byronic hero, at this point in its evolution anyway, is the gender binary of female softness and male hardness—the gentle female reflection of his masculine strength. The "Granite's firmness, and the Lily's growth," however, are both erased when his new love interest, Gulnare, acts as a man by killing Seyd. What is left is impossible to write, for "the gentle plant hath left no leaf to tell." The play on the word "leaf" for "page" suggests that the literal place of inscription, the page of the book, is a void. It is the same for the opposite side of the gender binary. The masculine "cold protector" is fragmentary words, shards of meanings, no longer mirroring any order, pieces of a value structure that cannot tell and pages that cannot be read.

For Conrad's escape from Medora to Gulnare and then from Gulnare back to a dead Medora, all point in the same direction: being a man means being a man for a woman. When that ends for Conrad, when Gulnare takes his place as a man and Medora stops waiting, he is left as a hero that cannot be written, at least not yet. Romance masculinity as it develops across the nineteenth century and the genres that come to surround it—adventure fiction, spy fiction, detective fiction—almost inevitably return to this potential for writing masculinity outside of female recognition. When we see what that writing looks like in the Byronic afterlife, Byron's failure to write it, which "leave[s] its hero incompletely resorted" (Wolfson 162), becomes the real heroism.

But writing does not fail Wentworth. Driven by fear of losing Anne to her distant, morally corrupt cousin, he writes her a desperate letter, a final plea, that fuses the language of Byronic romance with domestic education. In Wentworth's letter to Anne, Austen rewrites both the Byronic hero and the trajectory of feminization in *The Corsair* because Wentworth's romance agony functions as domestic education. There is surely a mending of the feminization and ultimate absence that marks Conrad. While Byron's "Granite's Firmness, and the Lily's growth" or love for Medora (3.673) is a breakdown of masculine value because women are not simply a reflection of men, Wentworth's pierced soul is mended through writing a new self: one that is capable of authentic marriage between equals. This moment of connection between Conrad and Wentworth, the disintegration of their masculine value, is a moment of deep generic disconnection between anti-domestic romance and the domestic novel's marriage plot. Instead of erasing power relations, the letter Wentworth writes to Anne places him inside a new domestic economy where she has the agency.

Austen metaphorically connects Wentworth, the writer, with Anne Elliot, the reader, by having her sink into the chair that he had occupied, "succeeding to the very spot where he had leaned and written" while she peruses his letter at Sir Walter's rented house in Camden-place Bath (158). The female reader "succeeds" to a position of power over the male writer. The substitution, the "succeeding," of Anne to the "very spot where he [Wentworth] had occupied," is the culmination of her piracy of Wentworth. Since the fall of Louisa, he has learned Anne's value, but the attentions of her cousin, Mr. Elliot, and his own behavior toward her has reversed the role of this man-of-action: he has become like an anxiously waiting woman. Just as Conrad became the waiting Medora, Wentworth becomes the self-conscious, worried Anne of the first half of the novel.

Ann has indeed "succeed[ed]" to the "very spot" of power that Wentworth once had over her. For in the letter, she reads that only she can mend him:

> You pierce my soul. I am half agony, half hope. Tell me not that I am too late, that such precious feelings are gone for ever. I offer myself to you again with a heart even more your own, than when you almost broke it eight years and a half ago. Dare not say that man forgets sooner than woman, that his love has an earlier death. I have loved none but you. Unjust I may have been, weak and resentful I have been, but never inconstant.... You do us justice, indeed. You do believe that there is true attachment and constancy among men. Believe it to be most fervent, most undeviating in F.W. [158].

Wentworth's letter uses the figurative "agony" of Byronic male representational crisis in order that it might be healed through female union. He "offers" himself that he might be completed. Austen's rewrites this Byronic crisis, the erasure of the divide between male and female subject positions, to rewrite Wentworth as a Byronic hero fit for an equitable marriage.

The piercing of his "soul," its splitting between "half agony, half hope," is the pulling apart of one form of male representation in order to introduce another. His desire to recreate himself in the language of a new romance domesticity employs *The Corsair's* tropes of constancy and agony for the sake of mending the pierced soul. At the center of Wentworth's reconstructed self is the concept of masculine consistency that, in many ways, defines the Byronic hero. It is through this consistency that Wentworth now inscribes himself as a feminized male—one that has been educated in a female subject position. The entire line of argument in his letter is that men can be like women in love. "Dare not say that man forgets sooner than woman," Wentworth writes, "that his love has an earlier death." This "true attachment and constancy among men," of which Wentworth is "the most fervent" devotee, makes him (in matters of love, at least) a woman. Wentworth has learned to write this new feminized masculinity necessary for marriage with a "rational" (45) woman like Anne Elliot because she pirates his masculine command at a moment of violent reversal and shifts the performance of gender values toward herself.

He is learning the language of domestic fiction—the proto-rhetoric of *Jane Eyre* and *Wuthering Heights*. Yet it is a transgeneric hybrid language. The poetic and figurative language "of being pierced, of being torn," moves beyond the realist presentation of subjectivity into a Romantic and particularly Byronic one. Wentworth thus re-creates himself in a figurative, poetic language that has the fleeting potential of transcending the cultural valuation of masculinity and the gender potential for the heroine, Anne. As he writes, "You pierce my soul. I am half agony, half hope." He turns himself into a poetic fragment, like Byron's "shiver'd fragments on barren ground!" (3.777), but one that "offer[s] myself to you again with a heart even more your own" (158) for Anne to put back together. He uses the language of Byronic agony, of masculine fragmentation, for the purposes of a perpetual domestic education. Wentworth's tearing and piercing of himself through transgeneric writing elucidates the way in which Austen uses the poetics of Byronic passion as a means toward a gender transformation which gives Austen's heroine agency in the bourgeois superstructure because she lacks any structural agency—legal, financial, or political. That is the real piracy in *Persuasion*. The new wealth generated by the Napoleonic wars will not be squandered in the old masculine pursuits of the gaming table and the hunt. For Wentworth to be the man for Anne Elliot, he must be persuadable; he must be domesticated.

The generic dangers of poetry are thus controlled in the domestic, realist reimagining of romance. Because "it was the misfortune of poetry, to be seldom safely enjoyed by those who enjoyed it completely" (68), Austen pirates the power of the new Byronic romance so that it might be "safely enjoyed." The "enigma" (Elfenbein 60) of the Byronic hero turns into the depth of feeling necessary for a new kind of domestic partner. Wentworth's violent male aggression and his new emotional depth are controlled by his love for Anne. Wentworth, therefore, is one of the first of many Byronic inspired male leads rewritten into the framework of the developing domestic novel. He should be understood in the developing genealogy of the Byronic hero, along with Emily Brontë's Heathcliff and Charlotte Brontë's Rochester, as not only capable of intense passion and violence, "but never inconstant" (158), as Wentworth writes to Anne. So while Byron would be exiled from England, the Byronic hero would find a home there. As we will see, the generic and gender de-limitation, the spirit of romance, which pervades both *The Corsair* and *Persuasion* will be replaced by works that were "calculated," as Austen writes, "to rouse and fortify the mind by the highest precepts, and the strongest examples of moral and religious endurances" (*Persuasion* 68) during the reign of Victorian domesticity.

Chapter Two

A House Fit for a Lady
Lord Byron's *Manfred* and Emily Brontë's *Wuthering Heights*

(How shall I sing her?) whose soul
Knew no fellow for might,
Passion, vengeance, grief,
Daring, since Byron died.

—Matthew Arnold,
"Haworth Churchyard" (159–62)

Perhaps it was Matthew Arnold in "Haworth Churchyard" who best phrased the textual similarities between the two writers that in life experience could not be more different—one a poor parson's daughter who died in utter obscurity, the other a worldly Scottish peer who was the first modern celebrity. *Wuthering Heights,* nevertheless, works to push out the "might, / Passion, vengeance, grief, / Daring," indeed, the Byronic inheritance, through a complex rewriting that turns Byronic liberation from individual opposition into the very ground on which to build a domestic enclosure. Superficially, the Byronic "might" and "daring," Heathcliff and the first Catherine, are replaced at the end of the novel by their domestic equivalent, the tamed versions of themselves: Hareton Earnshaw and the second Catherine. To show how Emily Brontë engages and transforms the Byronic inheritance, it will be necessary to show how it deeply informs the structure of her language and how the structure of her language undoes the very inheritance with which she is working. *Wuthering Heights* (1847) is set during the revolutionary upheavals at the end of the eighteenth century and the first three years of the nineteenth century, the French Revolution and the rise of Napoleon. The text reimagines the millennial impulses of that revolutionary moment inside the already closed domestic order of the mid-nineteenth century. It does this in large part through the vehicle of the commodification Byron's subjectivity. If we read closely, we will see how Emily Brontë uses the Byronic to textually bridge what Gérin sees as the "deep division in her mind" (94) between the Romantic and the Victorian, and how *Wuthering Heights* enacts this transformation through transgeneric language, turning Byronic rhetoric into one of the foundations of the domestic novel and the domestic order to which it is tied.

The world of religious observance, sexual rectitude, and the practice of domestic values, the rule of middle-class respectability, coalesced power at the end of the Regency. Lord Byron did not feel much at home here. The simplest reading of Conrad's unraveling masculinity is the desire to escape the "one virtue" (Byron *The Corsair* 3.696) of fidelity in marriage. That it must be played out through an elaborate gender reversal and a disappearance into the sea, a "death yet dubious" (3.694), suggests that the value of men beginning in the Regency is tied explicitly to their role in the developing industrial and domestic economy. As Byron himself would learn, escape is not an easy task; nor is it an easy task for the Byronic heroes that follow in the novels of the nineteenth century. The secret history of romance masculinity is the history of Byron's hero as he moves through the political and social enclosures initiated by the ruling middle class during the ubiquitous reign of Victorian respectability. At times, he will seem silenced to the point of extinction. A particular rhetoric will emerge, however, from the long and arduous journey of the Byronic hero inside the domestic novel as well as the adventure fiction of the 1880s romance revival. Created from the Byronic hero and the intense pressure of Victorian domesticity, by the fin-de-siècle this rhetoric had grown into a direct challenge to domestic values, particularly as they relate to masculinity. That is because at the heart of the Byronic hero is an open antagonism to the domestic values of family and home.

The articulation of the ascendant middle class domestic ideology over and against aristocratic libertinism played out on a national stage: the divorce proceedings of George IV and Queen Catherine. Their marriage had been unhappy one, and after George III died, the new king wanted to be rid of her. She was offered an increase in her income to remain abroad but she refused. She wanted to be the queen of Great Britain. George IV wanted a divorce. Initiated in the House of Lords on 17 August 1820, the divorce was conducted outside the ecclesiastical courts under a special bill of Pains and Penalties. It was an extra-legal affair, not a real trial, and it backfired on the king, for the divorce proceedings only served to consolidate the forces of middle class domestic virtue against eighteenth-century aristocratic privilege: "the high-class prostitutes, the boxes at the opera, the carriage drives in the park designed to advertise sexual wares, the life of ease and wit, the rude vigorous open enjoyment of sexuality, all this was anathema to serious Christians" (Davidoff and Hall 152). The public turned against George IV and rallied to the cause his estranged wife. She was cast as an emblem of embattled domestic virtue and womanhood. That Queen Caroline was none of those things, other than embattled, hardly mattered. George IV was forced to withdrawal the suit because of popular pressure. In newspapers, poetry, and sermons, the domestic values of the ascendant middle class, "the reaction to the whole episode marks one of the first *public* moments in which one view of marriage and sexuality was decisively rejected in favor of another" (Davidson and Hall 152).

The rebuff of George IV did have one notable public precedent, however: the exile of Lord Byron. Byron's disastrous marriage to Annabella Milbanke, their reputation wrecking divorce, and his flight to the Continent to avoid possible prosecution for sodomy and incest (all of which prefigured the Queen Caroline Affair) were very public. His marriage and scandalous divorce were really a catastrophe of Byron's own making. Rumors of incest with his half sister, Augusta, and his "unnatural" sexual exploration in the Eastern Mediterranean involving "sodomy & smoking ... the pipe and pathic" (*Letters* 1:239) were fueled by his own insinuations and aggravated by the antipathy of his recently slighted (and married) lover, Caroline Lamb. Byron and Augusta saw the dangers of scandal and ostracism if he continued "being Byron" under the tightening lens of celebrity. As Byron wrote to Lady Melbourne in April of 1814, nine months before his marriage, "she [Augusta] wished me much to marry—because it was the only chance of redemption for *two* persons—and was sure if *I* did not that I should only step from one scrape into another—particularly if I went abroad" (*Letters* 4:108). Byron's cover marriage had the exact opposite effect and his forced exile was a victory for domesticity and middle class respectability—for a little while, anyway.

On a "grim winter day" in Yorkshire, as Leslie Marscand describes it, Byron married Annabella Milbanke (191). Less than a year later, Annabella, now Lady Byron, decided her husband was mad. With the help of the *Medical Journal*, she diagnosed him with hydrocephalus—literally, "wet brain." He certainly gave her a lot of help with her diagnosis. Starting on their honeymoon and continuing throughout their short marriage, his drinking and his dark hints of past crimes, like sodomy and incest, were too much for her. The divorce turned into a public spectacle, a battle between middle class chastity and aristocratic lust, the virtuous maiden verses a lordly corrupter. It was like a Richardson novel in real time, played out over the gossip of drawing rooms, in newspaper innuendo, and, of course, through poetry. *Blackwood's Edinburgh Magazine* was the textual scene of one vicious attack against Byron's bisexuality that bordered on an incitement to violence (MacCarthy 276). At the same time, Lady Byron was defended and celebrated by middle class readers.

Mrs. Cookle's "Lines for Lady Byron" (1817) gives a sense of the public battle lines the couple's divorce drew. As she empathetically asks her readers:

> When suffering virtue heaves the secret sigh,
> ....
> Ask *where's* the heart, that is not prompt to share
> The wife's chaste sorrow, and the mother's care?
> Or *where* the breast, that is not quick to prove
> Its genuine sympathy with wounded love? [1–8].

Of course the answer is: "we" middle class, respectable defenders of domestic virtues are the hearts that are "prompt to share" and "quick to prove" our "sympathy." Mrs. Cookle's strained syntax is suggestive of the ideological mechanics through which one "view of marriage and sexuality was decisively rejected in favor of another" (Davidson and Hall 152) and the way in which Victorian domesticity became the center of English life. It is through the great "not," through excluding or repressing all difference as deviance, that Victorian middle-class domesticity became the only natural form of human life. Those that do not "share" or are not "quick to prove" the value of a "wife's chaste sorrow" have no place "*where*" we are— and we are in England. There was no place for Byron and the Byronic where the new, middle class order was articulating its particular form of social control—a moral and sexual panopticon—reified in the code of respectability.

The enraged public, incited by Lady Byron's persistent accusations of incest between Bryon and Augusta, drove him to Dover in October 1816. Ladies dressed as their chambermaids came to watch as "with haughty scorn" (134) as Matthew Arnold wrote in *Grande Chartreuse*, the disgraced poet took "the pageant of his bleeding heart" (136) to the Swiss Alps, Italy, and finally to Greece. It was a victory for the ascendant middle class, a preview of their cowing of the king four years later. At least, it seemed to be. But as Werner Huber points out, across the nineteenth century the specter of Byron and the Byronic hero became "the terror of bourgeois mediocrity" (93–94). As "the guilt-ridden cursed artist, the diabolical rebel," Byron and the hero that bears his name are "first and foremost 'the stuff of novels'" (Hurber 93–94). So while the forces of domestic virtue were pushing Byron into exile, the Byronic hero was on the verge of embedding itself inside the English domestic novel—the literary form of middle-class values.

The deep textual relationship between Byron's life, his hero, and the novels of the nineteenth century has a very specific material location: a biography printed in two volumes and published by John Murray in 1830. Commissioned by Murray and written by Byron's close friend Thomas Moore, the *Letters and Journals of Lord Byron with Notices of His Life* became an instant bestseller. Deeply researched and augmented by so many of Byron's heartrending journal entries and sparkling letters, Byron's biography became fundamental to the Byronic commodity's afterlife, even rivaling the poetry in popularity. "No book," Andrew Elfenbein argues, "had greater impact on Victorian perceptions of Byron" (*Byron and Victorians* 78). The biography was central to "the commodification of Byron's subjectivity [which] continued even without the presence of his poetry" (*Byron and Victorians* 78). In the end, the most lasting "Victorian perceptions" of Byron would rely neither on his poetry nor his life, but instead on the commodity of romance masculinity both his work and life inspired. Moore locates the lasting power of that commodity, Byron as his hero, at the moment of his leave taking. Moore is always at pains to disarm Byron's Victorian critics by painting the darker inflections of his character as the product of his genius. Byron's exile, however, is a moment of exaltation in Moore's biography. In fact, Moore explicitly connects Byron's mature genius to his rejection of a triumphant middle class domesticity. "He had," Moore writes, "in the course of one short year, gone through every variety of domestic misery" (14:53). The law had sought him and the society which had earlier feted him had then furiously turned against him. Moore characterizes Byron as a child that sees the mask he has been wearing in the "mirror of public opinion" and is wounded and "shocked"(14:54). This, Moore goes on, might have had a "softening and, perhaps, humbling influence ... on his spirit. But, luckily,—as it proved, for the further triumphs of his genius,—no such moderation was exercised" (14:54). "The storm of invective" forces him to turn his "youthful genius" into something "bolder and loftier" (14:55). In Goethe's words, Byron becomes the "Poet of Pain" (14:55). It was his transgressions that ultimately gave him his genius, his originality, and his authenticity. Transgression is necessary for authenticity and genius. In the nineteenth century novel, that transgression congealed into an anti domestic literary commodity: romance masculinity. Before Byron was congealed into the romance masculinity of the romance revival, the Byronic hero plays a role in creating the language of marriage and domesticity. Two of the earliest and most successful reproductions of the Byronic were written by two of the most important domestic novelists of the Victorian era, Charlotte and Emily Brontë. As I have said, it is a long story.

There is no doubt about Heathcliff's genealogy: he is a Byronic hero. He is either an orphan or the illegitimate child of the elderly Earnshaw. And like Conrad in *The Corsair*, "His heart was form'd for softness— warp'd to wrong; / Betray'd too early, and beguiled too long" (3.662–63). There are also glaring similarities not only to the Byronic hero, but to Byron's life. Though it is hard to trace the reading history of the reclusive Emily Brontë, it is certain that her father's library contained the *Complete Works of Lord Byron* (1833) edited by Thomas Moore, including Moore's biography of Byron. F.B. Pinion argues that Brontë's early writing, from the Gondal Poems up to *Wuthering Heights*, shows a deep conversance with both "Byron and *Paradise Lost* [for] in one dramatic situation after another they breath resolute defiance of the Byronic heroes and Milton's Satan" (56).

As Pinion meticulously details, there are obvious relationships between key elements of the biography and the arc of Heathcliff's character development. That Emily Brontë was deeply familiar with Moore's biography is, Pinion writes, "beyond doubt ... whether she realized it or not, she drew a number of suggestions from it for her novel" (206). Pinion goes on to detail both the obvious and the more arcane similarities between Heathcliff's history and Moore's *Life of Lord Byron*: deep seated anger born from "violent punishment in boyhood"; youthful unrequited love that leads to an anti social, often brutish self articulation; the cruelty with which Byron treated his wife; and such "minor parallels" as how Byron and Heathcliff handle unruly bulldogs (206–07). Ultimately it is the language of *Wuthering Heights* itself that testifies to the influence of Byron.

Specifically, Byron's *Manfred* (1817) and Brontë's *Wuthering Heights* use the sublimity of gothic incest to perform a desire that is transcendent, certainly beyond the bounds of life and death, but in *Wuthering Heights*, completely of this world. The arch gothic theme of incest, initiated by Horace Walpole in *The Castle of Otranto* (1764), became, in Byron's closet-drama and Brontë's novel, the sublime foundation of love. As David Morris notes, gothic incest is always connected to the terror of the sublime, the terror of Burke and later of Kant, but for the eighteenth-century gothic at least, the "sublime [is] utterly without transcendence" (56). It is a sublimity founded in the release of control that spirals downward into unsignifible, unspeakable desire—the infinity of mute drives. Thus "censorship" and "swooning" defined the eighteenth-century reaction to gothic texts (Morris 57). Nancy Armstrong suggests that the lasting power of Emily Brontë rests in "a meaning, or depth, that actually exists on the surface in the manipulation of signifiers" (*Desire* 187). *Manfred* and *Wuthering Heights* are about incest, but the real incest is textual and it is buried on the surface of both texts: in the trope of shared blood.

The Trope of Shared Blood: Manfred in Wuthering Heights

Wuthering Heights opens with a scene of spectral blood. After being put to bed where he should not have been, reading of the first Catherine's and Heathcliff's suffering at the hands of Hindley, the elder son, and fighting through a dream of an infinite sermon, Mr. Lockwood wakes to a knocking at the window. When he tries to stop the knocking, he grabs hold of and is grabbed by "the fingers of a little, ice cold hand" (32), those of a young and dead Catherine: "'Let me in—let me in!' 'Who are you?' I asked, struggling, meanwhile, to disengage myself. '[The first] Catherine Linton.... I'm come home: I'd lost my way on the moor!'" (32). Mr. Lockwood tries to "disengage" himself only to find it is useless. But the pane of glass is broken, and, "terror" making him "cruel" (32), he "pulled its wrist on to the broken pane, and rubbed it to and fro till the blood ran down and soaked the bedclothes" (32). Piling a pyramid of books against the broken pane, he still fights to keep the bleeding ghost out: "'Begone,' I shouted, 'I'll never let you in—not if you beg for twenty years.' 'It is twenty years,' mourned the voice: 'Twenty years. I've been a waif for twenty years!'" (32).

What is striking about this ghostly encounter is its physicality. The "manipulation of signifiers ... that actually exist on the surface" (Armstong *Desire* 187), the presence of blood that "ran down and soaked the bedclothes" in a ghost begins a genre transformation, a rewriting of the sublime gothic theme central to *Manfred*. Both Manfred and Heathcliff are seeking the body of the beloved beyond life. They are seeking to resurrect the dead because the dead, the sublime other, is really an image of themselves, feminized. This is something of a theme in Second Generation Romanticism. As Cynthia Baer points out, in Shelley's *Alastor* (1816),

Keats's *Endymion* (1818), and Byron's *Manfred*, "the protagonist's divided consciousness and the tension created in that division prompt a quest for wholeness, and in each the quest turns upon sexual counterparts and sexual union imagined and longed for as an ultimate oneness—in short, androgyny" (25). In his confession to the Witch of the Alps, Manfred outlines the unity of genders, "androgyny," as an incestuous sublime: "She was like me in lineaments—her eyes, / Her hair, her features, all, to the very tone / Even of her voice, they said were like to mine; / But soften'd all, and temper'd into beauty" (2.2.105–08).

The marriage of two subjects that Manfred outlines defines the sublime gothic fantasy of incest in both texts. Like Heathcliff, Manfred "loved her [Astarte] and destoy'd her!" (2.2.115). What remains is the trace of the transgression, the blood, which is also the very symbol of incestuous union, shared blood. As Manfred explains to the Witch, his murder of Astarte as literally in the blood. "I have shed / Blood, but not hers—and yet her blood was shed—/ I saw—and could not stanch it" (2.2.119–21). "Then whose blood is it? It was "not hers ... yet her blood was shed." It was not hers because it was his, and it was not his because it was hers. Manfred and Astarte are a single male / female subject and thus an image of prelinguistic wholeness and of connected bodies and blood—a sublime vision of the transcendent self. As Manfred makes clear:

> I say 'tis blood—my blood! the pure warm stream
> Which ran in the veins of my fathers, and in ours
> When we were in our youth, and had one heart,
> And loved each other as we should not love [2.1.24–27].

The blood is the material image of total subject-object union. Incest or shared blood is the projection of a fantasy of deeply Romantic fantasy, central in Hegel's Phenomenology of Spirit (1807) for example, of the completion of the self through the other, through "one heart."

Emily Brontë goes beyond Byron's metaphor of blood. In the first pages of *Wuthering Heights*, Lockwood is assaulted by Catherine the First's ghost and he "pulled its wrists on to the broken pane, and rubbed it to and fro till the blood ran down and soaked the bedclothes" (32). Brontë substitutes real blood for representational unity. She makes it material. The ghost bleeds. But the bleeding ghost becomes more complex when Heathcliff attacks the affected Lockwood for being in the room and his Manfredian passion emerges. With Lockwood, ever the snoop, looking on from a safe darkness beyond the chamber: "He [Heathcliff] got on to the bed and wrenched open the lattice, bursting, as he pulled at it, into an uncontrollable passion of tears. 'Come in! Come in!' he sobbed. 'Cathy, do come! Oh, do—*once* more! Oh! my heart's darling! hear me *this* time, Catherine, at last!' The spectre showed a spectre's ordinary caprice: it gave no sign of being" (36).

The question is: where is the blood? It would be too easy to fall into "sublimating strategies that conceal forbidden desires, including incest" (Armstrong *Desire* 187) or to simply discount Lockwood. There is undoubtedly sexual language: "he got on the bed ... wrenched open the lattice [so phonically near bodice] ... bursting ... into an uncontrollable passion"; and the presence of blood-soaked bedclothes tempts a connection to the breaking of the hymen. It is not a moment of sexual union, but instead a moment of retreat, withdrawal, of running away on the part of the disembodied Catherine. "It gave no sign of being"—no signs to whom? It gives no sense of being to Heathcliff. It leaves Heathcliff in an ecstasy of loss.

This is the real sublimity of the incestuous themes in *Manfred* and *Wuthering Heights*. Whether in Burke or Kant, the sublime is defined by pain and our inability to master it, to own it, to posses that limit. In the case of Astarte and Manfred, and of Heathcliff and Catherine the First, this painful and perpetual going away necessitates social transgression. In fact, social transgression is at the heart of the trope of shared blood. The taint of incest is both symbolic and historical, temporal and eternal.

"Adultery was not, bigamy was not, incest was not a temporal crime" (Pollock and Maitland 2:372) but a matter for the ecclesiastical courts, not the lay courts. From the twelfth century until the repeal of the Test and Corporation Acts of 1828 incest was a spiritual matter, not a legal one. In fact, it was not until 1906 that incest became a civil crime in England though it was a source of anxiety, particularly middle class anxiety, over the sexual practices of the rural and urban poor.[1] In Catholic cannon law, the Anglican ecclesiastical, "bawdy" courts, or the civil law, incest was a prohibition to marry, close cousins or a dead husband's brother for example, because incest was a transgression against the structure of the natural family. The seedier reality of rural poverty and urban squalor, of bodies crammed beside each other in drafty cottages in Yorkshire and tenements in Birmingham, the rape of younger children by older children—the genuine despair of it all is not part of *Manfred* or *Wuthering Heights*.

The trope of shared blood tells us far more about the development of domesticity than it does about the reality of incest in the early Victorian period. For above all, the trope of blood, with its sublime impossibility, defines both couples as anti domestic, as outside the economy of marriage, property, and respectability. These two seminal texts both deal with the sublime fantasy of gender erasure through unity. But how they construct the sublime absence so necessary for sublime love, and how they overcome, or do not overcome, this absence, represents a distinct literary and historical departure.

The rhetoric of Byronic resistance to a domestic trajectory creates the tension that defines the whole novel, the tension between Wuthering Heights and Thrushcross Grange, the gothic and the domestic. The first transgression is one of genre: Catherine the first wants to mix the gothic and the domestic. For after her first brush with the ideal middle class domesticity of the Lintons, she tells the family servant, Nelly (the real narrator of *Wuthering Heights*), "you think me a selfish wretch; but did it never strike you that if Heathcliff and I married, we should be beggars? whereas, if I marry Linton, I can aid Heathcliff to rise, and place him out of my brother's power" (101). Nelly calls it the "worst motive you've given yet for being the wife of young Linton" (101). The matronly nurse is, after all, the voice that transforms the novel from a Byronic Romantic to a Victorian domestic rhetoric. Catherine's answer to Nelly's remonstrance gives a sense of the generic divide:

> What were the use of my creation if I were entirely contained here? My great miseries in this world have been Heathcliff's miseries, and I watched and felt each from the beginning: my great thought in living is himself. If all else perished, and *he* remained, *I* should still continue to be, and if all else remained, and he were annihilated, the universe would turn to a mighty stranger: I should not seem a part of it.... Nelly, I *am* Heathcliff! [102].

It is tempting to read her claim of union figuratively, as an expression of undying love in the face of social difficulties, instead of literally, as what "actually exists on the surface" (Armstrong *Desire* 187). But if we follow the italics, Brontë gives us the linguistic equivalent of an equation: "*he*" + "*I*" + "*am*." Catherine is not simply sublimating their love, but in the most literal sense she is the same character framed by the social parallax of gender, but ultimately as Byronic as he. She even echoes Manfred's famous opening monologue, "Good, or evil, life, / Powers, passions, all I see in other beings, / Have been to me as rain unto the sands" (1.1.21–23). For the Byronic hero, the universe must always become Brontë's "mighty stranger." Even more, Brontë is retelling one of the key moments in *Manfred*, the fantasy of shared blood with its inherently sublime and transgressive union: "my great thought of living is in himself"; if all else is void, empty, "perished," I continue through him, for "Nelly, I *am* Heathcliff."

They have to die, of course. The Byronic heroes—Catherine the First and Heathcliff—must become ghosts of the sublime and transgressive trope of shared blood, the mixing of gender desire, the mélange of subjectivities. As perpetual exiles, they wander in the words of others: "the country folks, if you ask them, would swear on the Bible that he [Heathcliff] *walks*.... Yet that old man [Joseph] by the kitchen fire affirms he has seen two on 'em, looking out of his chamber window, on every rainy night since his death" (413–14). They are the disassembled signifiers of resistance to a developing culture of marriage, family, and respectability and thus exist through "chamber window[s]" and "on every rainy night since his death." The *Wuthering Heights* of the first Catherine and Heathcliff is a haunting. They are reminders of an enclosed Byronic rhetoric, canceled ways of speaking and being. That is why they both are so tragically defiant in language. They are like Manfred in the final scene, when facing death he refuses to acknowledge the demons of guilt that have come for him:

> *Thou* didst not tempt me, and thou couldst not tempt me;
> I have not been thy dupe, nor am thy prey—
> But was my own destroyer, and will be
> My own hereafter [3.4.137–40].

Or after Nelly comes to the dying Heathcliff with admonitions to turn back to the Bible because "from the time you were thirteen years old you have lived a selfish, unchristian life" (410), and he replies by demanding one last sacrilege "to the scandal of the whole neighborhood" (413), his burial beside Catherine. "No minister need come, nor need anything be said over me—I tell you I have nearly attained *my* heaven; and that of others is altogether unvalued and uncoveted by me" (410). It is the italicized "*my*" that is the final Byronic gesture: "*my* heaven," *my* desire over "*Thou*." Their shared defiance, however, hides a much deeper division between Byron's *Manfred* and Brontë's *Wuthering Heights*.

The Ghosts of Two Rhetorics

The tale of Heathcliff and the first Catherine's transgressive union is not as Byronic as it first seems. Though as we have seen, on one rhetorical level, the unimpeachable, transgressive unity of Catherine and Heathcliff forms a singular Byronic resistance to a domestic trajectory that finally marks the novel. On another rhetorical level, they form the foundation for their domesticated heirs, Catherine the Second and Hareton. So while Catherine and Heathcliff are ghosts of a historical, generic, and ideological shift, they are also the foundation and ideal of the domestic order. This is where Brontë rewrites the Byronic legacy and genealogy. For though both Manfred and Heathcliff are searching for ghosts, Byron's ghost is very different from Heathcliff's. In *Manfred*, Astarte is absence itself, an emptiness. When Manfred is able to resurrect her in the second act she comes as the "Phantom of Astarte" and gives him the prophecy of his death:

> PHANTOM: Manfred! To-morrow ends thine earthly ills.
>   Farewell!
> MANFRED: Yet one word more—am I forgiven?
> PHANTOM: Farewell!
> MANFRED: Say, shall we meet again?
> PHANTOM: Farewell!
> MANFRED: One word for mercy! Say, thou lovest me.
> PHANTOM: Manfred! [2.4.153–57].

Astarte turns into Gulnare; she fails at gender recognition. Manfred goes to Astarte so that she will "reflect or represent" the "postures of the masculine subject" (Butler 61), but instead of getting an "I love you so much. Of course I forgive you, my one true soul," only his name and his death are reflected. That is to say, he only sees himself.

Byron thus chooses emptiness instead of total union and wholeness with the female other; he negates Manfred's entire quest, his purpose. As Terence Hoagwood points out, Manfred's refusal to accept political and social reality as transcendental truth puts him in direct conflict with the emerging middle class Victorian reign of domesticity.[2] In the "mental theater" of *Manfred*, Hoagwood writes, "No transcendent voice is possible that would be able to make any answer absolute, and no means exist to make of any perspective or opinion (*doxa*) a transcendent truth" (42). The ultimate truth Manfred is seeking is the transcendental truth of love, the androgynous union of souls, and he is seeking it beyond life itself. Instead, he finds only his desire, his own empty fantasy. In this sense, Manfred is a retelling of Conrad's trajectory in *The Corsair*, but internally, in poetic language itself. As in *The Corsair*, the female object (Gulnare and Astarte) proves to be a literal "Phantom" of that fantasy.

Whether we call Manfred's quest "androgyny," like Baer, or the trope of shared blood, it is, as Hoagwood suggests, an "opinion (*doxa*)" transformed into "transcendent truth." According to Bourdieu, the doxa ("δόξα" or common opinion) expresses economic, class, gender order as a universal, natural ruling order. The doxa of domesticity is middle class

Victorian marriage turned anachronistically into natural law, the point and purpose of the social order. It becomes the means and ends of nature, history, and God. But the heart of the doxa (just like nature, God, and history) is always absent. Middle class domesticity "aims, without ever entirely succeeding at restoring the primal state of innocence of doxa,"(Bourdieu 169) pure union, where the mutilation of gendering, "the divided consciousness" (Baer 29), is transmuted by the alchemy of love into wholeness. Bourgeois marriage is the orthodox emanation of the unreachable innocence and promise of the doxa. It is a ghost in the text, a fleeting glimpse, and for Byron's aristocratic rebel, death.

Brontë gives us a very different kind of ghost. Heathcliff never gives up the dream of unity with Catherine, and in the end he gets it. The unity of Catherine and Heathcliff at the conclusion of *Wuthering Heights* is therefore both an exorcism of Byronic liberation—a grave in which to bury it—and one of the rhetorical foundations of middle class love and domesticity. In Heathcliff's confession to Nelly of his nearly necromantic intrusion into Catherine's burial site, there is a clear division between the Phantom of Astarte and Catherine. Byron's ghost is an empty poetic rhetoric; Catherine's ghost is a physical manifestation of the poetic language of gender unity. As Heathcliff wrenched at the coffin lid (as he previously wrenched at the lattice), the physical presence of Catherine returns to him: "There was another sigh, close at my ear. I appeared to feel the warm breath of it displacing the sleet-laden wind. I knew no living thing in flesh and blood was by; but as certainly as you perceive the approach to some substantial body in the dark ... so certainly I felt that Cathy was there: not under me, but on the earth" (356). Though he knows there is no "flesh and blood" nearby, there is the "approach of some substantial body." Again the question is: where is the blood?

The answer is: in the words. For what has outlasted the grave and cheated death is Heathcliff's and the first Catherine's figurative language, Byron's poetics of undying, eternal love, made into "some substantial body." In the plot of *Wuthering Heights*, the rewriting of Byron's "one heart" becomes material, like the bleeding ghost of Catherine. It transmutes Byron's poetic and figurative language into the emerging realist, domestic novel tradition. Brontë's poetics are drawn from Byron, but have a completely different trajectory. At the end of Manfred's search for forgiveness and love, he finds only empty words unable to hide his own name—"Manfred!" Brontë's Heathcliff and Catherine, however, speak Byronic tropes of societal opposition in order to subtly reinforce the very foundation of the Victorian doxa of domesticity—transcendent love as the union of man and woman. It is, as we see in movies, books, and TV shows today, the very foundation of the modern family.

Brontë's novel incorporates Byronic poetics in order to turn sublime transgression into the material and matrimonial language of Victorian domesticity. The full import of the transgeneric properties of *Wuthering Heights* is clear in how the oppositional tropes associated with Heathcliff and the First Catherine—total union versus the norms of society—will seamlessly become the structure of a domestic enclosure that marks the Victorian domestic space of their heirs, Catherine the Second (the daughter of Edgar Linton and Catherine the First) and Hareton (Earnshaw's son, adopted by Heathcliff).

In Catherine the Second and Hareton, the aggressive outside of the commercial, masculine world and the pacific, feminine home will exist in a parallax that is joined together by transgeneric language. For Brontë has transformed the figural poetic language of the Byronic into a domestic, realist language that transcends the limitations of *Manfred's* "mental theater" by "congealing" (Marx 316) its rhetoric into a new commodity—one that is ultimately defined by the values of the Victorian middle class. As the middle class was consolidating power inside its subjects by regulating desire through female moral surveillance, the language of matrimonial love turns into an orthodoxy, a discursive naturalization of a social and economic formula. Middle class marriage and all its virtues—thrift, cleanliness, sentimentality, and religious observance—came to reflect God's plan and nature's demands for everyone.

The trope of shared blood, one of the weirdest and most anti-domestic of poetic fancies, became a way to write the developing family under the regime of the middle class. "True love," and "family" join with nature and God in hiding the real productive power: capital markets, industrialization, and the growing nation state needed to manage a modern economy and the empire it created. Brontë uses the Byronic "us against the world" rhetoric in *Wuthering Heights* to enclose Heathcliff and Catherine the First's heirs in an insular and aggressive domesticity, the competitive family unit. This unit is all too familiar to us. It is embedded in seemingly infinite cultural manifestations—novels, movies, TV, political rhetoric, giant subdivisions and suburbs, government spending, and tax policy. Which brings us back to the question I have asked over and over: where is the blood? The intense violence and transgression that marked *Manfred* and the doomed lovers in *Wuthering Heights* hides the real blood of the working classes and imperial subjects. That is what it costs to build a house fit for a lady.

A House Fit for a Lady: The Inside and Outside of Love

In the closing chapters of *Wuthering Heights*, the sexual transgression that characterizes the Byronic gothic is displaced into moral education. It is the female supervision in the domestic sphere that transforms the space of the text from Byronic gothic into a domestic novel.[3] Ghosts, domestic abuse, and a textual space that has no inside / outside dichotomy start to change, not surprisingly, with reading. Like Wentworth, Hareton is domesticated through language, through the symbolic made material. For Hareton's and the second Catherine's relationship begins with an angry dispute over books. He is illiterate, and she mocks him for it. In an aggressively hectoring but also hopeful gesture, she makes her first real attempt at domesticating "a dog ... or a cart-horse" (382). She replaces the books he burnt after she mocked him for trying to read. But he does not take the bait, and refuses any of her gestures of reconciliation and domestication.

It is only when his gun backfires, splintering into his arm, and he is left defenseless by the fireside that Catherine's aggression begins to transform Hareton (whom Heathcliff tells Nelly is the personification of his youth) into a model of Victorian manhood—where aggression does not exist internal to the domestic, but outside it. Interestingly enough, it begins with an act of minor violence:

> "Let me take that pipe," she said, cautiously advancing her hand and abstracting it from his mouth.
> Before he could attempt to recover it, it was broken and behind the fire [385].

The breaking of the pipe, a purely masculine emblem, is the beginning of the transformation of the novel's space. It happens, as so much does in the novel, in the kitchen of Wuthering Heights. It is the first breaking of old habits—pipes, illiteracy, guns, and dogs—that changes the spatial landscape of the kitchen into a domestic space.

But the economy of domestication goes both ways. For after the short dispute, there is a minor sexual exchange that marks the new economy of domestication. On learning that Hareton had taken her part against Heathcliff:

> She returned to the hearth, and frankly extended her hand. He blackened and scowled like a thunder-cloud, and kept his fists resolutely clenched, and his gaze fixed on the ground. Catherine, by instinct, must have divined it was obdurate perversity, and not dislike, that prompted this dogged conduct; for, after remaining an instant undecided, she stooped and impressed on his cheek a gentle kiss [386].

Brontë's language is exquisitely employed in this scene of transition. There is an aggressively masculine, even Byronic, countenance "blackened and scowled like a thunder-cloud" with fists clinched. Domestic education is the goal and Catherine, by "instinct," understands that his "dogged" behavior—his association with beasts duly noted—must be transformed by a kiss. But not only a kiss: she "impressed on his cheek a gentle kiss." The impression of the "gentle" is what is key to the beginning of the transformation of Hareton from aggressive outside masculinity to domesticated inside masculinity—a Wentworth in training.[4] It is also here that the economy of sexual pleasure, even if it is but the impression "on his cheek [of] a gentle kiss," works to recreate Hareton. A gentle kiss replaces cheeks that were "blackened and scowled like a thunder-cloud." As with the breaking of the pipe and the aggressive insertion of the gentle, there is a more subtle violence, one that Armstrong sees as making up the structure of the ideology of the domestic that will mark Victorian domestic novels to come. It is the enclosure of desire into domesticated, controlled, respectable forms of individual performance. It is a domestic enclosure, where masculine aggression has no place and yet is indispensable.

In fact, the power of the domestic is inconceivable without masculine aggression. It is literally inconceivable because without the violent competition of the outside, the passive stability of the inside would become meaningless. In Armstrong's chapter on the Victorian domestic novel from *How Novels Think*, "Why a Good Man Is Hard to Find in Victorian Fiction," Freud's concept of displacement is brought to bear on the transformation of the aggressive male subject into the passive domestic partner that, one imagines, will be good for women readers. The displacement functions by projecting traits of masculine aggression onto female heroines, "where those features could be sensationally objectified and their potential for violence eliminated" (81). There is no better example of male violence being eliminated by projecting it onto female heroines than the second Catherine's taming of Hareton: breaking the pipe, impressing on him her gentleness, and eventually, most importantly, teaching him how to read and dress. Except here violence is neither sensationalized nor eliminated, but instead it is institutionalized as domestic economy. The relationship between Catherine Linton and Hareton Earnshaw is marked by a more specific, ideological violence: the domestic enclosure of the Byronic gothic.

That is to say, *Wuthering Heights* is transgeneric, rewriting Byronic gothic into domestic realism. Within the confines of Wuthering Heights before Heathcliff's madness and death, sexual desire and masculine (as well as feminine) aggression circulate freely, as openly as they do in *Manfred*. After his death, however, the domestic enclosure transforms the last bastion of gothic sensibility, the house atop the wild moor, into a typical Victorian home. But what makes this transformation important for us is the way in which the space and identity of the gothic is changed according to the necessary distinction between the pacific domestic inside and the masculine outside. This is borne out in the distinction between the Grange and Wuthering Heights, which are spatial metaphors for generic differences. The Grange is domestic while Wuthering Heights is gothic; eventually, the Grange will occupy its rival—Wuthering Heights will be domesticated. As Lyn Pykett points out in *Emily Brontë*, "embedded within this Gothic framework [of *Wuthering Heights*] … is a second narrative, which seems to move progressively in the direction of Victorian Domestic Realism" (76), one in which Hareton and the second Catherine find themselves in "a private realm of domesticity, where social, co-operative values are renewed within the bosom of the family" (77). In the move to "social, co-operative values" there is another violence, another kind of prison than the one Catherine experiences after her marriage to Linton Heathcliff. It is more subtle, more lasting, and more insidious because the making of the domestic demands a violence that is "embedded" in the creation of "a private realm of domesticity."

If we take an example of the Byronic gothic space of Wuthering Heights from Mr. Lockwood's first encounter with the house and juxtapose it with its domestication at the novel's close, we will see the constrictive violence of the inside / outside structure of the domestic enclosure. As with Byron's *Manfred*, Heathcliff's Wuthering Heights is a gothic space where the domestic inside and aggressive outside, comingle. Mr. Lockwood's initial encounter with the gothic space in the kitchen of Wuthering Heights still marks an uneasy, even violent, interchange between the outside world of masculine aggression and the inside world of domestic stability:

> I observed no signs of roasting, boiling, or baking, about the huge fireplace; nor any glitter of copper saucepans and tin cullenders on the walls. One end, indeed, reflected splendidly both light and heat from ranks of immense pewter dishes, interspersed with silver jugs and tankards, towering row after row, on a vast oak dresser, to the very roof. The latter had … a frame of wood laden with oatcakes and clusters of legs of beef, mutton, and ham…. Above the chimney were sundry villainous old guns and a couple of horse pistols: and, by way of ornament, three gaudily painted canisters disposed along its ledge…. In an arch under the dresser reposed a huge liver-coloured bitch pointer, surrounded by a swarm of squealing puppies; and other dogs haunted other recesses [5–6].

This passage is an explicit description of a domestic space where the inside / outside dichotomy is in abeyance. There are "no signs of roasting, boiling, or baking"—no signs of the domestic. There is kitchenware, but instead of genteel "copper saucepans" or "tin cullenders," hearty "pewter dishes" and "silver jugs and tankards" tower on an enormous oak dresser, which "reflected splendidly" the "light and heat" from the hearth fire, the ultimate symbol for domestic stability. At the beginning of the description it seems as if the domestic is utterly absent. Yet, in a reversal that maintains the ultimate instability of the gothic space where there is no clear distinction between inside and outside, there is food. The food, however, seems to have no relation to the preparation, and it is mostly meat: "legs of beef, mutton, and ham." In fact, if we simply follow Mr. Lockwood's descriptive associations, they are tied to the outside of masculine aggression. For "[a]bove the chimney were sundry villainous old guns and a couple of horse pistols," which suggest the external, aggressive world of masculine accumulation of means. Nor are these show-rifles traditionally placed above the mantle. They are villainous, sundry, and, one assumes, retired from service due to long usage.

But the guns' connection to the fire and the food again suggest the interrelation between the feminine domestic and the masculine outside. This is driven home by the passage's final image, "the liver-coloured bitch pointer, surrounded by a swarm of squealing puppies; and other dogs [that] haunted other recesses." With the dog and her puppies, we have a domestic scene traditionally anthropomorphized. But the language does not speak to stability and security. "The liver-coloured bitch" (again, associations of meat) is not surrounded by a merry or playful brood, but by a "swarm of squealing puppies." Even the sibilant consonants move the image to its baleful conclusion: the "other dogs [that] haunted other recesses." The dogs, associated throughout the novel with hunting and snapping at strangers, are part of the domestic as well as the aggressive outside. Throughout the novel, the gothic space engenders both male and female aggression that is neither purely masculine nor purely domestic.

This is not the case with domestic enclosure. In the conclusion to *Wuthering Heights*, when Mr. Lockwood returns to the top of the moor at the end of the novel, this witness to the bleeding ghost of Catherine discovers a definitive change wrought by the cultivating and civilizing power of the domestic:

> The male speaker began to read: he was a young man respectably dressed and seated at a table, having a book before him. His handsome features glowed with pleasure, and his eyes kept impatiently wandering from the page to a small white

hand over his shoulder, which recalled him by a smart slap on the cheek.... Its owner stood behind; her light, shining ringlets blending, at intervals, with his brown locks, as she bent to superintend his studies [378].

The passage playfully illustrates a restraint and control based on a strict maintenance of gender roles. The "male speaker" must be kept on task, kept from his impatient "wandering" by "a smart slap" from his female superintendent. In the newly domesticated kitchen "her light, shining ringlets [are] blending, at intervals, with his brown locks," suggesting the fantasy of the blended subjectivities, the trope of shared blood, the incestuous sublime realized by these first cousins. Their union is not, however, the wild spirits roaming the moors in a unity of Byronic defiance, but they are still dangerous.

As Lockwood finds out, this new domestic gentility does not exclude masculine violence. In fact, it creates that violence. Hareton's aggression maintains the enclosure, as Lockwood realizes when the two lovers leave for a walk on the moors: "I supposed I should be condemned in Hareton Earnshaw's heart, if not by his mouth, to the lowest pit in the infernal regions, if I showed my unfortunate person in his neighborhood" (379). The aggression Lockwood imagines will be his lot if he encroaches on the two lovers is created by the domestic enclosure itself. To have domestic intimacy, the "blending" (378) of locks, the enclosure must keep outside forces (whether a male rival or the larger pressures of social and economic life) away through aggression. The domestic enclosure needs external aggression to maintain its privileged position—whether in the local or transnational marketplace.

For Hareton Earnshaw, maintaining the domestic enclosure, "his neighborhood," means keeping the outside out; whereas for Catherine, it entails keeping intimacy and stability on the inside. Thus both subjectivities are defined and limited by roles that maintain the domestic enclosure. The forced limitations, the roles that must be played, are violent foreclosures of individual potentials; and, like steam pressure, the violence must go somewhere. Therefore, Armstrong is absolutely correct about the centrality of displacement in Victorian novels. But it is not fundamentally a displacement that hides a contradiction in masculine representation by superimposing it on feminine grotesques. The deeper displacement works to hide the violence of subject creation that the ideology of the domestic imposes on both men and women. This violence is displaced to an outside that threatens the domestic stability, which of course creates the dichotomy of inside / outside and thus the violence in the first place.

The transcendental love of Heathcliff and Catherine becomes the foundation for a new form of opposition in which the domestic enclosure protects against the aggressive outside. This inside / outside dichotomy is internalized and institutionally sanctioned through the union of Catherine the second and Hareton. As Lockwood "grumbled" to himself, watching Catherine the second and Hareton approaching him for the last time, "*They* are afraid of nothing.... Together they would brave Satan and his legions" (415).[5] Lockwood's final image and pronouncement on Catherine the second and Hareton is telling. It is not a picture of their abiding love, their mutual understanding "where social, co-operative values are renewed within the bosom of the family" (Pykett 77), but an image of violence, of braving "Satan and his legions." Their unity is one of opposition. A "*They*" (note again the italics) is created by their being "afraid of nothing ... together." They are a unity in opposition, both acting out aggression and passivity according to their appropriate gender roles: Catherine aggressively in control of Hareton's ongoing domestication inside the house and Hareton aggressively in control outside the home. The transcendental power of their love, symbolized by their upcoming nuptials and the blending of locks, unifies their gendered functions, making each a partner in a collective opposition to anything that threatens their developing domestic enclosure, even the sickly Lockwood. This final image of these Victorian heirs to Byronic passion, however reconfigured by Brontë, is one of opposition and violence, not bucolic love. In rewriting of the gothic and Byronic love of Heathcliff and Catherine the first Brontë uses the transgeneric language of poetry to unveil the ideological center of the doxa of domesticity: a transcendental love which promises unity while ossifying gender roles.

Brontë's writing on (and critique of) the domestic enclosure will resonate through the secret history of romance masculinity as it moves through domestic novels into the works of the romance revival.[6] Brontë's use of transgeneric, figurative language became a realist, material bridge between conflicting Byronic Romantic and Victorian value systems. It might be helpful, however, to stop and think about what that means for a moment, "a material bridge." I mean that the book(s), the material text, is a physical bridge, consumed by readers (up to today) that relives the transition from one kind of rhetorical being to another—Byronic Romanticism to domestic. This commodification of the text mystifies, however, another commodification, that of the Byronic hero and the rhetoric around him. As Elfenbein points out, what marks the Byronic after the death of the author is his monetization, his selling, and the potential return on investment he still offers authors and movie producers. Byron is forever, it seems, up for sale in the fantasy marketplace. That is because his commodification is part of the way we imagine masculine potential. He is part of our gendered fantasy economy.

This larger economy is divided into two self-labeled systems of value: domestic and adventure fiction. The rise of genres and book marketing in the nineteenth century was a testament to how this fantasy economy generated real money, and thus real power. But the history of these genres also frame what persons in any given historical moment think and feel about who they are in the world and what that person has the potential to do. As Marx points out in *German Ideology*, "language is practical consciousness" (158) and is thus a "social product," a commodity. As commodity its use value is in its practice. But like any other social product, it is in a constant state of exchange and transformation, repackaging and consumption. Byronic rhetoric circulates through different genres, and that circulation will elucidate a great deal about how the raw and infinite experience of being in the world is produced, sold, and used by real people. As we will see, two dueling concepts about how literary rhetoric circulates and what that circulation means will unsettle the literary marketplace of the late Victorian period. It will sever domestic realism from the romance revival, drawing clear distinctions between "women's writing" and "men's writing." Nor was it an abstract, academic conversation. In the grand Victorian style, it was a scandal of sorts, a story of wounded egos and dueling pens played out in periodicals for all to read. The players were serious and the game was deep. The defender of domestic realism was Henry James, and arguing for the revival of the romance was an upstart provocateur, Robert Louis Stevenson.

CHAPTER THREE

Bad Romancers

Domestic Enclosures
in George Eliot's *Middlemarch*
and H. Rider Haggard's *She*

> For in the multitude of middle-aged men who go about their vocations in a daily course determined for them much in the same way as the tie of their cravats, there is always a good number who once meant to shape their own deeds and alter the world a little.
> —George Eliot, *Middlemarch*

> English life is surrounded by conventionalism, and English fiction has come to reflect the conventionalism.
> —H. Rider Haggard, "About Fiction"

Today, looking back over more than one hundred years of literary and cultural history, it is easier to see how these nineteenth century genres—the domestic and the adventure—structure a still deeply gendered, media marketplace. The domestic and the adventure are more like supra genres because they form the linguistic foundations of so many other sub-genres: romantic comedy, the novellas of daytime television, and the classic family sitcom, or, on the other hand, spy, hard boiled fiction, and blockbuster summer action movies. The 1880s is a defining moment in the history of these supra genres. For their tropes are calcified at the start of the age of mass literacy and mass marketing. Unless we are willing to follow the path of endless regression back though the eighteenth-century novels of sentiment as well as the picaresque, back to the rebirth of comedic and tragic rhetoric on the French and Early Modern English stage, backward again to Dante, Medieval romances, the *lettres d'amour* of Abelard and Heloise, to Homer and to the Bible, the exchange between Henry James and Robert Louis Stevenson is a good place to start. It also is a good place for us to start because the argument between Stevenson and James highlights the rhetoric of romance and its relationship to domestic fiction. That relationship allows us to see the limits of the rhetoric of romance masculinity inside and outside the Victorian ideology of the middle-class family. Specifically, we will see how the rhetoric functions on the inside in George Elliot's *Middlemarch: A Study of Provincial Life* (1871–72) and how the rhetoric of romance masculinity is limited on the outside, literally, in H. Rider Haggard's *She: A History of Adventure* (1886–87).

In 1884, *Longman's Magazine* published two essays that encapsulated the division and interconnection between the Victorian domestic novel and the literature of the emerging romance revival. In September of 1884, *Longman's* published Henry James's essay "The Art of Fiction," which was in response to Walter Basant's lecture, "Fiction as One of the Fine Arts." The spat that followed had it its roots in the conclusion of the essay, where James claims that though Robert Louis Stevenson's *Treasure Island* (1883) is "delightful," he ultimately must say "no" to it as a work of art (403). It is not a work of art because it is not true *as* life. "George Eliot," James writes, "when she painted that country, I always said 'yes'" (403). For James, fiction is art when it becomes life and when it fails, he must say no. The next month Stevenson penned his reply, "A Humble Remonstrance," which also appeared in *Longman's*. Beneath these charming and virtuoso performances lie the defining philosophies of domestic fiction and adventure fiction—the way in which reality is commodified and sold back to us as our own thinking.

For Henry James, "the only reason for the existence of a novel is that it does compete with life. When it relinquishes this attempt, the same attempt that we see on the canvas of the painter, it will have arrived at a very strange pass" (378). According to James, the novel must hide its own historical reality in order to tell the story of its own transformation from human production (the text) to natural object. That is why James critiques Trollope for outing one of his narrators and thus disgracing his "sacred office" (379), of being a reality. The entire point of fiction is to show to the reader what reality is. This mystification of the difference between life and the novel, therefore, is not merely aesthetic—it is the *rasion d'être* of the novel's aesthetics. It is the "art of fiction" itself:

> I may therefore venture to say that the air of reality (solidity of specification) seems to be the supreme virtue of a novel—the merit on which all its other merits ... helplessly and submissively depend. If it be not there they are all as nothing, and if these be there, they owe their effect to the success with which the author has produced the illusion of life [390].

Three. Bad Romancers

The desire to both create the "air of reality," or the "solidity of specification," and at the same time hide its manufacture makes the novel into an organic object, "a living thing, all one and continuous, like every other organism" (392). For James, the organic reality of the novel "*does* compete" (James's italic) with life not only because of its organic reality—its formal components interacting in harmony—but because it is history (378). For James, "the only effectual way to lay it [suspicions against fiction as art] to rest is to … insist on the fact that as the picture is reality, so the novel is history" (379). The novel is the place where the history of human life is reproduced as harmony and beauty, as a painting. The "illusion of life," "the air of reality," "the solidity of specificity," in other words, the aesthetics of the novel frame, like a painting, a historical perspective only to transform it back though the mystery of art into and organic reality as life itself.

While James sees fiction as art, Robert Louis Stevenson sees it in more brutal terms: as an enclosure of life by the history of its own production, by genre. Fiction, for Stevenson, is nothing more than a way to reduce, to enclose, to trap the energy of life. That enclosure, the commodification of life in fiction, is narration. Rejecting the delineations between genres, for Stevenson, poetry, nonfiction, and fiction are "neither more nor less than the art of narrative" (366). And narrative is the only unifying function of literary art not because it replicates life, but because it seeks to contain and control it. Narrative does not "'compete with life'" (James qtd. in Stevenson 367), as James would have it, but works instead "to half-shut [the reader's] eyes against the dazzle and confusion of reality" (368). Life has little to do with art, painting or otherwise. For "life goes before us," Stevenson argues, "infinite in complication; attended by the most various and surprising meteors; appealing at once to the eye, to the ear, to the mind—the seat of wonder, to the touch—so thrillingly delicate, and to the belly—so imperious when starved" (368). Life is the silent drive of hunger, thunder claps of fear, unspeaking tastes and unspeakable feelings. Narratives, whether fictional or poetic, are not about the world, "infinite in complication," but about other narratives.

Stevenson argues that "our art is occupied, and bound to be occupied, not so much in making stories true as in making them typical; not so much in capturing the lineaments of each fact, as in marshaling all of them towards a common end" (369). This "common end" is not an "air of reality" or an "illusion of life" (James 390), but a substitution of the infinite real for the very finite enclosure of fictional narrative. "For the welter of impressions," Stevenson goes on to write, "all forcible but all discreet, which life presents, it [fictional narrative] substitutes a certain artificial series of impressions, all indeed most feebly represented, but all aiming at the same effect, all eloquent of the same idea, all chiming together like consonant notes in music or like the graduated tints in a good picture" (369). The narration speaks to its own limitations—the "same effect" and "same idea." But it is in fact these very limitations, this endless reproduction of infinite reality's simulacra, that makes narrative recognizable and even possible. And this reproduction is generic.

Henry James shrugs off the old eighteenth-century distinctions between novels of character and novels of incident because in genuine works of art both are so organically interwoven: incident is character and character is incident. For Stevenson, all that is real about fictional art is genre, and according to him there are three main genres,

> the novel of adventure, which appeals to certain almost sensual and quite illogical tendencies in man; the second, the novel of character, which appeals to our intellectual appreciation of man's foibles and mingled and inconstant motives; and third, the dramatic novel ... [which] appeals to our emotional nature and moral judgment [370].

By the 1880s, the novel of character and the dramatic novel seem to me elements of Victorian domestic realism. Whether it is an "intellectual appreciation" of our inconstant motives or an appeal "to our emotional nature and moral judgment," domestic realism is about social and moral conduct, which for James is nothing less than reality itself. "Grey" is how Franco Moretti describes domestic fiction, indicative of "something dark, cold, impassable, silent, heavy" (74). Romance, on the other hand, suggests heat and passion, movement, and explosions of violence that are accompanied by the lightness of the episodic. Elaine Showalter describes the sudden reemergence of romance after the publication of *Treasure Island* in book form in the fall of 1883 as a "men's literary revolution" (79), what Andrew Lang called King Romance.

This argument between James and Stevenson over the yes or no of romance is an argument about late Victorian life itself. Whether fiction is an organic representation of that totality as James would have it or genre is the enclosure of unrepresentable reality as Stevenson imagines, fiction takes part in the structuring of reality. It "substitutes," as Stevenson writes, "a certain artificial series of impressions, all indeed most feebly represented, but all aiming at the same effect, all eloquent of the same idea, all chiming together like consonant notes in music or like the graduated tints in a good picture" (369). For nineteenth-century middle-class men and women, the readers and writers of fiction, that "same effect, all eloquent of the same idea, all chiming together" is the domestic order, which animates every level of the Victorian life. It is a totalizing expression of society. Stevenson takes James's premise that fiction orders life and raises the stakes. It is not life, for Stevenson, but a simulacra of life, a mode of thinking that controls life. In the context of Victorian domestic orthodoxy, adventure fiction is "sensual and quite illogical" (370) because it is anti-domestic. For James, *Treasure Island* is a no and for George Eliot is always a yes because adventure fiction falls outside the shaping reality of domestic fiction. It is a form of thinking that does not fit. It is a rebellion.

Romance thinking is a heretical way to think inside of the Victorian domestic orthodoxy. It is a remainder of the Byronic hero, a particularly masculine voice of transgression and rebellion. We are going to look at that rebellion's failure in language, the victory of the domestic enclosure over romance thinking. But the repression of romance thinking inside domesticity only outlines a deeper historical failure to articulate masculine desire inside the dominant historical framework of domesticity. To Henry James in 1884, adventure fiction and its heretical romance thinking must have seemed an upstart compared to the fine art of domestic, realist fiction. That fantasy marketplace was here to stay. It is here to stay because masculine articulation inside domesticity means a subjection to "the air of reality" (James 390), the domestic enclosure. Whig history, capitalism, and its ideological personification, domesticity, fail to provide its promise of ever-greater happiness and fulfillment for those at the very top of its social construction, bourgeois men. That story is worth hearing because in the supra-genre of adventure fiction, this fissure in domestic ideology creates a commodified resistance that will repeat itself endlessly for the next hundred years. In George Eliot's *Middlemarch* and H. Rider Haggard's *She*, we will hear it.

Money and Marriage

A reading of *Middlemarch* begs a comparison to Pierre Bourdieu's "return of the *azal* [sheep]." For both the petit-bourgeoisie in Eliot's small town in the English Midlands right before the passage of the First Reform Bill (1832) and Bourdieu's description of Kabylia during the Algerian War for Independence (1954–62) are deeply concerned with the rhythm of a totalizing social order. Bourdieu describes the "return of azal," or sheep, from their pastures as an elaborate social movement, occupying every person. "Everything," Bourdieu writes, "without exception, in activates of the men, the women, and the children, is absolutely altered by the adoption of a new rhythm: the movements of the flock, of course, but also the men's work and the domestic activities of the women" (159). The total social experience is an interconnected movement, a ritual as well as a mode of production.

Eliot captures the same rhythm in the petit-bourgeoisie culture of rural England where "old provincial society had its share of this subtle movement."

> Some slipped a little downward, some got higher footing: people denied aspirates, gained wealth, and fastidious gentlemen stood for boroughs; some were caught in political currents, some in ecclesiastical, and perhaps found themselves surprisingly grouped in consequence; while a few personages or families that stood with rock firmness amid all this fluctuation, were slowly presenting new aspects in spite of solidity, and altering with the double change of self and beholder [95].

Eliot's brief Whig history of Middlemarch is suggestive of Bourdieu because of the totality of movement, the rhythm of human relations to one another and to the community. On the surface, the similarity ends there. For Bourdieu's Kabylia is a pastoral world with a direct relationship to its most important commodity, *azal*, where Eliot's Middlemarch is a world of investment, return, rise and fall, risk, failure, success, and class transformation, "the double change of self and beholder"—the world of capitalism.

Both rhythms, however, are reflections of the flow of commodities and fluctuations of exchange, for just as the "activities of the men, the women, and the children [are] absolutely altered by the adoption of a new rhythm" (159) so too do the inhabitants of the fictional Middlemarch adapt as "[m]unicipal town and rural parish gradually made fresh threads of connection—gradually, as the old stocking gave way to the savings-bank, and the worship of the solar guinea became extinct, while squires and baronets, and even lords who had once lived blamelessly afar from the civic mind, gathered the faultiness of closer acquaintanceship" (95).

The flow of commodities, the "return of *azal*," manifests in the social life of the village, in the transformation from an economy founded on land owning aristocrats to one based on consuming, exporting, and importing commodities worldwide—the usurpation of one ruling class by another. The First Reform Bill, which ended the rotten boroughs and the gerrymandered power of a few landed and titled families, was a political inevitability. It was the outcome of an economic movement because "land as a percentage of total national capital" decreased from more than half in 1798 to only seven percent by the beginning of the twentieth century (Kenwood and Lougheed 16) so that "even lords who had once lived blamelessly afar from the civic mind, gathered the faultiness of closer acquaintanceship."

In the town of Middlemarch, the symbolic reality accommodates the material reality, "the double change of self and beholder" (95), through marriage. That is why Eliot's brief economic and social history of her provincial, petit-bourgeois village is sandwiched between ruminations concerning love and marriage by "the young surgeon," Lydgate (95). For Lydgate fails in Middlemarch, and his specific failure, as well as the reasons behind it, illustrates the centrality of domesticity to the English middle class. Like Satan falling through the void, Lydgate illuminates the space where the individual subject is transformed into an objectification of and a commodity for the ruling orthodoxy. The social practices that developed around marriage in Regency and Victorian England were a way to maintain communal continuity through economic transformations and political upheavals (the English Civil War and the Glorious Revolution, the Industrial Revolution and the First and Second Reform Bills, for example) that were naturalized into the domestic doxa; marriage practices provided a middle-class origin myth and thus, anachronistically, the meaning and purpose of the entire Victorian social order. It is no wonder there was no place in the for a deviant poet, Lord Byron, and a lascivious king, George IV: the middle-class family is supposed to be God's reflection in human life, a divine order in itself.

This leads us back to the argument between Henry James and Robert Louis Stevenson in *Longman's Magazine*. For James, fictional language competes with nature, making a rival frame of it in history; for Stevenson, fictional language is an enclosure of life by genre. These two supra-genres make up an orthodox (domestic) and an interrelated heterodox (romance) ways of thinking. To apply Pierre Bourdieu's formulation of social structures, the domestic seeks, "without entirely succeeding," to "restor[e] the primal state of innocence of doxa" (Bourdieu 171), a utopia of harmonious united souls. Romance thinking, on the other, is a "heretical power," like the power of the "sorcerer who wields liberating potency—that of all logotherapies—in offering the means of expressing experiences usually repressed" (Bourdieu 171). The Byronic is a heretical rhetoric, a kind of saying that expresses fantasy practices which only exist in opposition to the domestic doxa. Lydgate's problem in *Middlemarch* is one of genre confusion—he thinks like a romancer inside a strict domestic economy.

Lydgate suffers from a lack of education. Like many characters from romance, Lydgate is an orphan and a dreamer. He's an unfortunate Edward Waverly because his domestic education will not be as romantic and nor will it end nearly as well. But his early life is a masculine idyll, filled with hunting, riding, and books: "He was a quick fellow, and when hot from play, would toss himself in a corner, and in five minutes be deep in any sort of book that he could lay his hands on: if it were Rasselas or Gulliver, so much the better, but Bailey's Dictionary would do ... and it had already occurred to him that books were stuff, and that life was stupid" (143). His valorization of books over the stupidity of life, even setting them apart, places Lydgate in opposition to Eliot's conception of domestic realism, where one learns life from hot play and from books ("German Life" 520). His choices, Johnson and Swift, are satiric romances; one even gets a whiff of an exotic and remote past from Bailey's etymological dictionary. The seed of Lydgate's disastrous marriage, dissolution, failure, and early death is contained in this passage. Because Lydgate is in the wrong genre. Like Byron's Conrad and Manfred, Scott's Waverly, Brontë's Heathcliff, and Dickens's Steerforth before him (as well as Conrad's Kim and Fleming's James Bond after), Lydgate's childhood places him distinctly outside domestic training. It is a recipe, as we shall see often enough, for the rearing of the male romance character.

An education in the domestic produces a very different kind of thinking. Jane Austen's Elizabeth Bennet, for example, is raised to understand how high the stakes are when creating one's own domestic enclosure. The indifferent husband, the neurotic wife, the willful and wayward girls, the endless clatter of the Bennets' house speak to the enclosure of the subject inside the very real walls of the domestic. For a lonely boy like Lydgate, his self-rhetoric is nurtured by his imaginative creation of himself through books. His own masculinity, developing outside of a domestic education, is driven by narrative: the narrative of a purely imagined self-becoming, a way to be an objective self in a world of men. Though this can happen in an infinite number of ways—desire to be a writer, a spy, or, in Lydgate's case, a doctor—it takes the form of a calling beyond the domestic to be more than the husband and wage earner. And Eliot is intensely aware of the relationship between vocation and romance. In Lydgate's case, the accidental discovery of an anatomy book boils into "an intellectual passion" (144) one that, for a time, wholly replaces the need for the domestic doxa to actualize Lydgate's masculinity. For when Lydgate takes the anatomy book from the shelf, "the moment of vocation had come, and before he got down from this chair, the world was made new to him by a presentiment of endless processes filling the vast spaces planked out of his sight by that wordy ignorance which he had supposed to be knowledge" (144).

Lydgate's almost instantaneous decision to become a man of science has the ring of religious conversion. The *tolle lege*, the "take up and read," that becomes the culminating moment in Augustine's conversion to Christianity is repackaged in the language of nineteenth-century science. Lydgate's masculinity is tied to his profession, medicine, and his own sense of his profession is tied to his ability to romance. The metaphoric associations Eliot uses to illuminate Lydgate's professional position are almost entirely drawn from romance: "We are apt to think it the finest era of the world when America was beginning to be discovered, when a bold sailor, even if he were wrecked, might alight on a new kingdom; and about 1829 the dark territories of Pathology were a fine America for a spirited young adventurer" (147). The relationship between adventure, (all male) professions, freedom from domesticity, and the fantasy of an all-masculine world will be emboldened by Muscular Christianity and ultimately coalesce at the end of the nineteenth century into genuine social phenomena: the obsession with field sport and Baden-Powel's Scouting Movement.

"*Middlemarch* is modeled on the sociologist's respect for individual fact," as J. Hillis Miller writes, which means the Midlands before 1832 (129). But when Eliot is actually writing her novel (1869–70), the heretical masculine rhetoric simmering just below the surface has already started bubbling up. Swinburne's *Poems and Ballads* was published to considerable handwringing by the middle-class literary establishment in 1866, and two years later the *Westminster Review* anonymously published Walter Pater's "Poems of William Morris," the first draft of his infamous "Conclusion" to the *Renaissance* (1868) By the romance revival of the 1880s, Lydgate's romance education, which lands him in a bad marriage and wreaked life, had become a way to escape from domesticity.

Romance Education

H. Rider's Haggard *She: A History of Adventure*, (1886) turns the figure of the lonely boy, free from women and domesticity, into the ideal of romance education.[1] In Horace Holly's account of young Leo's formative years at Cambridge, romance education means homosocial paradise. While other such openings for homosocial expression—Defoe's Caribbean island or Stevenson's endless hills of heather in *Kidnapped* (1893), for example—are created by accident, Holly's rearing of Leo is entirely premeditated. He wants a world without women, as he explains, so that "I would have no woman to lord it over me about the child, and steal his affections from me. The boy was old enough to do without female assistance, so I set to work to hunt up a suitable male attendant" (50). This desire for the love of a child to the expressed exclusion of any female caregiver by Holly, a man who defines himself by his acumen for high math, his immense physical strength, and his love of hunting, might suggest a contradiction in representation. However, it is not a contradiction; it is a departure. Historically, it is an inevitable manifestation of the public school system, which had been separating ambitious middle class and upper middle class families for two generations.

This system and its relationship to the fantasy of the Empire, however, congeal around a heretical rhetoric of anti domestic life. For throughout the novel, Horace Holly represents himself as absolutely masculine—indeed, he is so hairy and ugly women are repulsed by him—and as the absolute caregiver, becoming both mother and father to Leo: "We two grew dearer and yet more dear to each other. Few sons have been loved as I love Leo; and few fathers know the deep and continuous affection that Leo bears me" (51). It is a masculine utopia, and what makes this possible is not a radical re conception of the masculine, but a radical denial of the outside / inside dichotomy central to the domestic doxa.

The college, of course, was a place of scholarship, teaching, and competition. Within the traditional logic of the domestic doxa, it was definitively outside, beyond the bounds of the domestic. This is not the case with Haggard's fantasy Cambridge, for as Stephan Arata points out, "Cambridge itself is transformed into an extended domestic sphere, one reimagined on exclusively male terms" (97). They live in apartments very near Cambridge, and Leo grows up amongst the scholars and students of his adopted father's college. This is an idyllic, homosocial Cambridge, one Haggard could only imagine because his father had cut off his education, having decided his son was a dunce. The idyllic Cambridge becomes a masculine utopia by eliminating the inside / outside dichotomy essential to domesticity. As Holly recounts, "in a very short while ... the boy became the favorite of the whole College—where, orders and regulations to the contrary notwithstanding, he was continually in and out—a sort of infant libertine, in whose favor all rules were relaxed" (51).

Leo's movements "in and out" of the college as a young boy create an interconnection between domesticity and work. He is gendered as the classic middle-class Victorian child with hair "pure gold in color and tightly curled over his shapely head" (51). The Cambridge of Holly and Leo is evocative of Brontë's kitchen at Wuthering Heights under Heathcliff. It is a space of free symbolic exchange, where the hairy, ugly man becomes the ideal mother for the feminized child who is still, with golden locks and all, capable of thrashing his working class competition. Loving and gentle, Leo is the ultimate product of the domestic economy: a perfect English child. But the beautiful child is also violent. When Leo was nine or ten, the butcher's son had insulted Holly. Though the "strapping" butcher's boy was much bigger, Leo "thrashed him fairly" while his father cheered him to victory (52). This idyllic homosocial male space is unsustainable. The plot of the novel, the journey to the heart of Africa in search of the primordial She, destroys it.

As Norman Etherington points out, Haggard's "History of Adventure" is an inversion of historical evolution as the late-Victorian Englishman, Haggard, would have imagined it: they journey from "Cambridge, the epitome of high civilization, back though Islamic east Africa to a 'semi savage' people living among the ruins of Kôr, a civilization said to have flourished thousands of years before the rise of Pharaonic Egypt" (xvii). Leo and Holly's quest is to kill She, Ayeshe, or "she-who-must-be-obeyed," in order to settle Leo's family score that goes back to the time of the Ptolemies. These romancers' goal is to assassinate the transcendent figure of domesticity, emanating from her kingdom deep in the heart of ancient, mother Africa. They do not find a primordial femininity, but eternal domesticity. Though She is eternally youthful, capable of killing with her eyes, and able, with the help of a bowl of water, to read the thoughts of others, what she really wants is the perfect husband. It is also a retelling of the Empire's erotic history—Englishmen journeying toward unadulterated sexual pleasure with native women only to find, by the 1880s, their very British, very respectable wives waiting for them at their journey's end. In fact, the entire adventure—the ancient Egyptian legend, the cannibalism, the shipwreck—is merely a prelude for the domestic drama that Holly and Leo find at the end of their search, the totalizing power of the domestic doxa, embodied in "She."

It is just this totalizing power that J. Hills Miller points to as a central semiotic effect of *Middlemarch*'s narration, particularly in Lydgate's courtship and marriage to Rosamond. As Miller sees it, "the metaphor of a web ... is also used repeatedly in [the novel] to describe the texture of the smaller scale entities within the larger social fabric." The lovemaking of Rosamond and Lydgate, for example, is described as "the collective weaving of an intersubjective tissue" (130), or, as Eliot writes it:

> Young love-making—that gossamer web! Even the points it clings to—the things whence its subtle interlacings are swung—are scarcely perceptible; momentary touches of finger tips, meetings of rays from blue and dark orbs, unfinished phrases,

lightest changes of cheek and lip, faintest tremors. The web itself is made of spontaneous beliefs and indefinable joys, yearnings of one life towards another, visions of completeness, indefinite trust. And Lydgate fell to spinning that web from his inward self with wonderful rapidity.... As for Rosamond, she was in the waterlily's expanding wonderment at its own fuller life, and she too was spinning industriously at the mutual web [346].

Byron's and Brontë's trope of shared blood thus informs the language of Lydgate's and Rosamond's fantasy marriage: it is based on "visions of completeness [and] indefinite trust." It is a language that has been repackaged, appropriately, as natural doxa and thus as science.

Eliot's union of "fingertips," "rays" from eyes, and "changes of cheek and lip"—what Miller calls the "intersubjective tissue"—is Brontë's unity of souls and bodies socially merged by the staged process of courtship, engagement, and marriage. This weaving of "the gossamer web" with "subtle interlacings" is a totalizing process that should bring to mind the kitchen at Wuthering Heights where Lockwood sees the second Catherine's "light, shining ringlets blending, at intervals, with his [Hareton's] brown locks, as she bent to superintend his studies" (378). What is more, as Miller goes on to argue, the "parallelism between Eliot's aim as a sociologist of provincial life and the aims of contemporary biologists" (131) replicate human life as a biological interconnection, a manifestation of nature, a doxa. Living inside the totalizing web of the domestic doxa is the domestic enclosure, and Lydgate, with his romancer's flawed education, is bound to find himself inside it. He is, despite himself, a "spirited young adventurer" not in the "the dark territories of Pathology" (147) but in the totalizing web of the domestic doxa. Holly and Leo are right behind him.

Domesticide

As Holly waits for She to step from behind the veil, the tension builds into a string of questions, "Who could be behind it?—some naked savage queen, a languishing Oriental beauty, or a nineteenth-century young lady, drinking afternoon tea" (143), and, as Holly finds out, She is really a "nineteenth-century young lady" as eternal goddess. For her energy, which is connected to all of life's energy, and which gives her immortality and superhuman power, radiates Victorian respectability. She is, as Andrew Stauffer suggests, "perhaps a little ... like Queen Victoria in this regard" (22). Like Rosamond, She will come to exert absolute power over Holly and Leo. She comes to represent the "ominous and inexplicable authority" of the feminine, as Anne McClintock puts it (235–36). That authority is based on a late nineteenth-century British domestic power structure. After being in her presence, Holly, the self proclaimed misogynist, is domesticated: "I worshipped her as never woman was worshipped, and that would give my immortal soul to marry her" (182). He settles on begging for a kiss. She declines, and, as Holly narrates, "reaching out her hand, she held it over my head, and it seemed to me that something flowed from it which chilled me back to common sense, and a knowledge of propriety and the domestic virtues" (182). Distance, that is what Holly finds at the center of the domestic doxa, in the personification of its eternal and natural source, he finds something that "chilled [him] back" to the "domestic virtues."

Lydgate finds a distance, too, at the center of his domestic enclosure with Rosamond. For the illusion of totality, the harmonizing "gossamer web" enwrapping Rosamond and himself, comes to be defined instead by a total distance. After their flirtation is consummated, there is really nothing left: "between him and her indeed there was that total missing of each other's mental track, which is too evidently possible even between persons who are continually thinking of each other" (587). The total union of their courtship becomes a "total missing" because of genre confusion. Lydgate embodies Eliot's critique of Byronic romance masculinity inside the economy of the domestic enclosure, as well as the domestic enclosure itself. He follows the trajectory of Byron's *Corsair* in reverse.

Before his marriage, Lydgate imagines Rosamond as Medora in the first Canto of *The Corsair* and their future as an "ideal happiness ... of the kind known in the Arabian nights ... where everything is given to you and nothing claimed" (351). Rosamond seems to be the embodiment of perfect womanhood, and Lydgate anticipates that she will be a wife "who [would venerate] ... his high musings and momentous labours and would never interfere with them; who would create order in the home and accounts with still magic, yet keep her fingers ready to touch the lute and transform life into romance at any moment" (352). Similarly, Medora, sitting on "the summit of [Conrad's] tower-crowned hill" (1.342), reflects perfectly Conrad's masculine prowess and his vocation as a pirate, because her vocation is to reflect him. For Lydgate that means Rosamund's vocation will be to share his passion for science, "an ardour which he had fancied that the ideal wife must somehow worship as sublime" (587). She does not, and that is how the domestic enclosure kills Lydgate.[2]

Lydgate's heretical romance vocabulary ("magic," "romance," "ardour," "ideal," and "sublime") has no place in the economy of the domestic enclosure. Rosamond refuses "to reflect or represent the 'reality' of the self grounding postures of the masculine subject" (61), as Judith Butler puts it. For when Lydgate seeks his "sublime" image of himself in Rosamond, he finds only "the blank unreflecting surface her mind presented to his ardour" (587). Looking past the "interfering illusions" (581) of romance, he does not find his sublime self, but instead a nothing. Gradually, Lydgate's romance thinking ("spirited young adventurer" in "dark territories of Pathology") becomes bourgeois thinking.

Lydgate does lose himself, but it is not to love. He is totalized into the economy of the domestic enclosure. By the end of the novel, his mind totally occupied by debt. At Christmas, "with the year's bills coming in from his tradesman, with Dover's threatening hold on his furniture, and with nothing to depend on but slow dribbling payments from patients who must not be offended," one thousand additional pounds would give him the "time"—in the words of the hopeful mantra he repeats to himself in moments of strain—"time to look about him" (647). All he wants now is the freedom to be outside of the self, "to look about," because his mind is literally occupied by the alien rhetoric of money, furniture, home, wife, and material respectability. "'*This* is what I am thinking of; and *that* is what I might have been thinking of,' was the bitter incessant murmur within him" (648). "*This*" is the domestic orthodoxy, and "*that*" is the romance vocation of pure science; and *this* kind of generic thinking has replaced *that* kind. Money, accumulation, and debt, Eliot makes clear, are the realities behind the rhetoric of total union. The promising Lydgate that she presents to the reader at the beginning of the novel disappears.

Lydgate thus follows the trajectory of Byron's *Corsair* in reverse—and he should have known better. After all, he had seen a dead husband before. Just as Conrad had encountered "Gulnare, the homicide" (*The Corsair* 3.463), Lydgate had known "a Provençale, with dark eyes, a Greek profile, and rounded majestic form" (151). She had murdered her husband with a knife while onstage. After the fatal stabbing of her husband, Lydgate became an intimate of hers until she suddenly left. He tracks her down and sets the scene for a romantic recognition that will lead to a blissful domesticity. He proclaims his love, his willingness to wait, but also his desire for her promise to marry him alone. After this, she tells him that she "*meant to do it*" (153), to murder her husband, insisting, "I do not like husbands. I will never have another'" (153). She tried to teach him the lesson that Byron's Conrad learns in the closing Cantos of *The Corsair* and that Wentworth learns when he thinks he is losing Anne. She tried to teach him the foundation of a domestic education: women are real individuals, not merely reflections of men. He did not listen, and by the end of the novel he is lost.

Leo and Holly are met with another deadly fantasy of the female domestic inside: eternal constancy to a single masculine image. Medora made eternal. Whereas Rosamond cannot reflect the singular importance of Lydgate's masculine fantasy, She's entire life, all two thousand years of it, has been spent in a cold, maiden's waiting for one man alone. The irony is: the man she is waiting for is not Leo, but her reincarnated lover, Kallikrates, Leo's ancestor (she killed in a fit of anger because he would not leave his wife). It does not matter that Leo is not his ancestor. What matters is the transcendence of the doxa, the eternalness of its structure, the pure center of its power. This time the union will be forever. The insanity of the final scene with She is simply the fantasy of the doxa narrated.

Leo and She's marriage is not a figurative union of souls throughout eternity. It is happening in the text—Haggard goes to the transcendental center of the domestic doxa, nature itself, to seek the rhetorical heart of middle class marriage—eternal union. They are going to be wed in the "Fountain and Heart of Life" (257) so that Leo can be transformed, like She, into an immortal being, and they can be together forever, not as ghosts like Katherine and Heathcliff, but in the world of flesh and blood. It does not end well. In order to get Leo to follow her, She walks into the fire only to go backward through all the gruesome cycles of life and death, transforming from a beautiful goddess to an old woman to a child with an adult head. Her death completes the evolutionary regression which Etherington argues marks the novel's trajectory, and it is a reassertion of white, male imperial power that Arata argues defines the conclusion. It is also a moment of Byronic liberation and heretical freedom, a genuine domesticide, which turns monogamous marriage into bigamy.

It is, after all, bigamy, as Haggard argues in "About Fiction" (1887), that "is by custom conceded to the writer of romance," the one place they are free to speak back to the "English conventionalism" which "English fiction has come to reflect" (296).[3] Haggard's essay was published in the *Contemporary Review*, less than a month after *She* finished its six week run in the *Graphic*, and it makes sense that bigamy was on his mind. For as Holly says after She dies, "We both loved her now and for always…. As she told me, I was nought to her, and never shall be through the unfathomed depths of Time, unless, indeed, conditions alter, and a day comes at last when two men may love one woman, and three be happy in the fact. It is the only hope of my broken-heartedness, and a rather faint one" (267). It is a lovely image. Released from the domestic enclosure, "two men may love one woman," because "conditions have alter[ed]" so much that the jealousy that competition always creates has been transformed into acceptance and happiness.

Moreover, Leo and Holly, the two romancers, are in the same position vis-à-vis the unreachable innocence of the domestic doxa as Lydgate, Heathcliff, or Manfred (at least before he sees the emptiness of Astarte). All these men are searching for male wholeness through the disembodied female, chasing the image of their own empty desire. We are right back where we started: the ghost of a woman. Stauffer places She inside the quickly evolving gender politics of the fin de siècle, and as "a touchstone for many of the anxieties surrounding the New Woman in late-Victorian England" (22). For Sandra Gilbert and Susan Gubar, for example, "her powers illusively evoke the suffragists unfurling the 'maiden banner' of their rights," (7) a dangerous visitation from Herland, which both captivates and terrifies late Victorian men. She uses her power for the express purpose of realizing the totality of the domestic doxa—eternal marriage. But She fails to revive and reimagine domesticity inside of female power, for herself and for her lovers. The men are left again with ghosts of their own desire. But in the fin de siècle, it is a different kind of failure and a different kind of ghost. As Gilbert and Gubar argue in, *No Man's Land*, their history of women in the nineteenth century, text from this era reflected "male fears of a debilitating no man's land, showing that the rise of the New Woman was not matched by the coming of a New Man, but instead ... with a crisis of masculinity" (2:vii).

The failure of Lydgate, Holly, and Leo to establish an autonomous masculinity inside the domestic enclosure elucidates just such "a debilitating no man's land." Even Holly's and Leo's radical dream of a bigamous union with the "entirely New Woman: the all-knowing, all-powerful ruler of a matriarchal society" (Gilbert and Gubar 6) ends as a shared broken heart. They end up back in the college, Leo's hair white, and Holly without his animal masculinity. They are aged and half-broken down. The novel's final image is not of romance possibility but of a domestic doxa that is timeless and absolute: "I have no doubt it [the marriage] must and will occur, in obedience to a fate that never swerves and a purpose that cannot be altered" (280). Holly and Leo end up back in their rooms at Cambridge, bad romancers that cannot be wholly inside the domestic enclosure, nor find a genuine space outside it.

That is not the end of our story however. For "the rise of the New Woman" at the end of the nineteenth century is "not matched by the coming of a New Man," but by the return of the rhetoric of the Byronic hero warped by the language of domestic fiction and Victorian domestic orthodoxy. The rhetoric of romance masculinity is the literary marketplace's monetized answer to the fin de siècle's crisis of masculinity. But it is not created out of thin air. It is the product of the Byronic afterlife inside the domestic novel. Romance masculinity is a villain in the domestic novel. To find it and unearth its commodity structure, we have to go backwards to the birth of Victorian domestic masculinity's coming-of-age, we have to go back to Charles Dickens's *David Copperfield* (1849–50).

Part II. The Rhetoric of Romance Masculinity

CHAPTER FOUR

A Secret History
The Byronic Hero in Charles Dickens's *David Copperfield*

He beat me then, as if he would have beaten me to death.
—Charles Dickens, *David Copperfield*

In *The Novel and the Police* (1988), D.A. Miller sees *David Copperfield* as a text that is defined by secretiveness: "The manuscript to which ... he [David] *commits his secrets* is precisely that: the place where he encrypts them" (199). This secretiveness defines the act of subjectivity in *David Copperfield*, an economy of hoarding. It is "the hidden innerness," Miller writes, "that like the miner's hoard must never see the light of day. Just as we can say of this hoard in a capitalist economy that it is *worth nothing* as soon as it has been removed from circulation and exchange, so we might not wonder at an innerness that is never recognized in intersubjectivity" (204), a self that is never joined with others. According to Miller, David announces his secret self through his inability to tell "at the time of narration" (Miller 199). Recounting his time at Murdstone's and Grinby's, for example, David writes "that I suffered in secret, and that I suffered exquisitely, no one ever knew but I" (144). Miller reads this as another moment in *David Copperfield* where "the self is most itself at the moment when its defining inwardness is most secret" (200). Miller's insight into the economy of hoarding the self in *David Copperfield*, helps us see clearly another level of intersubjective circulation of desire. For David is almost always the good, bourgeois subject; David is almost always most himself when his "defining inward is most secret," when he is under the supervision of domestic orthodoxy: of Aunt Betsey and his future wife Agnes. There is one exception in the novel, J. Steerforth. When he narrates the death of J. Steerforth, he casts off his secretiveness. "As plainly as I behold what happened," David explains, "I will try to write it down. I do not recall it, but see it done; for it happens again before me" (660). Like Poe's purloined letter, the real secret always hides in plain sight. For there is another novel inside the first novel, a black market economy of desire and recognition. The first novel is the familiar story of David's journey to successful Victorian, middle-class masculinity, and it is defined by an economy of hoarding. The other novel, told on the surface, is the story of David's fantasy life, the black-market economy of romance masculinity. This secret history is not about what happened to David and his inability to write it, but how what happened to David creates his desire—not the secretiveness of memory but the secretiveness of wanting. It is not the secret of the masculinity he becomes, but the secret of the masculinity he wants to be. In the illicit, black market novel, David rejects his inevitable journey to domestic masculinity. In the secret history, the real hero is J. Steerforth, and he is a Byronic hero.

It is through a heavy storm that desire returns: J. Steerforth is brought back to David. Standing helpless on the shore at Yarmouth, David watches a ship coming apart and men trying to save it and notices "especially one active figure with long curling hair, conspicuous amongst the rest" (667). It is J. Steerforth, with "long curling hair" reminiscent of his Byronic forbearer, performing his last act for his always admiring and almost always helpless friend, David:

> I saw that she [the ship] was parting in the middle, and that the life of the solitary man upon the mast hung by a thread. Still, he clung to it. He had a singular red cap on ... and as the few yielding planks between him and destruction rolled and bulged, and his anticipative death-knell rung, he was seen by all of us to wave it. I saw him do it now, and thought I was going distracted, when his action brought an old remembrance to my mind of a once dear friend [668].

Wearing a singular red hat, Steerforth's blithe gesture of greeting as he sinks into the "rolling abyss" (663) is the final act of defiance in his history of defiance. For David, Steerforth, "the old remembrance," is to remain as he always was, "the solitary man" wearing the "singular red hat" and meeting "his anticipative death-knell" in the most romantic of ways: by waving his hat at death. Though Ham, not to be outdone, emerges from the crowd of onlookers and tries to save the drowning man, he is buffeted by the waves. These two rivals for the love of Emily meet in the raging sea and both are drowned. And yet, for all of David's handwringing over Ham before he dies, he is instantly and automatically forgotten once "the active figure with long curling hair" washes ashore (667). For on the beach, as David relates, "among the ruins of the home he had wronged—I saw him lying with his head upon his arm, as I had often seen him lie at school" (669).

The Problem of Steerforth

It is at Mr. and Mrs. Creakle's school, Salem House, that David first meets Steerforth. Salem House is a common Victorian middling prep school for the aspiring classes, filled with child abuse, malnutrition, and religious hypocrisy. It also has a Byronic hero as a fellow student, and in David's first encounter with Steerforth, almost all the tropes of the Byronic hero are applied. Like Byron himself, and his heroes Conrad or Manfred, there is a mélange of beauty, bearing, and violence that surrounds Dickens's Steerforth. David, sitting in the dark after their first meeting, is "thinking of his nice voice, and his fine face, and his easy manner, and his curling hair" (81), which corresponds to the common description of Byron's "remarkable delicate features ... his fine blue eyes ... [and] head of curly auburn hair that emphasized the uncommon beauty of his face" (MacCarthy 120). There is also the violence. When asked what he would do if Mr. Creakle "ventured to lay a hand on him" (80), Steerforth replies by "dipp[ing] a match into a phosphorous-box on purpose to shed a glare over his reply" and he "said he would commence by knocking [him] down with a blow on the forehead" (80). The threat knocks the other boys "breathless" (80).

After most of the boys had "gone to bed" the rest, including David, "remained whispering and listening half undressed" (81), Steerforth asks David if he has a sister and David says no. "'That's a pity,' said Steerforth. 'If you had had one, I should think she would have been a pretty, timid, little, bright-eyed sort of girl. I should have liked to know her'" (81). Of course, the "pretty, timid, little, bright-eyed sort of girl" is David. This homosocial exchange is a new kind of intersubjective recognition, a different way of being a man for David. And David answers Steerforth's feminization as he does throughout the novel, by making Steerforth an object of romance:

> I thought of him very much after I went to bed, and raised myself, I recollect, to look at him where he lay in the moonlight, with his handsome face turned up, and his head reclining easily on his arm. He was a person of great power in my eyes.... No veiled future dimly glanced upon him in the moonbeams. There was no shadowy picture of his footsteps, in the garden that I dreamed of walking in all night [81].

When David looks at the drowned Steerforth on the beach at Dover "lying with his head upon his arm, as [he] had often seen him lie at school" (669), he is returning to a nest of emotions and impulses that his hetronormative domestic discipline, almost the sum total of his life, was constructed to resist. But David never escapes the fantasy space where Steerforth "lay in the moonlight, with his handsome face turned up, and his head reclining easily on his arm," in fact, he sees it inscribed on Steerfourth's dead body. Dickens's bildungsroman is a narration of David becoming the bourgeois father and successful professional—the ideal embodiment of domestic masculinity. It is also the secret history of another kind of masculine articulation: the pleasures of Steerforth's body, the pleasures of Byronic liberation, "the garden that I dreamed of walking in all night." These two ways of being a man, David's bourgeoisie domestic masculinity, and transgressive romance masculinity represented by Steerforth, elucidates a pattern of masculine possibility that will echo throughout romance revival and on.

The tug-of-war between romance masculinity and domestic masculinity that marks David's coming into being is chronicled in his naming and renaming. The importance of proper signs—the naming and renaming of David—relates, as signs always do, to their referent, David. He is David, Trot, and Daisy. David's names have very little to do with him, the signified, and everything to do with those doing the naming. The name-givers, and this should not be surprising, are placeholders for the antithetical possibilities of masculine representation. In a diametric opposition of representational possibilities, David's Aunt Betsey is the domestic pole and Steerforth is the romance pole. This has everything to do with masculine recognition: the giving of names is the outward manifestation of that recognition.

So it is no surprise that when David seeks refuge with Aunt Betsey after having left the wine warehouse of "Murdstone and Grinby" and romancing his way across the English countryside, her first recognition of David is a return to the fantasy of his femininity, that he should have been born a girl. At David's birth as a biological boy, Aunt Betsey left disgusted. She wanted to help raise a girl and nothing else. That fantasy is very much still alive when David returns to her seeking shelter from his stepfather. As she tell Mr. Dick "'he has done a pretty piece of business. He has run away. Ah! His sister, Betsey Trotwood, never would have run away.' My aunt shook her head firmly, confident in the character and behaviour of the girl who never was born" (169). Though Aunt Betsey does not have a girl, she works to create the next best thing—a man dedicated to the values of home and hearth, a domesticated man. According to Gareth Cordary, "in this disciplining.... David imbibes the values and practices of mid–Victorian bourgeois liberalism, which enables him to achieve a position of respectability and power" (71–72). Aunt Betsey even replaces David's natural father's name with her own, calling him "Trotwood" or simply "Trot." She reaffirms her disciplining power by giving David her name and then making him the perfect product of a domestic education—almost, at least. David's masculine recognition will depend his entire life on domestic women—first Aunt Betsey, then his first wife Dora, and finally the ideal of Victorian womanhood, his future wife Agnes. Of course, she calls him Trot.

After all, Aunt Betsey is not the only name-giver in the novel. The other is aristocratic, confident, sexually promiscuous, vain, and intensely alluring to David: J. Steerforth. Bestowed upon him during their second meeting at a roadside inn, Steerforth's name for David is Daisy. Aunt Betsey thus gives him a masculine name, "Trot," with its hard consonants and suggestions of movement and action, whereas Steerforth, on the other hand, conjures up "the pretty, timid, little, bright-eyed sort of girl" of their shared school days—that persistent figure of homosocial desire. There are two economies of recognition in *David Copperfield*. One is domestic, where David's value must be validated by women, where being a man means being the man for a woman inside reproductive heterosexuality. In the other economy of recognition, the black-market economy, being a man means being for other men. What it means to be a man changes between David and Steerforth throughout the novel. But their recognition always circulates in a romance economy, and it is dangerous to the domestic enclosure for which David is disciplined and destined.

In the course of David's domestic trajectory, Steerforth's influence must be mitigated, controlled, and (perhaps) overcome by David's future wife, Agnes. And she, according to Cordary, plays a large part in David's "disciplining, which is due in no small part due to the invisible influence of Agnes Wickfield" (71). In this case, she is far from an "invisible influence"; rather, the perfect emblem of Victorian female felicity and domesticity must break Steerforth's romancer's spell. Yet even after Agnes finds David and Steerforth drunk in the theater, even after she confronts David the next morning, he still defends Steerforth. David calls him "a guide, a support, and a friend to me" (312). Agnes's response suggests the bipolarity between the domesticated masculinity David has been educated to be and the romance masculinity that Steerforth represents and David desires to be. Agnes explains to David that "I feel as if it were someone else speaking to you, and not I, when I caution you that you have made a dangerous friend " (312–13). Agnes's invisibility is really the power of the doxa itself, the "someone else speaking" is to the voice of the middle-class values she and David shared in childhood. That is what makes her come to David and denounce Steerforth as his "bad Angel" (313) from Shakespeare's Sonnet 144. But as the "good Angel" (313) she explicitly connects David's affection for her with his renouncement of Steerforth's friendship: "'I only ask you, Trotwood, if you ever think of me—I mean' with a quiet smile, for I was going to interrupt her, and she knew why 'as often as you think of me—to think of what I have said'" (313). What is so striking is how the long dash works textually to divide and connect her and Steerforth, "as often as you think of me—to think of what I have said" that Steerforth is a "dangerous friend." For if David is to think of her—he must think ill of Steerforth. By connecting her "quiet smile" to her denunciation of Steerforth, Agnes is trying to replace Steerforth as "a guide, a support, a friend." There is no way to replace Steerforth: Dickens will have to kill him off.

For David is always the lonely boy and can never quite overcome his desire to articulate himself in opposition to the family. This desire to be freed from the domestic enclosure is the product of patriarchal violence itself. After David's mother marries Murdstone, he is shunned from the life of the family and left with a "sense of my being daily more and more shut out and alienated from my mother" (53). The Oedipal drama between son and stepfather pushes the lonely boy into the rich arms of romance rhetoric. In his dead father's small library, that "blessed little room," he reads Roderick Random, Peregrine Pickle, Humphrey Clinker, *Tom Jones, Don Quixote, Gil Blas,* and *Robinson Crusoe, Arabian Nights,* and "Tales of the Genii," romance texts all, and spends the rest of his time "impersonating [his] favorite characters," including a week as Tom Jones and over a month as Roderick Random (53 54). He cannot escape the rhetoric of romance masculinity as an adult because it is the life of the lonely boy. "When I think of it," David recalls, "the picture always rises in my mind, of a summer evening, the boys at play in the churchyard, and I sitting on my bed, reading as if for life" (54). This masculine romance rhetoric is a commodity that David consumes "as if for [his] life," because it promises a practice of being masculine inside of his deteriorating domestic environment through whose porous walls David's mother has let seep in the competitive, violent, outside world of masculine aggression. The violent competition that marked (and still marks) bourgeois life—the competitive exams, imperial postings, commerce, marriage market, and the battle for respectability—is inscribed on the body of the boy.

This is the secret at the center of the secret history of romance masculinity: male bodies hurting other male bodies. In David's case, romance fantasy is beaten home. Dickens's history of the lonely boy culminates in the morning that he is flogged for failing at his lessons. His mother, looking on helplessly, asks to be taken away as Murdstone takes hold of the boy. David bites him and, as he relates, his stepfather "beat me then, as if he would have beaten me to death.... Then he was gone; and the door was locked outside; and I was lying, fevered and hot, and torn, and sore" (56). Left in the room for five days, his face "swollen, red, and ugly" and his "stripes ... sore and stiff." David confesses to the reader that the wounds "were nothing to the guilt I felt" (56). Murdstone likewise tells David's mother, "I have been flogged myself," suggesting that this guilt runs both ways (55). This violence, of course, is the purest product of masculine competition; it is simply the sum of a male education, the outside turned inside.

Like generations of boys before him, David is beaten for poor performance at his studies, for not competing at a high enough level. As George Ryley Scott writes in the *History of Corporal Punishment* (1889), "beginning in the present century, the birching of boys has been inseparable from the discipline of nearly every school in Great Britain.... So general was the practice of corporal punishment that not so very long ago the teacher was popularly and vulgarly referred to as the 'bum buster'" (Scott). Competition and obedience to competition was beaten into the English boy body and it was internalized as guilt. It is Nietzsche in the "Second Essay" of the *Genealogy of Morals* who best explains the relationship between guilt and capitalism. In fact, guilt for Nietzsche is the genealogy of capitalism itself, the internal remainder of the violent exchange between creditor and debtor. "The major moral concept *Shuld* [guilt]," Nietzsche argues, "has its origin in the very material concept Schulden [debts]" (63). David's punishment, his physical pain, is a payment for the debt that he must pay for his failure at his studies; it is nothing more than the "contractual relationship between *creditor* and *debtor*, which is as old as the idea of 'legal subjects' and in turn points back to the fundamental forms of buying, selling, barter, trade, and traffic" (63). David *owes* his stepfather success.[1] For Dickens, guilt is what remains after the outside of masculine competition (buying, selling barter, trade, and traffic) has been internalized and connected with the deepest voice of the individual—the guilt of the I is David's real secret self. Internalized shame and guilt is a weight that David says lies "heavier on my breast" than the pain itself (56). David *owes*, and he will always owe.

That is also why David loves Steerforth: he is never beaten. According to Dickens, there was at Salem House "one boy on whom he [Mr. Creakle, the school master, the father, the boss] never ventured to lay a hand, and that boy [was] J. Steerforth" (80). Steerforth represents freedom from the violence of male gendering: freedom from the father, the "bum-bust[ing]"-teacher, and most of all the internal shame their violence leaves on us. It is a freedom I cannot imagine, and David cannot stop himself from loving Steerforth for it. He is not the same kind of debtor that David is.

The problem Agnes faces when she tries to replace Steerforth's romance thinking with her domestic thinking ("as often as you think of me—to think of what I have said") (313) is a problem other critics have struggled with as well. David's oscillating allegiances to these potential models, domestic thinking and romance thinking, seems like a failure of growth. According to Mary Poovey, "*David Copperfield*, then, is a novel in which the identity of the 'hero' is never completely stabilized or fully individualized because the main character is split" (119–20). This division plays out, for Poovey, over the body of Emily, the niece of David's nurse and his working class, childhood crush. Steerforth absconds with her to Italy and then abandons her while she is pregnant. David's unwillingness to denounce Steerforth, according to Poovey, suggests a connection that undermines the entire project of the domestic bildungsroman, where "transgressive desire [can be] neutralized in the safe harbor of marriage" (Poovey 90). For Badri Raina the problem is more straightforward: Dickens knows Steerforth is bad, but is as enamored with him as David is. Raina traces David's constant defense of Steerforth: when Agnes recognizes his danger, Steerforth's absconding with Emily, his past brutality toward Rosa Dartle, and a death that also leads to the irreproachably loyal Ham's drowning. "As David grows, allegedly, into an independence of mind," Raina concludes, "his view of Steerforth remains uncorrected, not because he fails to see as much as because he *chooses* not to see. Throughout his life David wishes nothing better than that he were Steerforth" (84).

The problem with Steerforth is that he is a Byronic hero packed up from the Regency and reintroduced in the middle of a Victorian bildungsroman. Edgar Johnson, Mario Praz, and Steven Harvey[2] have all noted "Steerforth as a Romantic poet in disguise—Byron in particular" (Harvey 305). Why that arch Victorian Dickens chooses the Byronic character, for Harvey, comes down to simple economics: "as a shrewd business man ... if his readers were fascinated by the kind of sensationalism inherent in the Byronic hero, Dickens would certainly give it to them" (316). Once we understand Steerforth as a Byronic hero, the problem Steerforth presents to David's growth into an ideal Victorian father and husband becomes a generic problem. Steerforth represents heretical romance thinking inside a domestic enclosure. David, the lonely boy, can never give up Steerforth because he cannot give up the rhetoric of romance masculinity commodified in the Byronic hero.

The Object of Gratification

Dickens's audience was "fascinated by the kind of sensationalism inherent in the Byronic hero" (316) and wanted to consume Byronic heroes as much as David. In *David Copperfield*, the black market of masculine desire is transacted through the body of the other, the female, working-class body of Emily. In this sense, David and Steerforth's relationship follows Eve Sedgwick's classic reading of male homosocial desire in *Between Men* (1985) in which Sedgwick employs René Girard's structuralist theory of the European novel in order to read "the politics of male homosociality" (17). For Sedgwick, David's infatuation with Steerforth is "part of David's education ... the painful learning of how to triangulate from Steerforth onto women, and finally, although incompletely, to hate Steerforth and grow at the expense of his death" (177). For Sedgwick, Emily's body, the object, stands in for the illicit exchanges of male desire: masturbation, mutual male masturbation, anal eroticism, and perhaps even love. It is through Emily (the object) that David (the subject) writes his desire for Steerforth (the mediator). (See figure 1):

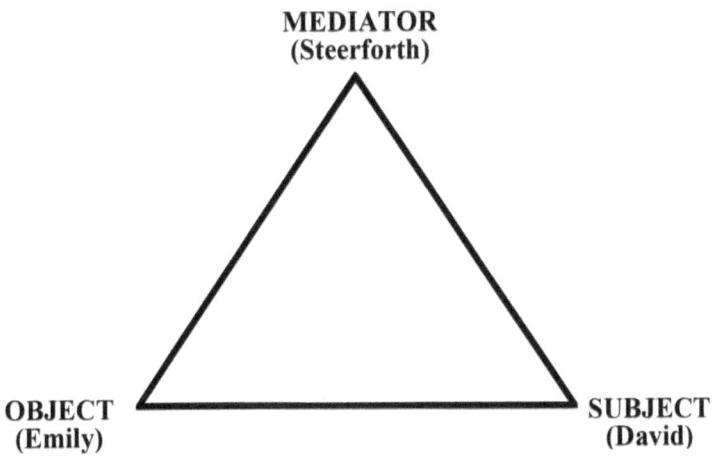

Figure 1

But this triangulation is incomplete, as Sedgwick points out, and though David does grow beyond Steerforth, he is never able to hate him. The incompleteness points to another element of David's and Steerforth's relationship, another triangular structure.

If we return to René Girard's earliest formulation of triangular desire, we can see David's and Steerforth's relationship in terms of consumption and commodification.

In this triangular structure of commodification and consumption, David is the subject/consumer and Steerforth is the object, but what he is mediating is the rhetoric of romance masculinity itself, a historically produced way of being a man. (See figure 2):

In *Desire, Deceit, and the Novel* (1965), Girard's reading of Don Quixote's relationship to the fictional knight-errant, Amadis, outlines the way that Byronic romance masculinity functions in *David Copperfield*. It fills in the incompleteness Sedgwick sees in David's overcoming of Steerforth and answers why "David wishes nothing better than that he were Steerforth" (Raina 84). For David has surrendered to the Byronic hero, Steerforth, what

> Don Quixote has surrendered to Amadis[,] the individual's fundamental prerogative: he no longer chooses the objects of his own desire—Amadis must choose for him. The disciple pursues the objects which are determined for him.... By the model of all chivalry. We shall call this model the mediator of desire. Chivalric existence is the imitation of Amadis [34].

Romance masculinity's "existence is [an] imitation" of the Byronic hero. David cannot fully give up Steerforth because it is not Steerforth that he

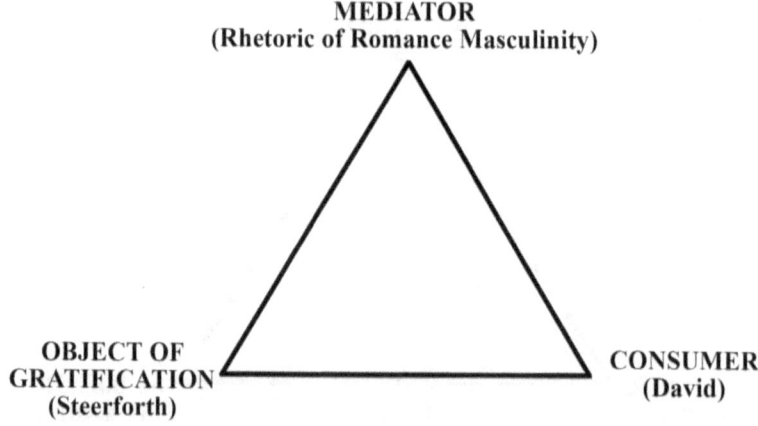

Figure 2

loves, but the mimetic potential Steerforth represents. And Steerforth represents mimesis of a subjectivity, a way of being a man that's "existence is the imitation" of the rhetoric of romance masculinity. It is in some ways a perfectly mystified commodity because, like Amadis, "the mediator is there, above that line, radiating toward both subject and object" (34).

Like any commodity, romance masculinity's value is both social and direct. It is created socially and consumed directly. Books are printed, movies are made, as Marx puts it in the *Grundrisse* (1939), because they are "particular products into which the individual desires to convert the portion which distribution has assigned to him; and finally, in consumption the products become objects of gratification, of individual appropriation.... The thing subjectifies itself in the person" (227). For example, when a young man, a twenty-first century David Copperfield, wants to exist as a romance male, he desires a certain kind of car or perhaps his choice of sexual partners, but "that line" between subject (our young man) and object of desire (cars, sexual partners) is mediated by the rhetoric of romance masculinity, by a historically generated thinking, a rhetorical and mimetic commodity. Perhaps it is James Bond or 2 Pac that radiates through the object, but they are merely placeholders, contemporary packaging of a rhetoric of male becoming that was born alongside and against the concept of the modern bourgeois family.

The commodity, in this case Steerforth, mediates the desire congealed in the Byronic hero: to be totally self-created and thus completely free from the alienating guilt of gender, history, and class, and to really be his own man. This is its fantasy value: romance masculinity is a commodity that rebels against commodification. As Steerforth will show us, it is a mode of masculinity created by transgression. And as we have seen in *Wuthering Heights* and *Manfred*, transgression is a ghost. "'You come upon me,'" he [Steerforth] said almost angrily, "'like a reproachful ghost'" (274) when David interrupts Steerforth staring at the fire in the Peggottys' empty sitting room. Steerforth is almost ready to abscond with Emily, and David's interruption allows Steerforth to act out his transgression in front of the always admiring David. David sees "a passionate dejection in his manner that quite amazed me. He was more unlike himself than I could have supposed possible" (274). Steerforth is at the place where his desire is meeting social reality, and it is filled with Byronic melodrama: "'It would be better to be this poor Peggotty, or his lout of a nephew,' he said, getting up and leaning moodily against the chimney-piece, with his face towards the fire, 'than to be myself, twenty times richer and twenty times wiser, and be the torment to myself that I have been, in this Devil's bark of a boat, within the last half-hour!'" (274–75). He would rather be this "poor Peggotty, or his lout of a nephew" because "to be myself," in Steerforth's case, means being a romance masculinity and, which means transgression and violence.

By taking Emily away unmarried, he is socially killing her, forcing her to live on the outside of Victorian life. She is to become a ghost, like Catherine at the upper window of Wuthering Heights, forever tapping against the glass. Exactly like Manfred and Heathcliff, Byronic self-dramatization of guilt turns the internal pain into an external specter, a ghost. Unlike Byron's Manfred or Brontë's Heathcliff, Steerforth is overcoming a ghost of his own violence, *before* the act. What Steerforth is commodifying for David and what David cannot ever give up is the transgression past guilt itself. As Steerforth explains to David,

> "I told you, at the inn in London, I am heavy company for myself, sometimes. I have been a nightmare to myself, just now—must have had one, I think. At odd dull times, nursery tales come up into the memory, unrecognized for what they are. I believe I have been confounding myself with the bad boy who 'didn't care,' and became food for lions—a grander kind of going to the dogs, I suppose. What old women call the horrors, have been creeping over me from head to foot. I have been afraid of myself" [275].

This exchange between the "I" and "myself," four times in the short passage, suggests the same split that defines David throughout most of the novel. The distance between the "I" and the "myself," between internal fantasy life, the secret-self to use D.A. Miller's formulation, and the social realities of mid-Victorian masculinity: being and representation, voice and words—all of it is mediated by guilt.

Steerforth is a torment to "myself," "heavy company" for "myself," "a nightmare to myself." It is the same guilt that rests, "heavier on my breast than if I had been a most atrocious criminal," on David after Murdstone beats him (56). It is the same guilt that transcendentally defines Manfred, even in defiance, for "what I have done is done; I bear within / A torture which could nothing gain from thine" (3.4.27–28), a guilt that is carried forever inside the "Mind which is immortal" (3.4.29). The guilt, the material inscription of patriarchal violence, is masculinity itself. As Steerforth tells David, "'it would have been well for me (and for more than me) if I had had a steadfast and judicious father'" (275).

By overcoming the guilt he feels toward Emily, the ghost of his transgression, Steerforth is able to uproot and overcome the guilt he feels for failing the fantasy of a judicious father and the competitive regulations of masculine gendering. There is no way to ever please the father that never was, the invisible power of patriarchy itself. The "reproachful ghost" (274) Steerforth sees in David is not only the guilt of his future crime, but the guilt of a desire that will take him outside the respectable world of masculine accumulation—the success that David prizes above all things—outside the domestic enclosure. Steerforth just leaves it: "'So much for that!' he said, making as if he tossed something light into the air, with his hand. 'Why, being gone, I am a man again,' like Macbeth" (274–75). And here is yet another ghost—the ghost of Banquo, whom Macbeth had murdered. Steerforth uses Macbeth's lines from Act III, when the ghost of Banquo has left Macbeth, to reflect his own "horrors" leaving him.

Being the Man: Rewriting Macbeth in David Copperfield

But the reference to *Macbeth* in *David Copperfield* suggests a larger violence, the shift from an ideal homosocial world of romance, to the bourgeois world of paired domestic units competing for money and status. The quote from *Macbeth* speaks to more than the "horrors" of guilt leaving him, but the historical roots of that guilt—the transition of masculine value by a capitalist economy. It brings us back to Lady Macbeth's plea for her husband to kill his king, Duncan:

> What beast was't then
> That made you break this enterprise to me?
> When you durst do it, then you were a man;
> And to be more than what you were, you would
> Be so much more the man [1.7.49–53].

Inside Lady Macbeth's plea for Macbeth to kill his king is the historical transition from the homosocial space of hunt and battle, hounds and retainers, "the beast" to the competitive economic unit of the family. As Lady Macbeth makes clear, domesticity's role in defining masculinity is dependent on accumulation. Her accusatory question in response to Macbeth's chivalric definition of the male is pregnant with the language of capitalism and domesticity: "What beast was't then / That made you break this enterprise to me?" The domestic is constructed on a strict outside / inside dichotomy. The dichotomy is formed by the outside "beast," with all its connotations to the king's hunt and the homosocial pleasure of male sport, set in opposition to the language of law and capitalism. "Break" suggests legal default and "enterprise" suggests capital accumulation. As

Lady Macbeth has made clear, "From this time / Such I account thy love" (1.7.38–39). The "account" of her "love," the ledger of their union, is dependent on Macbeth's willingness to accumulate for the internal domestic—and so is his status as a man. It is his desire to accumulate the kingdom for his own house by killing Duncan that makes him a man, not the prosecution of his duty as a nobleman. In fact, Lady Macbeth argues the fulfillment of that desire would make him so "much more the man." The move from the indefinite "a man" to the definite "the man" is the recognition of masculine value by the female, which is necessary for the formation of a new capitalist masculine identity. For "a man" to be "the man," the outside action must further the accumulation of the domestic inside.

Lady Macbeth's language goes on to conflate capitalist "enterprise" with heterosexual reproduction. In a telling and violent metaphoric shift, the enterprise of the outside becomes the ultimate symbol of the domestic inside: the suckling babe. Lady Macbeth vividly describes "how tender 'tis to love the babe that milks me," yet she is only too ready to pluck its "boneless" gums from the nipple and dash "the brains out" (1.7.53–57) if she had sworn to accumulate for the internal domestic and failed to carry it out. Macbeth's state as "the man" is utterly dependent on Lady Macbeth's recognition, and that, in turn, is dependent on his willingness to privilege the new domestic masculinity over the older forms of masculine chivalry. To save his baby, his family, he must betray his king.

But to understand the phallic recognition that Lady Macbeth threatens to withhold if Macbeth does not choose the domestic over the chivalric masculine as well as Steerforth's rejection of that same phallic recognition, it will help to look more closely at the mechanics of gender construction that Judith Butler lays out in her discussion of Lacan's notion of masquerade. According to Butler's reading:

> Women are said to "be" the Phallus in the sense that they maintain the power to reflect or represent the "reality" of the self-grounding postures of the masculine subject, a power which, if withdrawn, would break up the foundational illusions of the masculine subject position.... Hence, "being" the Phallus is always a "being for" a masculine subject who seeks to reconfirm and augment his identity through the recognition of that "being for" [61].

In the historical, material development of gender, this recognition (and representation) of the phallus (symbolic masculine value) has been sanctioned and promoted by the state through the institution of marriage. As the exchange from *Macbeth* underlines, however, the defining of masculinity by the domestic enclosure was the product of a burgeoning capitalist economy, one that needed to replace more traditional alliances to clan and locality. Macbeth's implied defense of his unwillingness to murder his king hearkens back to a chivalric masculinity in which the recognition of the phallus was, at least ideally, dependent on homosocial rituals: the hunt, the games of war, and battle itself. It is a conception of masculinity in which masculine value is mirrored by men. Whether or not there was ever a historical moment where phallic recognition occurred outside the "being for" the female is not at issue here because, either way, it exits in the rhetoric of romance masculinity. In fact, we see it in *David Copperfield*. At the moment of Steerforth's leave taking there is a rewriting of what it means to be a man, and it is a return of the repressed fantasy of pre-capitalist masculinity: "'Why, being gone, I am a man again,'" like Macbeth (274–75).

Steerforth goes backward: from being "the man" through the domestic recognition of the husband to being "a man" inside the fantasy space of romance. Dickens's Steerforth rewrites Macbeth as a return to romance masculinity. Being gone from the domestic economy means being gone from the institutionalized gaze of women who are, as Butler puts it, "said to 'be' the Phallus ... the 'reality' of the self grounding postures of the masculine subject" (61). Central to the rhetoric of romance masculinity and its appeal as a commodity is this "being gone" from domestic economy, and that means no longer needing a female to "augment his identity through the recognition" of his phallus, no longer needing a woman "being [his masculinity] for" him (Butler 61).

Being Gone as Romance Commodity

This fantasy of freedom from the female gaze is central to the male culture industry today—in first person shooters, summer action blockbusters, and the exponentially growing and ever-more violent pornography marketplace. The heroism in Byron's *Corsair* and *Manfred* is in dying with the guilty mark of gendering, carrying it inside—usually into oblivion—without again violating the female body with self authenticating desire. *David Copperfield* is a moment of departure. The "afterlife" (73), to use Benjamin's formulation, of the Byronic hero has a "history of its own" (71), is a living thing, an updating commodity. It becomes something different as it moves through the nineteenth-century novel. It becomes a rhetoric of romance masculinity: a fantasy of wholeness beyond domesticity and the gaze of the authenticating female. In *David Copperfield* the fantasy of male wholeness is "up there," as Girard writes, "above that line, radiating toward both subject and object" (34), toward David, Steerforth and toward men today. A contemporary masculine subject might be transformed into a unified, confident, authentic masculine subject, "a man again" (Dickens 474–75), for a moment at least, by consuming the rhetoric of romance masculinity, by following the consumptive triangle through to gratification. The irony is: that consumption is only a repackaging of the violence at the center of male gendering—the outside competition of the patriarchal order as masculine interiority. This authentic, masculine interiority is created through violence.

That is why, in *David Copperfield*, articulating romance masculinity means physically transgressing across the body of Emily, taking her away and socially killing her. Mary Poovey recognizes that "Steerforth acts out the complex of desire and punitive anger of which hostility toward sexuality is the cause and Emily the object" (98). This "hostility toward sexuality" echoes different meanings when we look at it in the context of the living history of romance masculinity, and it takes on deeper more ominous shades. This violent articulation of romance masculinity, Steerforth's escape from the domestic enclosure, externalizes the guilty remainder of male gendering into an object outside the self, Emily, and then kills it, figuratively or literally. The "I" and the "myself," the inside of desire and the outside of social life, are thus united in transgression against an object like Emily. She is made to stand in for an entire superstructure mechanic implicit in the guilty mutilation of the bourgeois, male subject and then she is killed. Romance masculinity commodifies the guilt of competitive male gendering by externalizing it, overcoming it, and thus reproduces the original violence as freedom from that guilt. The romance masculinity becomes free, real, and authentic by reenacting its own violation on an object outside the self: by reproducing competitive patriarchal violence as rebellion. As I said before, romance masculinity is a commodity that rebels against commodification: it is the violence of the symbolic father perfected in the fury of the son.

The perfect romance masculinity, therefore, is a dead one—the totalized commodity. And so we are back to where we started, David on the beach looking at his dead friend Steerforth. He is no longer a challenge to David's goal, or least the goals of his domestic educators. In fact, he is the best kind of Victorian commodity, one of remembrance and sentiment, a human one void of its freedom and danger. In the first lines of the chapter following Steerforth's death "The New Wound, and the Old," Dickens interjects an apostrophic elegy: "No need, O Steerforth, to have said, when we last spoke together, in that hour which I so little deemed to be our parting-hour—no need to have said, 'Think of me at my best!' I had done that ever; and could I change now, looking on this sight!" (669).

Steerforth is translated by death into poetry. Milton's *Lycidas* (1645) comes to mind immediately. Dickens uses trimeter and pentameter lines to elegize David's drowned friend. By becoming poetry, Steerforth is transformed into the realm of art and thus is safe for consumption, idealization, erotic longing—since he is out of circulation.[3]

Steerforth will not be our last dead body.

CHAPTER FIVE

"Hey you, there!"
Transforming Dickens's Domestic Masculinity into Romance Masculinity in Stevenson's *Treasure Island*

> *"It was I!"*
> —Robert Louis Stevenson,
> Treasure Island

The earliest works of the romance revival function to avoid male enclosure simply by "being gone" from Great Britain—geographically, imaginatively, and historically. Robert Louis Stevenson's *Treasure Island* (1883) and Haggard's *King Solomon's Mines* (1885), two early examples of the genre, both avoid an inevitable clash with orthodox domesticity by creating, through the expanded generic parameters of romance in the 1880s, a space in which to exercise romance fantasy without political and social danger. *Treasure Island* was a departure from the domestic fiction that preceded it simply by being gone from the domestic.[1] This being gone allows for a romance masculine world, one where the demands of wife and work, the inside and outside of the domestic enclosure, are totally nonexistent. The space, the island itself, is entirely outside Victorian domestic control. And what such early works of the romance revival lack is any tension between domestic masculinity and romance masculinity, as we have seen in the previous chapter, between what David must be and what Steerforth wants to be. Jim Hawkins is both David and Steerforth.

Jim Hawkins is a new commodification of the Byronic hero in the 1880s, a romance masculinity. But this Byronic commodity is retooled and reproduced for the new economic and ideological realities of the 1880s. It has also been transformed by its journey through the domestic novel and its rebirth in the romance revival. This rebirth of the rhetoric of romance masculinity is drawn from the Byronic hero, but as we have seen, it is also deeply connected to the Victorian bildungsroman and the values that structure it. In Jim Hawkins, Stevenson rewrites narrators of Dickens's classic bildungsromans, David and Pip from *Great Expectations*, as the romance masculinity of Steerforth. But Steerforth, the romance masculinity, is being repackaged as well. By following this repackaging of romance masculinity, we will be able to see an ideological transformation of masculinity, of what Great Britain wants its young men to be. Though Stevenson reimagines the classic Dickens narrator as an anti-domestic, violent, competitive masculinity, Jim is also deeply, deeply obedient. The anti-domestic violence has not been lost on critics; however, it has often passed as amorality.[2]

According to G.K. Chesterton, Stevenson "was appealing to a sort of sanguinary innocence against a sort of silent and secretive perversion" (83).[3] Diane Simmons calls *Treasure Island* a "moral duty free zone" (46), and for John Seelye "it is amorality that lends special interest to *Treasure Island* for adult readers, given that Stevenson wrote during a time when Victorianism was in full funereal flower" (xii). What looks like amorality in Jim Hawkins is the return of romance masculinity as hero. But it is a return with a difference. In the 1880s, romance masculinity is driven by a retracting economy, hyper-competition in world markets; it is the product of the Long Depression (1873–96). The text is not amoral at all, as we will see, but a work of pure obedience. What looked immoral in Dickens's novels at mid-century became obedience in Stevenson's tales by the fin de siècle. As I said, Stevenson's Jim Hawkins is a rewriting of the classic Victorian Dickensian male narrator and romancer, the developing bourgeois heroes of *David Copperfield* (1849–59) and *Great Expectations* (1860–61). The difference is: the world has changed.

The Long Depression and Romance Masculinity

Scholars like Bradley Deane have located *Treasure Island* inside late-Victorian imperial policy, the realpolitik of New Imperialism, where the civilizing mission of the mid–Victorian period, the empire that Gladstone and J.S. Mills had imagined, was being replaced by the greedy land grabs of Cecil Rhodes and Alfred Beit. The drive to make the empire pay, realpolitik, was driven by the contraction of the global economy which had been initiated by the collapse of the U.S. based multinational bank, Jay Cooke and Company, and which was sustained by the saturation of global markets brought on by overproduction during the Second Industrial Revolution. The United States, France, and a newly united Germany were all seeking new markets for their underpriced commodities (the price of steel was slashed by a half during this time period). As Eric Hobsbawn describes, the British economy did not collapse as dramatically as the United States' and Germany's, but the effects were more lasting and intense.

> Unlike the other industrial powers, the British boom would not really revive. Prices, profits and rates of interest fell or stayed puzzlingly low. A few feverish little booms did not really halt this long and frustrating descent.... And when the economic sun of inflation once more broke through the prevailing fog, it shone on a very different world [104].

It shone on a very competitive marketplace, and Great Britain was not winning.

It is perhaps easier for those of us who have lived through the Great Recession (2007–) to see how retracting economies can make cultural institutions, seemingly overnight, more brutal and competitive. Both the realpolitik New Imperialism codified at the 1884 Berlin Conference, and the emergent works of adventure fiction were ideological and policy proscriptions to the contraction of the global economy through the last quarter of the nineteenth century. It is in this sense that the publication of *Treasure Island* is an ideological moment. Bradley Deane places the phenomenon of *Treasure Island* in a developing "imperial play ethic" where "persistent boyishness put a more beguiling face on the new imperialist ideology … transform[ing] aimless process into endless adventure and the absence of universal law into a profusion of possibilities for exhilarating play" (690). The "endless adventure" and "the possibilities for exhilarating play" have a particular purpose: return on investment. *Treasure Island* is a bildungsroman for the Long Depression.

"Hey you, there!" Great Expectations *and* Treasure Island

The figure of the lonely boy, made familiar to readers through Dickens's *David Copperfield* (1849–59) and *Great Expectations* (1860–61), became the foundation for the developing history of romance masculinity: David and Pip were thus rewritten in Jim Hawkins. Dickens's narrators in *David Copperfield* and *Great Expectations* accumulate value by transforming the competitive violence at the heart of male gendering and the guilty reminder, into a mature, ethical, and domesticated subjectivity. The pain and guilt of male gendering, in the classic Christian ontology of suffering, becomes decency and humaneness in the heroes of Dickens's bildungsromans. Stevenson reproduces Dickens's boy narrator and romancer, ruminating on his youth from the privileged position of the adult, but Jim never "grows up." He never becomes the unified Christian, domestic masculinity of Dickens's David and Pip. It is not because of the narrator's boyishness, but because Jim grows up *to be* the outside violence of masculine marketplace completion. In Stevenson's narrator Jim, the outside becomes his interiority. It is the commodification of the violence of patriarchy as the rage of the son. It is the story of the Dickensian hero becoming Steerforth—a romance masculinity. The conflicting and interconnecting relationship between Dickens's bildungsromans and Stevenson's *Treasure Island* becomes clearest when we look specifically at Pip in *Great Expectations*. That is because both Pip and Jim get ahead in life because of criminals.

Both Pip and Jim are products of illicit economic accumulation by first working for an absent, criminal father. The entire plot of Pip's rise to the rank of gentleman, the opportunities, betrayals, pain, and reversals which mark Pip's narration, begins with a transgression, his feeding and freeing of the convict Magwitch, and the guilt that it summons from him. I say summons because Magwich is calling forth the guilt that lies at the heart of competitive masculine gendering in the Victorian period.[4] As Michal Peled Ginsburg writes, "it is clear ... that the encounter with the convict does not simply create, or originate the feeling of guilt; rather, it confirms a feeling of guilt which predates it and which is equivalent with life itself" (116). Dickens suggests that "guilt ... is equivalent with life itself" through the stratagem Magwitch uses to induce Pip to steal food and a file: the omnipresent "young man." As the desperate criminal Magwitch tells the terrified young Pip,

> There's a young man hid with me, in comparison with which young man I am an Angel. That young man hears the words I speak. That young man has a secret way pecooliar to himself, of getting at a boy, and at his heart, and at his liver. It is in wain for a boy to attempt to hide himself from that young man ... that young man will softly creep and creep his way to him and tear him open.... I find it wery hard to hold that young man off of your inside [11].

The great irony in this passage is that the only "young man" with Magwitch is the young man Pip will become. The eloquence he uses to control Pip rests in the violent metaphor of the "secret way" the "young man" has "of getting at a boy." For the young man does not kill the "boy," he becomes his "inside" through his "secret way" of getting at "his heart, and at his liver," his ability, "pecooliar to himself," to "tear him open," to take over the boy. This is what Magwitch does: the "young man" that Pip will become is meant to be a social and class revenge for Magwitch's own poor expectations. By making Pip a gentleman, Magwitch turns him into the guilt-ridden, self-conscious, bourgeois subject, and Pip "find it wery hard to hold that young man off of your inside."

The function of guilt in *Great Expectations* is then the internal reproduction of the ideology of competition: the ethic of striving, social mobility, and success that define the representation of ideal bourgeois masculinity inside middle-class Victorian Britain. It is the guilt of social striving that marks almost all of Pip's relationships—whether to his abusive sister, the loving Joe, or even the cruel Miss Havisham. But for the Dickens of *Great Expectations*, capital accumulation can be a means or an impediment to reaching the real goal of this moral masculinity. That is why Pip is only free when he gives Magwitch's money away. To be Dickens's unified moral masculinity, one of the more radically progressive Victorian masculine ideals, he must refuse Magwitch's money—dirty money—and make his own way in an imperial trading house.

Trade was certainly booming after the economic calamities of the 1840s and 1850s, and Great Britain is the most dynamic economy in the world. The rejection of a tainted patrimony makes sense to middle-class readers raised in an era marked by Britain's ever rising economic tide and exposed to the liberal and ethical ideals that growth afforded them. It made sense in 1860, but that does not last. It is the "sudden transformation," as Eric Hobsbawm writes, "of the leading and most dynamic industrial economy into the most sluggish and conservative, in the short space of thirty or forty years (1860–90/1900)" (156) that helps explain the central difference between the trajectory of Dickens's and Stevenson's bildungsroman. "Conscience," Pip narrates, "is a dreadful thing when it accuses man or boy" (16), and in the end, he can afford to pay his off. By the 1880s that price is too dear.

At the beginning of *Treasure Island*, there is the same complicity with a convict, but without the guilt. For Bill (or Billy Bones), the old pirate hiding out in his family's tavern, pays Jim "a silver fourpenny" to "look out for 'the seafaring man with one leg'" (4–5). Although, like Pip and his "young man," Jim is haunted by the specter of the one-legged man, unlike Pip he has no moral qualms about helping a man who is clearly on the lam. In fact, he openly acknowledges his complicity: "For me, at least, there was no secret about the matter; for I was, in a way, a sharer in his alarms" (4). But Jim does more than simply become "a sharer in his alarms." From the beginning of *Treasure Island* to the end, the real "story" of Jim's maturation into a romance masculinity is mediated not by patriotic, class, or paternalistic loyalties, but by the desire to compete like his pirate "father," Billy Bones, by beating his father's pirate competitor—Long John Silver and his crew.

Like almost all romance masculinities, from Scott's Waverley to Byron's Conrad to Brontë's Heathcliff to Dickens's Steerforth, Jim has no father figure. He is absent from the text; dying in his room, he is never given a voice in dialogue or a place in the action. He is, therefore, a dying model of masculinity for Jim, its "full funereal flower" (Seeyle xii) of Dickens's domestic and moral masculinity. Jim's father cannot compete in the new economy; he is a failed bourgeois—he cannot even collect the rent from his tenants. After Billy Bones had long overstayed his welcome and his "money had been long exhausted," Jim recounts, "still my father never plucked up the heart to insist on having more. If ever he mentioned it, the captain [Billy Bones] … stared my poor father out of the room. I have seen him wringing his hands after such a rebuff, and I am sure the annoyance and the terror he lived in must have greatly hastened his early and unhappy death" (6). He is a model of failure in the recessionary marketplace transposed conveniently onto the eighteenth century world of high stakes seafaring.

What his father lacks, and what Billy Bones and Jim Hawkins share, is signified in one word: "pluck"—the late Victorian male code word for male completion internalized as the male subject. Jim's real father is Billy Bones. Thus Jim is the perfect reflection of masculine gendering—the commodification of the enraged son staring back at the violent father and thus becoming him. *Treasure Island* is ultimately the story of Jim Hawkins proving himself to the invisible father Billy Bones, proving he has pluck. So when Billy Bones dies of "thundering apoplexy," it is no surprise Jim is moved: "it is a curious thing to understand, for I had certainly never liked the man, though of late I had begun to pity him, but as soon as I saw that he was dead, I burst into a flood of tears" (18).

Both Pip's and Jim's "expectations" are created by transgressions on behalf of the adoptive father—in both cases, a violent male convict, representative of the ultimate outside of the domestic, the ultimate figure in the violent world of male competitors. The adoption of Pip and Jim by the violent father are moments of recruitment into the violence of the outside economy. They are taken out of the home and made to enter the world of completion. Through their transgression, each boy is recruited and transformed from an individual into a competitive masculine subject, from boy to man. But because their adoption is also a transgression there is an ideological hailing in the text. In Althusser's famous formulation of hailing, which is "*interpellation* or hailing, and which can be imagined along the lines of the most commonplace everyday police (or other) hailing: 'Hey, you there!'" (163). This hailing announces them as a subject, as a part of ideology. For when and how the hailed subject reacts highlights "the existence of ideology" through the interpellation of the subjects, which is "one and the same thing" (163). As we will see, the moments of theft in *Great Expectations* and *Treasure Island* are thus moments of "hailing or interpellation" (163), and as such they tell us something real about the fabric of masculine potential in the 1860s as opposed to the 1880s. But what tells us more is the gap between the two, between Pip and Jim, because that gap gives us a glimpse at how the unrepresentable totality of the historical movement, capital, national, and cultural, is producing bourgeois masculinity at very different global economic moments. This difference shows itself in the way they steal.

The difference between Pip's stealing for Magwitch and Jim Hawkins's stealing of provisions and a boat in order to adventure across Treasure Island against the express orders of his business partners, suggests how far Jim has departed from the moral coding of Dickens's male narrators. When Pip is stealing Magwitch's food he is in a state of hallucinatory guilt-ridden panic. Dead rabbits wink at him. He hears alarms of "Stop thief!" everywhere (18). "I had no time for verification," he tells the reader, "no time for selection, no time for anything, for I had no time to spare. I stole some bread, some rind of cheese, about half a jar of mincemeat" (18). What defines Pip's theft of the food for Magwitch is the phrase "no time." His frequent repetition of the phrase suggests more than Pip's fear and worry, but also the dread conscience of his misdeed as if they were right behind him, bearing down on him. Jim, on the other hand, takes his time. Washing up dishes, working as the cabin boy once more, he plans an escape—what he refers to as "my escapade":

> I was a fool, if you like, and certainly I was going to do a foolish, over-bold act; but I was determined to do it with all the precautions in my power. These biscuits [Jim's first theft], should anything befall me, would keep me, at least, from starving till far on in the next day.
>
> The next thing I laid hold of was a brace of pistols, and as I already had a power horn and bullets, I felt myself well supplied with arms [118].

The "precautions in [his] power" that Jim utilizes at the start of this "escapade" are the opposite of Pip's guilt-ridden grabbing. Where Pip has "no time," Jim takes all the "precautions in his power." Althusser understands "guilty feelings" (163) as a part of interpellation, as part of the process of turning the individual into the subject, yet they remain distinct from the ideological hailing of the subject. He is not sure where they come from—"despite the large numbers who 'have something on their consciences'" (163). Nietzsche places guilt at the heart of capitalism's transformation of individuals to subjects, in the relationship between debtor and creditors. I have argued this guilt is the historical reminder of the gendering of young men in the nineteenth century, of the outside of competition internalized: "I am my debt." We see a shift in what the debt means between these two texts. In the genealogy of the bildungsroman, Jim is almost recognizing Pip. They almost seem to be hailing each other as they pass. And we can see one historical ideal of British masculinity taking the place of another. That is to say, there is a shift in the ideological recruitment of masculinity: the transformation from Dickens's domestic masculinity to Stevenson's romance masculinity. We should not confuse this transformation with freedom. It is not. The debt has simply compounded.

The Words of the Father

Still, like Steerforth, Jim must overcome the guilt of male gendering in order to be authentic, to be a genuine romance masculinity. Guilt, the pain of the boy's debt to the patriarchy, functions as labor in *Treasure Island*—female labor. After he passes the treasure map Squire Trelawney and Dr. Livesey, Jim is immediately relegated to domestic labor—the exact work he had preformed at the Admiral Benbow. He effectually becomes the only woman in a world of men and, in the total patriarchy of Treasure Island, he ceases to really exist. Even after the attack on the redoubt, Jim returns to being a cabin boy, that is, he returns to traditionally feminine labor that has marked his career as a romancer up to this point. For "all the time" that Jim was "washing out the block-house, and then washing up the things from dinner, this disgust and envy kept growing stronger and stronger, till at last ... [he] took the first step towards [his] escapade" (118). The domestic labor of "washing out" and "washing up" creates a "disgust and envy" that keeps growing "stronger and stronger" until it must be met with theft, piracy, and killing. It is this guilt or "disgust and envy" as Stevenson calls it, that puts Jim's plan into motion.

This, however, is not an escape from the patriarchal power structures represented by Dr. Livesey, Squire Trelawney, and Captain Smollett. Jim's disobedience is actually a deeper level of obedience. He is doing their will because he is competing violently for the best of all natural resources: gold, pure specie. He is acting unconsciously for the competitive masculine outside by going to the outside. He is paying his debt, not to the squire and the doctor, but to his real creditor, the one who gave him the map and set him on his path. He is obeying his symbolic father, Billy Bones. As in any other bildungsroman, Jim is searching for masculine identification, to be named and thus recognized. As Althusser reads Freud, it is the Father's Name that locates the individual, "always-already," in the world as a singular subject inside a particular ideology—the subject "will bear the Father's Name, and will therefore have an identity and be irreplaceable" (164). Jim is looking for patriarchal recognition, which will grant him a real masculine "identity" and thus make him "irreplaceable." His search tells us how Great Britain's domestic and imperial ideology was hailing bourgeois male subjects at the end of the 1880s.

This figure of the lonely boy or the orphan, like Kipling's Kim, illuminates the social and economic values of the British ruling class at this moment by giving us a sense of what this class needs boys to become. Having no earthly father, they must get recognition from the symbolic father, the ruling patriarchy and competitive outside of capitalism. Patriarchal values were in flux between the 1850s and the 1880s. David's journey in *David Copperfield* to the "Father's Name," to masculine recognition, is an extended domestic education, while Pip renounces dirty money and practices ethical capitalism. With intense global competition spurred on by the Long Depression and personified in the European "Scramble for Africa," Jim must speak the language of the symbolic father to become a man. He must learn to speak the vicious code of late–Victorian masculinity: "Dead men don't bite."

He hears these words for the first time while inside the womb of the apple barrel. Tucked away in the damp and dark, he hears the ghostly words of Billy Bones. He is listening for his life. Long John Silver is planning a mutiny, and his co-conspirators are trying to decide whether or not to kill Jim's partners and the loyal crew. In this "parlyment" of pirates around the apple barrel there is a "vote" on whether to put "'em [non-pirates] ashore like maroons … or cut 'em down like so much pork" (60). Israel Hands wins the short debate: "'Billy [Bones] was the man for that,' said Israel. 'Dead men don't bite,' says he" (60). As we will see, these words define the destination of Jim's romance and his place among men. When Jim leaves the redoubt after his disgust with domestic labor, he starts the process of acting out the words of Billy Bones. But this process is not a conscious or deliberate one. Like Althusser's hailing, it activates another voice speaking inside Jim.

During Jim's adventure across the currents of Treasure Island in Gunn's small boat, "a most cross-grained lop-sided craft to manage" (122), he "kept [his] head" (127) by totally surrendering control of the craft, for the "coracle, left to herself, turning from side to side, threaded, so to speak, her way" (127). Jim realizes that he "must lie where [he is], and not disturb the balance" (127). Though he is hoping to reach shore, the unguided boat leads him to the *Hispaniola* and the real reason he left: to speak the words of the ghostly father back to his competitor for those same words. The competition begins when Jim finds Israel Hands wounded on the deck. But Israel is not badly wounded, and he is able to steal a knife and hide it. After that, he throws the spectral words of Billy Bones back at Jim, like a challenge: "Well, now I tell you, I never seen good come o' goodness yet. Him as strikes first is my fancy; dead men don't bite; them's my views—amen, so be it" (137).

Both Jim and Israel Hands are obedient to those words, to the competitive system of male recognition and reward. After a back and forth fight, Jim gains the upper hand, loading his two pistols and taking aim at Hands, he turns Bones back on him: "'One more step, Mr. Hands,' said I, 'and I'll blow your brains out! Dead men don't bite, you know,' I added, with a chuckle" (140). He does not, however, fire the gun intentionally. Rather, as Jim relates, "in the horrid pain and surprise of the moment—I scarce can say it was by my own volition, and I am sure it was without a conscious aim—both my pistols went off." This moment of transformation is a moment of recruitment for Jim. He is being "hailed" and named as an ideological commodity of the masculine outside—he has value and he is real. His "volition" and his "conscious aim" are no more his in this moment than his words and his chuckle. He is a commodity of patriarchal violence. In pure obedience, he is an unconscious and alienated reproduction of Billy Bones. Jim's "chuckle" is the dark laughter of the old sea-song Jim used to hear Bones singing at the Admiral Benbow:

> Fifteen men on the dead man's chest—
> Yo-ho-ho, and a bottle of rum! [3].

The pirates have returned. We have heard their song before. The real voice that is hailing Jim is the voice of romance masculinity.

We have heard it in the "Pirate Song" from *The Corsair* and have seen it in the aggressive masculine representations that were produced during the intense national competition that marked the Napoleonic Wars (1803–15). The outlaws and pirates have returned as the sons of innkeepers, the sons of the bourgeoisie. And this moment has all the promise of danger and reward. The spirit of adventure has returned, and we can hear Byron's "dark blue seas" from *The Corsair* and the new romance masculinity that wants to

> feel—to the rising bosom's inmost core,
> Its hope awaken and its spirit soar?
> No dread of death—if with us die our foes—
> Save that it seems even duller than repose;
> Come when it will—we snatch the life of life—[1:21–25].

Unlike Byron's Conrad, Jim never grows beyond this spirit of adventure. The Byronic hero comes to learn the alienating limits of his masculine posturing, which is why that hero is so often tragic or comic. It seeks its own destruction. Romance masculinity, however, has been repackaged inside the realist presentation of subjectivities throughout the domestic novel, and it does not destroy itself with its own language. It simply lives to again and again "snatch the life of life."

Romance Masculinity

To "snatch the life of life," to not fear death if it means the death of competitors or "foes"—the rhetoric of romance masculinity has returned in *Treasure Island*. There is no domestic education. Whether it is Byron's seaman jeering at the man that "cling[s] to his couch, and sicken[s] years away" while he with "one pang—one bound—escapes control" (1:28–32) or the ominous laughter in Billy Bones's and Long John Silver's "Fifteen men on the dead man's chest—/ Yo-ho-ho, and a bottle of rum" (3), romance masculinity is hailed, or recognized, through transgression. So when Jim meets Long John Silver again, facing death or torture, he speaks the words of romance masculinity: "Let the worst come to the worst, it's little I care.... But there's a thing or two I have to tell you ... here you are, in a bad way: ship lost, treasure lost, men lost; your whole business gone to wreck; and if you want to know who did it—it was I!" (151).

"It was I" is the simplest definition of romance masculinity, where transgression across the body of the competitor creates wholeness, authenticity, and masculine value: "*I* was in the apple barrel.... *It was I* who cut her [the ship's] cable ... *it was I* that killed the men you had aboard of her, and *it was I* who brought her where you'll never see her more" (151–52, my emphasis). The formula for romance masculinity is simple enough. "It was I": the transgression (it) creates the freedom and wholeness of the subject (I). At this moment, Jim grows up. If he remains "boyish," like Kim and Lord Jim after him, it is because this is the end of maturation— he has reached his purpose. Jim Hawkins is now a commodification of masculinity that can win wars and secure treasure. What looks like boyishness is the apotheosis of the Long Depression's masculinity: his only purpose is to win in a competitive marketplace, not to become a reflective ethical agent. Nor is Jim amoral. He transgresses against a stated prohibition (killing) because it is the secret law (killing). Men are not supposed to kill, but the social and economic demands of imperialism and capitalism demand just that—killing. He is the obedient son and is rewarded. In fact, all of his partners are rewarded with the only real value in *Treasure Island*—gold.

Monetarists

There is a very simple moral code in *Treasure Island*: get the gold. When Jim looks into Tom Gunn's cave, it is like he is looking into the fantasy at the heart of the national banks of Germany, France, the United States, and Britain and the fantasy at the heart of nineteenth century capitalism and classical economic theories of the gold standard:

> I beheld great heaps of coin and quadrilaterals built of bars of gold. That was Flint's treasure that we had come so far to seek, and that had cost already the lives of seventeen men from the *Hispaniola*. How many it had cost in the amassing, what blood and sorrow, what good ships scuttled on the deep, what brave men walking the plank blindfold, what shot of cannon, what shame and lies and cruelty, perhaps no man alive could tell [182].

In 1844, the Bank Charter Act pegged all British paper currency to gold. The British adoption of the gold standard was a means for creating and controlling world markets. As Giulio M. Gallarotti, citing the work of Robert Gilpin, puts it, "the British state 'desired' a global economic system organized around British industry, finance, and economic philosophy (lassie-faire)," and the central focus of British foreign polity was the maintenance of "free capital movements and a unified monetary system" (86). But British monetary hegemony never became political hegemony. Gladstone's "splendid isolation" ended with the creation of a unified Germany after the Franco-Prussian War (1870–71). The newly minted German Empire adopted the gold standard in the early 1870s, as did the furiously industrializing United States. By the end of the decade "gold had become extremely scarce owing to expanded use and declining supply" (Gallarotti 68). This scarcity of gold raised interest rates and reduced the circulation of money, shrinking economies worldwide and threatening British global monetary hegemony. Whoever found the Treasure Island would win.

Reality followed fantasy: the treasure was discovered after the treasure books, *Treasure Island* and *King Solomon's Mines*, had been written. The discovery of the Witwatersrand Lode in South Africa is itself an adventure tale. In 1886 an Australian wanderer, George Harrison, came upon an outcrop of gold veined stone, filed his claim, and initiated, one of the largest gold rushes in world history. In the article "New African Gold Fever," published in the *Dundee Courier* in 1887, one "Visitor to the Diggings" recorded the sweeping transformation gold had brought to the sleepy veld only a year after Harrison had filed his claim ("New African" 4). The correspondent found "Pretoria the head center of the gold mania. All the men of capitol and means interested in these fields are to be found there, and the telegraph is largely monopolized by them. The pestle and mortar are heard at work in almost every other house" ("New African" 4). With organized camps and processing mills relying on cheap labor, black and white, the special correspondent concluded that "the best things are yet to come" ("New African" 4).

There was certainly more to come. Less than a decade later, Cecil Rhodes and Alfred Beit, owners of the De Beers Mining Company, organized and carried out the Jamison Raids (1895–96), and three years later the Second Boer War (1889–1902) began. The Empire simply could not turn away from the immense wealth South Africa promised. Jim sees the cost of the nation's amassing of gold and diamonds when he looks into Tom Gunn's cave: "How many it had cost in the amassing, what blood and sorrow, what good ships scuttled on the deep, what brave men walking the plank blindfold, what shot of cannon, what shame and lies and cruelty, perhaps no man alive could tell" (182).

CHAPTER SIX

Being Home
The Schizophrenic Enclosure as Dr. Jekyll and Dorian Gray

> *He that has found the sin has bought it.*
> —Oscar Wilde, *Regina v. Wilde*
>
> *He was looking on the body of a self-destroyer.*
> —Robert Louis Stevenson, *Strange Case of Jekyll and Hyde*

Division and splitting, dualities and doubles, British masculinity in the last two decades of the nineteenth century is schizophrenic. One of its earliest cultural historians, Holbrook Jackson, separated the decades between the early aesthetic decadence that ended with the trial of Oscar Wilde in 1890 and the hyper-masculine imperial jingoism that replaced it. Stephan Arate, on the other hand, sees this masculine duality, the aesthetic and the jingoistic, as an interconnected manifestation of late nineteenth century masculinity, where "the masculine imperialist adventure was in large part a response to the perceived dangers of Wildean aestheticism" (7). He is right, but in this chapter we will search for a deeper interconnection. For both the decadent and the imperial adventurer are also articulations of masculinity outside the domestic enclosure of the middle class family, ways of being a man that exclude the wife and the child. The decadent and the adventurer are returns of repressed masculine rhetorics, various guises of romance masculinity.

Though decadence seems entirely distinct from the violent, antidomestic fantasies of imperial adventure fiction, like Byron's "pirate's song" from *The Corsair*, they are another way of being gone from domestic control, of snatching the "life of life" (1:25).[1] Whether one chooses the symbolic, un-reproductive pleasures of the anus or the ecstasy of being close to death in the deserts, jungles, and dark forests of the imaginary empire, the middle-class family is not a part of the storyline. By the end of the nineteenth century, the interconnected romance rhetorics of decadence and adventure had been commodified for all time in the serial characters of Sherlock Holmes and A.J. Raffles. But, despite these literary representations, the crisis was real, it was schizophrenic—and it is with us still.

Because "Victorian culture was of one mind in maintaining both the continuity and incompatibility of the two aspects of British masculinity," as Nancy Armstrong puts it, marketplace aggression ("completion, aggression, and dominion") and the social laws of Victorian respectability came to co-exist in "one mind" (*How* 81). In Robert Louis Stevenson's *Strange Case of Jekyll and Hyde* (1886) and Oscar Wilde's *Picture of Dorian Gray* (1890), there is genuinely "one mind" existing in "both continuity and incompatibility," which is why Richard Dellamora classifies *Jekyll and Hyde* and *Dorian Gray* as part of "a literature of masculine crisis" (196).[2] This crisis is really a reckoning.

Between the passage of the First Reform Bill (1835) and the end of the Franco Prussian War (1871) the real driver of the British economy was domestic railway construction and industries like iron and coal. The spike in the GDP and the capital accumulation generated by heavy railroad investment, along with enormous stock dividends, created the illusion of an ever advancing liberal economy.[3] The gold standard, the empire, international trade, ethical individualism, and the middle class family were seen as the fulfillment of God's dispensation, the domestic doxa—at least, as long as the capital flowed. By the start of the 1880s, however, the bullish economy at the heart of David Copperfield's and Pip's world had been replaced by international competition and internal capital constriction. As I said, the crisis of masculinity at the end of the nineteenth century was an economic and social reckoning. The accumulated wealth of the ruling class, its real *raison d'être*, was destroying it. By following the rhetoric of romance masculinity in *Jekyll and Hyde* and *Dorian Gray*, it will become clear that the privileged power of commodity purchase, the ability to buy and sell anything, is eating patriarchy up from the inside.

The Body Without Organs

This masculine crisis is also a crisis of hiding and the failure to hide. It is the crisis of the desire to maintain the respectable exterior of bourgeois rule, which is its ideological rationale, while indulging in the decadent luxuries that rule afforded. The fundamental crises of *Jekyll and Hyde* and *Dorian Gray* are about lusts and desires in conflict with respectable appearances. That is why it is best to leave things alone, not to look too closely. As Enfield reminds Mr. Utterson, while taking one of their customary "Sunday walks" (8), that is why detection is so dangerous:

> "You start a question, and it's like starting a stone ... and presently some bland old bird (the last you would have thought of) is knocked on the head in his own back garden and the family have to change their name. No, sir, I make it a rule of mine: the more it looks like Queer Street, the less I ask."
>
> "A very good rule, too," said the lawyer [11].

In *Jekyll and Hyde*, detection is a form of transgression. They both agree there is a prohibition against seeking the internal structure of desire ("Queer Street") behind outward respectability. It is a cultural prohibition in the elite middle-class patriarchy, "a very good rule," against detection inside their closed world. It is also an acknowledgment of the decadence hiding underneath the "bland old bird." They are, however, to protect their own. And Utterson breaks the rule for good reason. He connects the unseemly Hyde to his eminently respectable friend, Dr. Jekyll. After Utterson hears Enfield's tale—Hyde's trampling a little girl and Dr. Jekyll's rescue of Hyde with an enormous check—he must uncover the secret. As Utterson tells Enfield, "Richard, your tale has gone home" (12). After its fantasy of treasure islands, romance masculinity "has gone home," but it has gone home schizophrenic.

Enfield's description of Mr. Hyde, the first, is repeated almost verbatim throughout the novella by others. And it is one defined by satanic and by schizophrenic disjunctions. As Enfield tells Utterson,

> He is not easy to describe. There is something wrong with his appearance; something displeasing, something downright detestable. I never saw a man I so disliked, and yet I scarce know why. He must be deformed somewhere; he gives a strong feeling of deformity, although I couldn't specify the point. He's an extraordinary looking man, and yet I really can name nothing out of the way.... I can't describe him. And it's not want of memory; for I declare I can see him this moment [11–12].

The simultaneous attraction and repulsion that he feels makes it impossible for Enfield to record and code Hyde, to place him. Enfield defines Hyde by what Deleuze and Guattari named in *Anti-Oedipus* as the disjunction of the schizoid: "he's an extraordinary looking man, and yet I really can name nothing out of the way."

He sees Hyde as disjunction because the "schizo has his own system of co-ordinates for situating himself at his disposal, because, first of all, he has at his disposal his very own recording code, which does not coincide with the social code, or coincides it with only in order to parody it" (Deleuze and Guattari 15). As Enfield explains to Utterson, after Hyde runs over the child, the crowd that gathered around and threatened to ruin Hyde, "killing being out of the question." The women gather around like "harpies. I never saw a circle of such hateful faces; and there was the man in the middle, with a kind of black, sneering coolness—frightened too, I could see that—but carrying it off, sir, really like Satan" (10). Like Milton's Satan, Byron's hero, and Deleuze's and Guattari's schizo, Hyde is a partisan of chaos and desire. As Utterson apostrophizes to Jekyll after getting his own glimpse of Hyde, "If ever I read Satan's signature upon a face, it is on that of your new friend" (17).

Hyde's satanic deformity is both historic and metaphoric: Byron had a clubfoot and the Byronic hero (at least in the mode of Manfred) wears the mark of sin—the blood of Astarte. Most significantly, Hyde's satanic "signature," including his status as a deformed Byronic romance hero, is his definitive trait: he is a form of rebellion. Hyde represents the outer limit of Byronic romance masculinity, what Peter Thorslev, in his conclusion to *The Byronic Hero*, argues is the most enduring element of the Byronic hero: "total rebellion" (197). As Thorslev defines it, the Byronic hero is "most intimately related to ... the tradition of 'metaphysical' or 'total' rebellion. It is total rebellion not only on a political level, but also on the philosophical and religious level—and sometimes, in nihilistic extremes, against life itself" (197). We can thus see Hyde as a deformed derivative of the Byronic hero pushed to "nihilistic extremes," to an opposition "against life itself."

Being home, this romance masculinity becomes the demonic, deformed, and "evil" in the domesticated men around him. Utterson cannot record, code, and thus order Hyde inside of the same elite, patriarchal structure in which he and Jekyll belong. What makes Hyde schizo is just that: his place inside the respectable middle-class patriarchy, inside Jekyll. It is because he is the unlimited romance masculinity (Hyde) hidden at the center of a domesticated, respectable ideal patriarch (Jekyll). Together Jekyll and Hyde become a schizo "code of delirium or of desire," and thus he (Jekyll as Hyde or Hyde as Jekyll) "deliberately scrambles all the codes" (Deleuze and Guattari 15) for the mature, sober patriarchy of Utterson. This is a dark secret at the heart of the fin de siècle crisis of masculinity—unlimited desire trapped inside of a respectable limit.

This same secret lies between Dorian and his picture. It is not much of a secret though. At his last sitting, Dorian is shown his picture. "As he stood gazing at the shadow of his own loveliness, the full reality of the description flashed across him" and he instantly hates the picture for the contrast between the timelessness of its beauty and the reality of his own mortality:

> His face would be wrinkled and wizen, his eyes dim and colourless, the grace of his figure broken and deformed. The scarlet would pass away from his lips, and the gold steal from his hair. The life that was to make his soul would mar his body. He would become dreadful, hideous, and uncouth.
> As he thought of it, a sharp pang of pain struck though him like a knife [25].

It is one of Shakespeare's favorite themes in the Sonnets: this division between art and reality, between artifice's lasting perfection and human life's fleetingness. For Dorian, art awakens in him a desire to triumph over reality. And he gets what he desires—he buys it. "If it were only the other way! If it were I who was to be always young, and the picture that was to grow old! For that—for that—I would give everything! Yes, there is nothing in the whole world I would not give! I would give my soul for that" (25). Dorian and his picture live on as property in a schizo form of self-recording. The body of the picture, to be hidden in the lonely boy's memories of his schoolroom, becomes a kind of capital. Deleuze and Guattari describe it as "a perverted, bewitched world quickly comes into being, as capital increasingly plays the role of a recording surface that falls back on (*se rabat sur*) all production" (Deleuze and Guattari 11). The picture becomes the place where Dorian's sins are recorded: his cruelty to Sybil Lane; his murder of Basil Hallward; his blackmailing of the young chemist to remove Basil's corpse; and his murder of Sybil Lane's brother. All are recorded on the painting (the body of capital itself) hanging in the vault, the locked schoolroom: "a perverted, bewitched world."

Hyde is supposed to function like Dorian's picture: they are both Deleuze's and Guattari's body without organs, the ideal body of capitalism.[4] Hyde and the picture are supposed to "serve as a surface for the recording of the entire process of the production of desire" (Deleuze and Guattari 11). Like Dorian's picture, Jekyll's Hyde is meant to consume without the consequences of consumption. Jekyll's "beloved daydream" is that a body could be produced in which "each [romance and respectable] could but be housed in separate identities," literally different bodies, so that "the unjust might go his way ... and the just could walk steadfastly and securely" (49). But, Jekyll asks himself, "how, then, were they [to be] dissociated," the consumption from the consumer (49)? Through purchase of course: Jekyll "purchased at once, from a firm of wholesale chemists, a large quantity of a particular salt ... the last ingredient required" (50).

Both Dorian's picture and Jekyll's Hyde are purchased bodies that are meant to free their owners from the social world of scandal that haunts both Dorian and Jekyll. These bodies without organs, like money itself, allow for transactions that transgress the moral and social realities of late Victorian bourgeois society, and thus perform at home its real ethic—the desire for unfettered and total consumption, what Jekyll calls his "vicarious depravity" (53).

In *Jekyll and Hyde* and *Dorian Gray*, it is the privileged that are the offenders. As Simon Joyce argues, the characters of Hyde and Dorian Gray are "privileged offenders" and represent a "cultural fiction, the product of a wish fulfillment which had the useful effect of diverting attention away from genuine social problems of poverty, unemployment, and labor unrest that had recently begun to reassert themselves" (503). I would add their purchasing power, their social positions, and their greed for ever more create "the genuine social problems of poverty, unemployment, and labor unrest." In the fin de siècle, the reassertion of social ills brought on by the Long Depression and the continued decline in the British Isle's share of world exports from 30 percent in 1876–1880 to 19 percent by 1913 (Kenwood and Lougheed 89) threatened the stability of Britain's ruling elite and the "privileged offenders" of the bourgeois that justified its rule in terms of thrift, endless labor, and Christian purity. The violent competition and unquenchable desire for ever more luxury, ever more money, ever more power called for its own destruction, its own masculine crisis.

In the fin de siècle and today, this crisis has been read in terms of anal pleasure and un-reproductive economies of desire. That, of course, suggests a relationship to Byron and his hero. As Elfenbein put it, public men like Bulwer Lytton, Benjamin Disraeli, and Wilde (before his prosecution) all "represented themselves as ersatz Byrons, whom they knew as a great celebrity and as one who committed the most unspeakable sexual crimes" (206). Linehan calls these "unspeakable sexual crimes" the "speaking absence" (204) in *Jekyll and Hyde*, and they have led scholars such as Vladimir Nabokov and Elaine Showalter to argue that "Jekyll's secret adventures 'were homosexual practices so common in London behind the Victorian veil'" (Nabokov qtd. in Showalter 183). But Wilde outstripped them all in his Byronic "posing" (Elfenbein 230).

The sexual milieu of *Dorian Gray* was so clear that Edward Carson, rising for the defense of Lord Queensbury in Wilde's first trial, argued that Queensbury, based on "Wilde's literature alone" (Hyde 166), had been justified in accusing the author of being a "posing somdomite [sic]" (Holland xix). On 3 April 18995, during the *Regina v. Wilde* trial, when Carson asked him point blank if Dorian's "sins" were not anal, Wilde did not deny it:

> CARSON: Then, you left it open to be inferred, I take it that sins of Dorian Gray, some of them, may have been sodomy.
>
> WILDE: That is according to the temper of each one who reads the book; he who has found the sin has bought it [Holland 78].

He does not deny it, but instead he points us in another direction, away from the late nineteenth century obsession with the pleasures and poses of sodomy evidenced by the enormous attention the trial generated. He points us instead toward purchase and exchange: "he who has found the sin has bought it." By forcing first Carson and now us to look at the sin in terms of buying (the privileged power of commodity purchase), Wilde gives a radically different way to read the crisis of masculinity as well as the romance rhetoric inside of both *Jekyll and Hyde* and *Dorian Gray*.[5]

Problems of Production

Jekyll's purchase of another body (by extension through his purchase of salts) and Dorian's purchase of the painting with his soul allow for the most intense forms of consumption. Their new bodies create consumption without, or so they think consequence, and that is the highest pleasure for Dorian and Jekyll. They literally consume their privileged position as it is mirrored back to them. For example, each time Dorian returns from one of his "mysterious and prolonged absences," he would go up to the old dusty schoolroom "and stand, with a mirror, in front of the portrait that Basil Hallward had painted of him, looking now at the evil and aging face on the canvas, and now at the fair young face that laughed back at him from the polished glass" (106). Jekyll, too, turns to the mirror after first taking the draught, and "when [he] looked upon that ugly idol in the glass, [he] was conscious of no repugnance, rather of a leap of welcome" (51). In both cases, we can see the mutual mirroring of distinct and yet identical subjectivities inside the same identity. "The schizoanalytic argument," Deleuze and Guattari write, "is simple: desire is a machine, a synthesis of machines, a mechinic arrangement—desiring-machines. The order of desire is the order of production; all production is at once desiring-production and social production" (296). Looking in their two mirrors, it seems that both Dorian and Jekyll have been freed from the "order of production," the unity of their desire-production and their social production, what they want from the social consequence of what they want. They are wrong. It is the *illusion* of privileged purchase, the funhouse mirror of purchase without consequence, that is breaking down and turning on the late Victorian patriarchal order—ironically, the very privileged purchase power that is meant to control and maintain its class position. For the purchased bodies have minds of their own.

Hyde becomes desiring-production and is immediately outside the control of Jekyll (social-production). Thus, the body without organs, the commodification of his privileged purchasing, turns against Jekyll. This purchase becomes the most dangerous of Romantic transgressions: independent human creation outside of nature. Like Frankenstein's monster, another deformed Byronic hero, Hyde is the child of economic advantage trumping the natural order. Both monsters are the product of privileged doctors, the wealthy Dr. Frankenstein and the wealthy Dr. Jekyll, who are able to purchase a means of conquering death (Dr. Frankenstein) and the limits of the body (Dr. Jekyll). Both, like Manfred, use their privileged position to transcend human limitations. There is, however, one stark difference. Frankenstein hates his monster; Jekyll *is* his monster. "[W]hen I looked upon that ugly idol in the glass," Jekyll recounts, "I was conscious of no repugnance, rather of a leap of welcome. This, too, was myself. It seemed natural and human. In my eyes it bore a livelier image of the spirit, it seemed more express and single, than the imperfect and divided countenance, I had been hitherto accustomed to call mine" (51). Jekyll immediately associates himself with his creation because "the ugly idol" is the face of his real desire. It is not something outside of him like Frankenstein's monster, but a "livelier image of the spirit" than he "had been hitherto accustomed to call mine." He is creating a better, realer self and in this creation, Jekyll sounds much more like Byron when he creates his Byronic hero, Childe Harold.

As Byron writes of creating a Byronic hero in the famous stanzas of *Childe Harold's Pilgrimage* Canto III,

> 'Tis to create, and in creating live
> A being more intense, that we endow
> With form our fancy, gaining as we give
> The life we image, even as I do now.
> What am I? Nothing: but not so art thou,
> Soul of my thought! with whom I traverse earth,
> Invisible but gazing, as I glow
> Mix'd with the spirit, blended with thy birth
> And feeling still with thee in my crush'd feelings' dearth [6.46–54].

Both Byron's hero and Jekyll's Hyde are the creation of "crush'd feelings' dearth." They are "a being more intense" or, as Jekyll describes Hyde, "a livelier image of the spirit, it seemed more express and single" (31). Hyde is the "life we image" whereas Jekyll is divided between his desires and his duties to the code of respectability. There is, however, an historical ocean dividing Childe Harold and Hyde—the end of Romanticism, the coalescence of middle-class power and its domestic doxa, the Byronic heroes' warping journey through the domestic novel. Hyde is thus deformed and satanic but still "the diabolical rebel, the terror of bourgeois mediocrity" (Herber 93–94). Where Childe Harold is always the exile, the wanderer far from Great Britain and the regulations of respectability, Hyde is in the middle of it. Hyde is not a Byronic hero, but one of romance masculinity derived from the Byronic hero. At its most Byronic, romance masculinity seeks to uproot the gendering that gave its guilt in exchange for power, respectability for its desire, it seeks to unify Jekyll's "imperfect and divided countenance." Inside of the domestic enclosure of the late Victorian bourgeoisie, that means "total rebellion" (Thorslev 197) against patriarchy. It is a kind of homecoming.

I am not alone in seeing the real setting of *Jekyll and Hyde* as patriarchy itself. William Veeder places the textual space of *Jekyll and Hyde* neither in "London or Edinburgh but the larger milieu of Late Victorian patriarchy" (108). Jerrold E. Hogle locates Hyde inside a struggle for "power [that] has been culturally set up as a legitimized object of exclusively male desire, then men have been urged to pursue that end in conflict with virtually every other male ... this violent rivalry is the foundation of the social order" (165). The foundation of the social order for Hogle is the "Father's Dictum (with phallus)." But it is also something simpler: it is the outside of capitalist competition. The foundation of the social order is the violence of accumulation, and its ethic is the violent completion meant to ensure that accumulation. This code of completion is inscribed onto the male body by every social institution of Victorian middle class life. The satanic Hyde is the creation of the outside of masculine completion: he is the commodification of romance masculinity, the rage of the son, now being visited on the father.

In Hyde, the violent reality of male gendering returns for revenge against patriarchy and the domestic enclosure. Stevenson textually recreates the inside / outside dichotomy of the Victorian domestic social order only to destroy it. And that space is a home overseen by a woman: the only witness to Hyde's murder of Carew is "a maid servant" watching from inside a house (21). As she looks down out upon the "lane ... brilliantly lit by the full moon," she feels all the peace and protection of the internal inside, or the pacific, domestic enclosure: "Never (she used to say, with streaming tears, when she narrated that experience) never had she felt more at peace with all men or thought more kindly of the world" (21). It is a moment of perfect connection between the ideal domestic space and the patriarchal power meant to protect and provide for it—Carew steps out of the fog and into the moonlight. For Carew, an "aged and beautiful gentleman" with a "very pretty manner of politeness," comes to represent for her "something high too, as of a well-founded self-content" (21). Carew represents "something high"—patriarchy has a top-down vertical construction—and he is at the same time "well-founded," which echoes all the tropes of the "foundational," "organic," "natural" patriarchal order that bestows on him a "self-content": the projection of the completeness of masculine, class power. It is not Carew in particular that attracts Hyde, but the veridical and natural construction he represents—patriarchy. Hyde brings him "to the earth."

The maid's ideal connection between the inside of domestic peace and the outside of masculine power is "shattered." "Mr. Hyde broke out of all bounds and clubbed him to the earth. And next moment, with ape-like fury, he was trampling his victim under foot, and hailing down a storm of blows, under which the bones were audibly shattered" (23). By attacking the very image of the respectable gentleman, Hyde's attack on Carew is an attack on the "well-founded" world of late Victorian patriarchy. It repays the aggression of masculine gendering by re-inscribing on the body of the image of masculine power with its own brutality. It repays David Copperfield's beating at the hands of Murdstone, when he is beaten within an inch of his life because he fails to meet up to the father's expectations and then defends himself. The image of Carew, the ideal patriarch, drives Hyde mad. In "Henry Jekyll's Full Statement of the Facts," Jekyll describes the beating of Carew as return of Satan, the demonic, the deformed romance hero, for "the spirit of hell awoke in me and raged" (56). It is also pure pleasure: "I mauled the unresisting body, tasting delight from every blow" (56).

Hyde's murder might first seem like a purely Oedipal act—the son killing the father in order to take his place, the ultimate reaffirmation of patriarchal transformation. Ironically, however, it is not, because the murder of Carew creates a return to Jekyll's Victorian father. After Jekyll takes the draught, fearing for his life as the murderer Hyde, he suddenly "saw [his] life as a whole ... when [he] had walked with [his] father's hand, and through the self-denying toils of [his] professional life" (57). Jekyll tries to escape Hyde and return back to the symbols of patriarchy that secure his position. "Life as a whole" means his position as a bourgeois man, his relationship to his father and his profession. His privileged position cannot save him, however, because of his position as privileged purchaser, his ability to buy anything is what is destroying him. What endangered his very subjectivity (Hyde) was his ability to buy his way out of consequences (Hyde). It is not the Oedipal rage of Hyde that does Jekyll in: it is a scarcity of recourses.

His power of purchase fails him. What ultimately undoes Jekyll is what lent him his power to create the body of Hyde—the power of purchase. In the end, "[his] provision of the salt ... began to run low" (61). He tries desperately to buy more. He sends his servant to every chemist in town and back again, but to no avail. It cannot be bought because there was an "unknown impurity" in the first salts that had caused the initial formula to work (61). Jekyll's privileged power of purchase bought him Hyde, and it is the failure of that power that kills him. Total consumption of the body without organs, the body of capitalism, ultimately ends as "the body of a self-destroyer." Utterson's detection leads him to Jekyll's laboratory, where he finds his friend has killed himself.

"The living death of his own soul"

As in *Jekyll and Hyde*, the killing of a patriarchal figure only works to reinforce the power of the patriarchal order in *Dorian Gray*. Hearing the rumors that are circulating around London, Basil confronts Dorian about his reputation for vice, refusing to believe it because "sin is a thing that writes itself across a man's face. It cannot be concealed. People talk sometimes of secret vices. There are no such things" (126). Basil demands that Dorian remain the perfect commodity. He is supposed to exist like one of Ruskin's gothic cathedrals or Morris's Arts and Crafts cabinets, a commodification of the human spirit. And Dorian is—he is his picture, Basil's picture. After Dorian rips the tapestry covering his portrait, Basil begs him to repent. Dorian does not. Instead,

> Dorian Gray glanced at the picture, and suddenly an uncontrollable feeling of hatred for Basil Hallward came over him, as though it had been suggested to him by the image on the canvas, whispered into his ear by those grinning lips. The mad passions of a hunted animal stirred within him.... Something glimmered on the top of the painted chest that faced him. His eye fell on it. He knew what it was. It was a knife.... He seized it and ... rushed at him, and dug the knife into the great vein that is behind the ear, crushing the man's head down on the table, and stabbing again and again [132].

While Dorian is killing the father of the painting, the real father is the picture itself, and it is mediating his desire and directing his violence. The picture does not exist for Dorian. Dorian exists for the picture. The "image on the canvas" is more than a mere repository for Dorian's sins. The "image" suggests the hatred and the murder, "whispered in his ear" through "those grinning lips" (132). Dorian's murder of the painter does nothing to free him from the father, from his commodification. It only highlights the reality: the commodity itself is in control. That is the opposite of what Dorian wanted, the opposite of his deal.

Dorian imagined his purchase of the picture would grant him freedom from the loneliness of the creeping consumerism of modernity. In this sense, *Dorian Gray* anticipates the alienation and loneliness that will inform the Modernist project after World War I. Dorian's ruin of Sybil Vane and Lord Henry's sister, all the young men he ruins, and his life of "creeping at dawn out of dreadful houses and slinking in disguise into the foulest dens in London" (127) are attempts to find a "new spirituality" (108). He embarked on a search for "the true nature of the senses [which] had never been understood" because "they had remained savage and animal merely because the world had sought to starve them into submission or kill them by pain" (108). When he looked back "upon man moving through History, he was haunted by a feeling of loss" (108). But the revolution of the senses, the freedom from haunting emptiness, cannot be realized through transgression without consequences; there is a cost to almost infinite wealth and endless youth. Sheldon W. Liebman places Dorian's failure at the feet of "modern life,"[6] but we can be much more specific. Dorian's inability to create in his own ideal of the "new spirituality" is actually the product of history itself. He is "haunted by a feeling of loss" because he is himself simply another commodity in the developing consumer culture of the late nineteenth century, an empty product of his class and gender.

It is the emptiness, that feeling of loss that kills Dorian Gray. Dorian finally realizes his life has been "the living death of his own soul." He does not blame himself for killing Basil because Basil painted the picture that destroyed him. "It was the portrait that had done everything" (295). The portrait was always in control, "had done everything." For as Dorian takes up the knife, "bright, and glisten[ing]" from his repeated cleaning, he imagines that, in destroying the painting, "it would kill the past, and when that was dead he would be free. He seized it, and stabbed the canvas with it, ripping the thing right up from top to bottom" (297). In trying to "kill the past" and "be free," however, Dorian only cuts away the real secret of his history—that he is controlled by the desire of his class: by Henry, Basil, and the privileged purchasers, the one percent that ruled fin de siècle Great Britain. He was made to taste everything, every possible pleasure, and lets everyone else—the working-class Sybil Vane and brother, the clever chemist Alan Campbell, who commits suicide after helping Dorian get rid of Basil's body—pay the real bill. He tries to kill the picture, to slash it, and it kills him.

The dark irony of Dorian's concern for his soul is that it was dead long ago. In the end, he is nothing but the sum of all the purchases of his class. When the servants finally entered the classroom, they find "lying on the floor was a dead man in evening dress, with a knife in his heart. He was withered, wrinkled, and loathsome in visage" (298). This is the same face that Dorian had seen sitting in the studio when he was a young man, a face "wrinkled and wizen, his eyes dim and colorless, the grace of his figure broken and deformed" (25). It was the face of the privileged purchaser. He ends up identical with the picture, a commodity of a developing consumer culture: "the living death of his own soul" (295).

All of Dorian's sins are merely the commodification of the privileged power of purchase in late Victorian patriarchy. "If Byron's poetry," Elfenbein writes, "offered the reading public a commodified subjectivity, *The Picture of Dorian Gray* offered a commodified sexuality that was worth commodifying because it represented itself as deviant" (230). That is certainly, as we have seen, how Carson read *Dorian Gray* at Wilde's trial on 3 April 1895—and, to make my point again, Wilde did not deny it. After Carson read a homoerotic excerpt between Dorian, Lord Henry, and Basil, he asks him again if the book is not merely a cover for sodomy,

> CARSON: Do you mean to say that that passage describes a natural feeling of one man towards another?
> WILDE: It describes the influence produced on an artist by a beautiful personality.
> CARSON: You prefer person?
> WILDE: I said Dorian Gray's personality. You can describe him how you like [Holland 89].

The passage Carson reads is about the meaninglessness of bourgeois life. Using one of Lord Henry's epigrams, Basils tells Dorian: "a really *grande passion* is the privilege of those who have nothing to do, and that is the use of the idle classes in a country. Well from the moment I meet you, your personality had the most extraordinary influence over me" (qtd. in Holland 87). As Dorian finds out, personality cannot be purchased by the privilege ... of the idle classes." In fact, *Dorian Gray* is a cautionary tale about he possibilities of becoming a personality through consumption.

Personality, which Wilde insists on using with Carson, is the utopian promise of a classless society. Because, as Wilde writes in the "Soul of Man Under Socialism" (1891),[7] developing a personality is the entire point of human life and should be the entire point of our collective human society. In Wilde's essay, the ideal human society, the point and purpose of all social and economic life, serves the collective goal of Individualism—the development of every person's personality. As Wilde tells his readers in 1891 and the future readers,

> "You have a wonderful personality. Develop it. Be yourself. Don't imagine that your perfection lies in accumulating or possessing external things. Your affection is inside of you. If you could only realize that you would not want to be rich.... And try also, to get rid of personal property. It involves sordid preoccupation, endless industry, continual wrong. Personal property hinders Individualism [the collective form of personality] at every step" [1180].

This is Oscar Wilde's reading of the Gospel, a kind of aesthetic Sermon on the Mount, spoken by Wilde's Jesus to nineteenth-century readers. And they are meant as directions for human freedom, a map to utopia. That utopian impulse is what connects Lord Byron and Oscar Wilde beyond commodified deviance. They are both personalities in Wilde's sense of the word. They are both searching for an escape from commodification of masculinity itself, "sordid preoccupation, endless industry, continual wrong." The two great male liberators, one at the start of the nineteenth century and one at its end, were both vilified and forced to die in exile.

Wilde seems to see it coming. "Most personalities," he writes, " have been obliged to be rebels. Half their strength has been wasted in friction. Byron's personality, for instance, was terribly wasted in its battle with the stupidity and Philistinism of the English" (1179). He could be writing his own epitaph.

CHAPTER SEVEN

Writing the Rebel into Shape
Schizophrenia as Form in
Sir Arthur Conan Doyle's *Sign of Four*
and E.W. Hornung's Raffles Stories

"For me," said Sherlock Holmes, "there still remains the cocaine-bottle."
—Sir Arthur Conan Doyle,
The Sign of Four

The American publisher of *Lippincott's Monthly Magazine* (1868–1915), J. M. Stoddart, had Oscar Wilde and Arthur Conan Doyle out to dinner. "It was indeed a golden evening," Conan Doyle dutifully recorded in his *Memories and Adventures* (1924), noting that Wilde's "conversation left an indelible impression on [his] mind" (94). The topics veered from genuine virtue to the wars of the future to stories of murder and detection. Stoddart's ears must have perked up when the conversation turned sensational. Conan Doyle outlined the complex plot of his second Holmes novel and Wilde followed suit with his own tale—the killing of Basil and the acid bath prepared by the blackmailed chemist. Stoddart ended up buying both. Conan Doyle's *The Sign of Four* was published in *Lippincott's* in February of 1890, and Wilde's *The Picture of Dorian Gray* followed in July. The dinner and the shared publication history suggest another, deeper structural intersection between the arch aesthetic and one of the creators of modern detective fiction. Conan Doyle's Sherlock Homes oeuvre is part of the literature of masculine crisis that pitted romance masculinity against domestic values.

Sherlock Holmes and Dr. Watson are products of the same crisis of masculinity that bred Stevenson's romance monster and Wilde's tragedy of consumption. In fact, they are commodifications of the conflicting, destructive, and utopian energies. Except, they sell the crisis back as the cure: Sherlock Holmes and his loyal chronicler, Dr. Watson, function as an answer to the schizophrenia of desire that circulates through *Jekyll and Hyde* and *Dorian Gray*.[1] The crisis of masculinity (romance desire versus domestic duty) created a rupture in the symbolic manufacturing of masculinity, and it generated a utopian critique of capitalism and consumerism—Wilde's ideal of personality development. This crisis of masculinity is replicated in the Watson-Holmes dynamic. But it is replicated in terms of a complex interchange between utopian detection and middle class surveillance.

That interchange is also seemingly endless in its reproducibility, from the detective's first appearance in print to as recently as the latest resurgence of Holmes films and television shows. Starting with the release of the motion picture *Sherlock Holmes* in 2009 along with its sequel, *Sherlock Holmes: Game of Shadows* (2011), there has also been a BBC series, *Sherlock* (2009), an American counterpart, *Elementary* (2012), and another major motion picture, *Mr. Holmes* (2015). The return of Sherlock Holmes during the midst of our own Long Recession should not be a surprise. The economic and social dynamics of a retracting economy in the face of intense global competition is the natural milieu for the world's only "consulting detective" (17). The character was born in the Long Depression (1873–96), which, as I pointed out in chapter 5, marks a more than twenty year decline in British productivity: "prices, profits and rates of interest fell or stayed puzzlingly low" (Hobsbawm 104), along with the unemployment and under-employment such stale economic output inevitably creates.

The Holmes-Watson narration is marked not by internal masculine violence, with its critique of male patriarchal power and its ethos of competition, but by an exchange system through which domesticated masculinity consumes the romance rhetoric. But the consumption of romance rhetoric works to correct violence inside of domestic enclosure. Holmes uncovers perverted domestic spaces and class bounding, super-criminals (as in *Hound of the Baskervilles* [1902]) or corrects the flow of wealth from the international marketplace to the domestic economy (in *Sign of Four*). The rips and fissures Holmes and Watson identify and correct through Conan Doyle's novels and short stories are almost endless when we imagine them remitted over one hundred years of cultural history. What remains stable, however, is the form itself—a figure of romance masculinity detecting crime while a domestic, respectable form of masculinity monitors, chronicles, and controls the outcome.

"Haughty and aristocratic"

Sherlock Holmes also marks a return of the aristocrat and is thus connected to the Byronic hero through class performance. While Holmes shares a privileged position, it functions in a much different way than Dorian Gray's and Dr. Jekyll's bourgeois privileged power of purchase. That is because Holmes is a symbolic return of the aristocratic ideal that was replaced by the middle class during the first thirty years of the nineteenth century. The aristocratic ideal does not return as the sexual profligate or the champion of the landed tradition and feudal right. The aristocratic ideal that survived and ultimately thrived inside late nineteenth-century bourgeois print culture and into our own twenty-first century post-industrial manifestations is romance masculinity as Byronic distance. Whether descended from Conrad, Manfred, Childe Harold (or Byron's own posing), the aristocratic ideal that survives the bourgeois revolutions of the nineteenth century is characterized by *distance from middle-class values*. That is exactly how William Hazlitt described Byron and, by extension, his heroes. The poet, according to Hazlitt, is "like a solitary peak, all access to which is cut off not more by elevation than distance. He is seated on a lofty eminence, 'cloud-capt' taking up ordinary men and things in their hands with haughty indifference.... He exists not by sympathy, but by antipathy. He scorns all things" (120). Hazlitt sums it up: "Lord Byron, who in his politics is a *liberal*, in his genius is haughty and aristocratic" (122).

This same distance from middle-class values defines the relationship between Holmes and Watson. In the *Sign of Four*, Holmes shoots up his difference and consumes it in the face of the concerned, middle-class Dr. Watson. He

> took his bottle from the corner of the mantelpiece, and his hypodermic syringe from its neat morocco case. With his long, white, nervous fingers he adjusted the delicate needle and rolled back his left shirtcuff. For some little time his eyes rested thoughtfully upon the sinewy forearm and wrist, all dotted and scarred with innumerable puncture-marks. Finally, he thrust the sharp point home, pressed down the tiny piston, and sank back into the velvet-lined armchair with a long sigh of satisfaction [123].

For Holmes, romance masculinity exists in antipathy to the economy of respectability: he is the decadent junkie with both his "neat morocco case" and "innumerable puncture-marks" on his muscular forearms. The hero's mainlining of cocaine functions like the gothic sorcery and themes of incest in *Manfred* or the secret sin in *Childe Harold*: they create a different mental space in which romance masculinity can exist. With "a long sigh of satisfaction," Holmes drifts away from Watson's world and values.

This otherness of romance masculinity manifests itself as an aristocratic aura—distance as power. For "there was that in the cool, nonchalant air of my companion" Watson admits, "which made him the last man with whom one would care to take anything approaching to a liberty. His great powers, his masterly manner, and the experience which I had had of his many extraordinary qualities, all made me diffident and backward in crossing him" (123). In Holmes's world, "diffident and backward" defines the bourgeois in the face of aristocratic distance.

Holmes's "cool, nonchalant air" and "masterly manner" create a distance from Watson, and that distance allowed for a serial consumption, which is a development in the history of media. Holmes takes the enormously successful commodification of the Byronic subjectivity and multiplies it *ad infinitum*. He became a marketplace innovation that fueled an entire industry: Agatha Christie's Poirot and Miss Marple, Sapper's Bulldog Drummond, Ian Fleming's James Bond, Raymond Chandler's Philip Marlowe, and Sue Grafton's Kinsey Millhone, to name just a few. The serial consumption of Holmesian romance masculinity is based on the success of its Byronic hero because Conan Doyle repackaged what Elfenbein argues is the central structure of the Byronic hero. "This invisibility of origins," Elfenbein writes, "is the critical turn that Byron's rhetoric performs on the tradition of sensibility and its representation of the inner self.... Byron foregrounds this lack of access as the dominant characteristic of the Byronic hero. All that remains visible is a superstructure built upon baffled desire" (20). It is the "baffling of desire" that makes serialization a possibility, keep Watson and the reader returning to discover the mystery of Holmes's romance masculinity. It is the Byronic, aristocratic distance that makes Holmes so tantalizing and so reproducible. Hazlitt hints at this secret potential in the Byronic hero, realized anew in Sherlock Holmes: "his genius is haughty and aristocratic" (122).

Detecting the Totality

Like Charles Dickens's David Copperfield (the domestic masculinity) watching Steerforth (romance masculinity), Holmes represents the possibility of a different kind of male articulation, an entirely different economy of the male subject. Holmes's rhetorical commodification denies the dictum to accumulate, and thus the violence of the outside of capitalism that defines male, bourgeois gendering. Like our own culture's fetishizing of the addict's body,[2] like Sid Vicious or Kurt Cobain's bodies, Holmes's drug use functions as a fantasy of escape from the reality of late nineteenth century bourgeois London. He needs the cocaine solution to give his existence meaning. For "what else is there to live for?" Holmes asks Watson (130). "Stand at the window here. Was ever such a dreary, dismal, unprofitable world? See how the yellow fog swirls down the street and drifts across the dun-colored houses. What could be more hopelessly prosaic and material?" (130). The world of exchange and reward, the world of middle-class life is "unprofitable." What he wants is transcendence. Holmes uses drugs to transcend the part and touch the whole, to be exalted. As he tells Watson before shooting up, "I abhor the dull routine of existence. I crave for mental exaltation" (124).

The real exaltation he craves is the detective's case: the murder or mystery. It pulls him into London itself. The case that Miss Morstan brings to him will allow him entrance into London's totality. "'Rochester Row,' said he, 'Now Vincent Square. Now we come out on the Vauxhall Bridge Road. We are making for the Surrey side apparently,'" and Holmes "muttered the names as the cab rattled through squares and in and out by tortuous by-streets" (140). For the case becomes the opening through which he will once again enter the body of the immense city with its endless squares, alleys, and wide boulevards, where he uncovers its taverns and street-walkers, mansions and tenements, its bankers, fishmongers, carpenters, lawyers, its gold buried deep in the vaults of the Bank of England. The case opens the gap that pulls him into the pulsing, living body of late nineteenth century capitalism.

Watson's entry into the totality, into London and the world beyond his rooms at Baker Street, on the other hand, is defined by recognizable, middle class domestic accumulation. In the *Sign of Four*, after Miss Morstan consults Holmes about the death of her father, Watson and Holmes argue about her merits. For Holmes, any client is "a mere unit, a factor in a problem" (135); they are a possible entry into the teeming totality of London and, through its ports, to Britain's global empire. Watson's perception of Miss Morstan is no less of a "unit" and no less of an entry into a totality. For Watson, "her smiles, [and] the deep rich tones of her voice" automatically interpolate him into the totality of late nineteenth century capitalism (136). As another doctor, Lydgate from *Middlemarch* discovered, love and desire are merely economic structures. Watson, however, already knows the price of the domestic enclosure—"What was I, an army surgeon with a weak leg and a weaker banking account, that I should dare to think of such things?" (136). "Such things" are marriage and domesticity with Miss Morstan. Watson, the practical, middle-class man, understands his position "What was I[?]") as an always-already: the competitive outside internalized as the male self. And in the competitive marketplace of the fin de siècle, Watson has no illusions about what he is: a "weak leg and weaker banking account," that is to say, a "weaker" competitor. He is the debtor, to use Nietzsche's formulation from *Genealogy of Morals*, and his desire manifests itself as guilty accusation, "that I should dare to think of such things?" Watson's "what was I?," his internalized guilt, is the exact opposite of romance masculinity's articulation of masculine value, the "It was I" from Stevenson *Treasure Island* (151), where the transgression creates the freedom and wholeness of the subject.[3] Thus it is easy to see why Watson and the modern media consumer are mesmerized by Holmes. He escapes the inadequacy and the guilt that comes with the internalization of competitive capitalism, Nietzsche's creditor-debtor relationship, Watson's weak leg and weak bank account. He instead finds his value in the outside world, not the inside world. He finds himself by going out there, to the mystified, distant body of the totality.

Holmes uses the classic formulation of Scholastic philosophy, developed by Saint Augustine, the "Great Chain of Being," to describe the historical production of late nineteenth century capitalism. "From a drop of water," Holmes writes in his article, "The Book of Life," "a logician could infer the possibility of an Atlantic or a Niagara without having seen or heard of one or the other."

> So all life is a great chain, the nature of which is known whenever we are shown a single link of it.... By a man's fingernails, by his coat-sleeve, by his boots, by his trouser-knees, by the callosities of his forefinger and thumb, by his expression, by his shirt-cuffs—by each of these things a man's calling is plainly revealed. That all united should fail to enlighten the competent inquirer in any case is almost inconceivable [16].

As Jean-Paul Sartre describes this totality in *The Reprieve* (1945), "a hundred million free consciousnesses, each aware of walls, the glowing stump of a cigar, familiar faces, and each constructing its destiny on its own responsibility. And yet of each of those consciousnesses, by imperceptible contracts and insensible changes, realizes its existence as a cell in a gigantic and invisible coral" (326). It is not a metaphysical, spiritual, or national realm that creates a web (to use Eliot's language from *Middlemarch*) through which individuals enter into the life of the whole.[4] In Holmes's "Science of Deduction," his "Book of Life" is a manifestation of class and the power of class. The body of the individual, the make of his boots, his fingernails, the wear of his coat—"by each of these things a man's calling is plainly revealed," and it is that calling through which the individual "realizes its existence as a cell in a gigantic and invisible coral," as part of the "great chain" (72).

Holmes, and in many ways the figure of the detective, is always-already the discoverer of the violence at the center of the economic totality because the detective represents a submerged and alienated historical subjectivity, the Byronic aristocrat. That is because he is in part the creation of the violence of bourgeois rule—he is one of its exiles. And he must always remain on the outside of its central ideological manifestations: marriage and accumulation. Thus Holmes is hostile to the great bourgeois passions of love and money: he "never spoke of the softer passions, save with a gibe and a sneer," and his only pleasure is in exaltation or drug use (239). He is not, for all that, a figure of Byronic sexual and political liberation. His aristocratic distance is mediated through a superhuman power, not through sexual and political danger. Like Conrad, that man of "loneliness and mystery," Holmes "sways their souls with that commanding art / That dazzles, leads, yet chills the vulgar heart" (*The Corsair* 1:173–78); and he is like Manfred, who claims "in my mind there is / A power to make these [all of life] subject to itself" (1.1.13–16). Pasquale Accardo suggests how the Byronic aristocrat could become a hero again for in "the golden age of Victoria Regina with its vicious underworld, crass commercialism, sexual perversion, and child prostitution" (18). With the failures of Whig history and bourgeois rule to produce an ever more virtuous, prosperous, and democratic nation, fin de siècle readers might "encounter a Sherlock Holmes as adversarial hero, a countercultural phenomenon" as Accardo suggests (18), especially if we see him as an aristocratic return. Homes is not simply "a countercultural phenomenon," an avenging aristocrat, he is also the ultimate product of the specialized and competitive labor market of the late nineteenth century and the early twenty-first.

Holmes is made for the modern labor market. He is totally dedicated and completely specialized: he is his job. He rejects love and marriage because of its potential to become "a distracting factor which might throw a doubt upon all his mental results" (239). It would be like "grit in a sensitive instrument, or a crack in one of his own high power lenses" (239). As Watson makes clear, Holmes is a machine, but more than just a machine, he is a labor specific machine, a detection machine. With his absolute dedication to a single form of labor, Holmes is the opposite of the aristocratic ideal. In fact, he is the opposite of the gentlemanly ideal as it was formulated by the public school focus on classical languages and moral development. Holmes lacks all "viewness," to use Cardinal Newman's term for the moral and mental purpose of a liberal education in his classic *The Idea of the University* (1852). Holmes is a product of the new economy of specialization and production, an economy that needs engineers for railroad, mines, and steel factories. Watson's ledger of Sherlock Holmes's abilities makes this specialization clear:

Sherlock Holmes—his limits

1. Knowledge of Literature—Nil.
2. "   " Philosophy—Nil.
3. "   " Astronomy—Nil... [13].

Or on the other side of the ledger, there is his labor potential:

7. Knowledge of Chemistry.—Profound.
8. "   " Anatomy—Accurate but unsystematic.
9. "   " Sensational Literature.—Immense [14].

And Holmes is also a master of stylized masculine violence, "an expert singlestick player, boxer, and swordsman" (14). As Holmes tells Watson, "it is of the highest importance, therefore, not to have useless facts elbowing out the useful ones" (135). What Sherlock Holmes knows is his job, and it is that knowledge which allows him to corner the labor market inside the recessional economy of the Long Depression. He is, as he makes clear to Watson, the "last and highest court of appeal in detection," "the only one [consulting detective] in the world" (124). He is the market. And that market turned the hyper-competitive world of late Victorian capitalism into romance. This is particularly clear in *The Sign of Four*, when Mrs. Forrester exclaims that Miss Morstan's search for her patrimony "is a romance!... An injured lady, half a million in treasure, a black cannibal, and a wooden legged ruffian" like Long John Silver from *Treasure Island*. "They take the place of the conventional dragon or wicked earl" (188).

The case takes Holmes into the totality of London, and ever further, to the center of the colonial trade with India. Watson, Holmes, and Miss Morton's dark cab ride through the labyrinthine streets of London brings them to Mr. Thaddeus Sholto, a personification of Anglo-Indian wealth. Inside the claptrap house they find that the "richest and glossiest of curtains and tapestries draped the walls," with "Oriental vase[s]" along the walls and carpet as soft as "a bed of moss" (142). The "two great tigerskins" and "huge hookah" both "increased the suggestion of Eastern luxury" (142). The case is opening up for Holmes not only London, but Great Britain's global trade, its "Eastern luxury."

The mysteries of the anonymous pearls sent to Miss Morstan and her father's disappearance are all connected to the wealth of imperial India and how that wealth is going to be distributed (or not going to be distributed) in Great Britain. And in the 1890s the distribution of Indian wealth goes to the core of the Empire's place in the world economy: its trade balance, and thus its gold flow. Starting in the 1880s and continuing to 1914, India balanced the books in the City of London. India "offset approximately 40% of Britain's total [trade and thus gold] deficits" by exporting heavily to Continental Europe as well as Japan and the United States (Kenwood and A.L. Lougheed 98). So when the Indian treasure goes missing, someone must find it. That someone is Holmes.

Yet for Holmes, the figure of romance masculinity, the object of detection is merely a means of transgressing the bowels of London, the docks of the Thames, deeper into the totality of late nineteenth-century capitalism. It starts by his search for a boat, the *Aurora*. But the trade of the river is so dense below London Bridge that there is "a perfect labyrinth of landing-places for miles" (181). After waiting for word and not getting any, Holmes decides to look for the boat himself. Watson finds him "standing by [his] bedside, clad in a rude sailor dress with a pea jacket and a coarse red scarf round his neck" (191). He disappears into the depths of London. The reader and Watson are left with only "a long chain of curious circumstances" (191) because the act of detection leads Holmes to the very foundations of British middle class consumption: Dockland, Port of London, at the end of the nineteenth century, the largest harbor in the world. Wilde's description of Dorian Gray's hansom ride through Dockland to Chinatown in Limehouse gives us a sense of where Holmes is going. "A cold rain began to fall, and the blurred street-lamps looked ghastly in the dripping mist."

> The public-houses were just closing, and dim men and women were clustering in broken groups round their doors.... Then they passed by lonely brickfields. The fog was lighter here, and he could see the strange bottle-shaped kilns with their orange fan-like tongues of fire.... Here and there a lantern gleamed at the stern of some huge merchantman. The light shook and splintered in the puddles. A red glare came from an outward-bound steamer that was coaling. The slimy pavement looked like a wet mackintosh [Wilde 153–55].

In Docklands, the pacific inside and the violent capital outside have broken down. It is a place of interpenetration, where the working-class and the poor live in the reality of late nineteenth-century capitalism. Where "dim men and women" spilling out of pub are surrounded by "strange bottle-shaped kilns," "lonely brickyards," and the coal fire burning on "outward-bound steamer." At Dockland, the "perfect labyrinth" (Conan Doyle 181), the immensity of London opens to an ever larger, ever expanding totality. It opens to the oceans of the world. The sailor is the human image of those oceans with all its riches and perils.

It is in one of the dark and narrow alleys that Dorian Gray meets Sybil Vane's brother, James, a sailor bound for India. And it is as an old sailor that Sherlock Holmes returns to Watson, "clad in seafaring garb, with an old pea-jacket buttoned up to his throat ... a respectable master mariner who had fallen into years and poverty" (194). The old seaman is, of course, Sherlock Holmes. The inane fantasy that an upper-class subject can inhabit working-class consciousness (never the other way around), can take their knowledge and stalk their communities without living their lives is the least interesting part of class passing in the Holmes stories. Holmes's journey as a young sailor and his return as "a respectable master mariner who had fallen into years and poverty" is also a fantasy of transgression and transformation, where the romance hero enters into the living organism of capitalism, its veins running across oceans and continents and across the entire globe, in order to dig up, to detect, one of its secrets.

The Sepoy Rebellion

In the *Sign of Four*, the secret Holmes digs up is the Sepoy Rebellion of 1857 (in Conan Doyle's time called the Indian Mutiny), a vast rebellion that pitted "the colonial regime" against "over 120,000 trained professional soldiers from the Bengal Army ... with tens of thousands of armed rebels reinforcing and aiding them" (Habib 60). Significantly, the man Holmes is searching for in Dockland is Jonathan Small, one of "the sign of four" that found the treasure—a treasure that was won from a rich rajah during the mayhem surrounding the siege and battle of Agra (May–September 1857), one of the most vicious encounters of the war. John William Kaye describes the opening of the rebellion at Agra as pure chaos in his meticulous detailed and jingoistic *History of the Sepoy War* (1864–76), the definitive history at the time Conan Doyle was writing: "All discipline, all fidelity, all loyalty were blown into the air.... There was a scene of terrible confusion" (3:214). Kaye goes on to quote "a brave-hearted Englishwoman['s]" letter to her brother: "The panic here exceeds any thing I have ever witnessed. Women, children, carts, gharries, buggies [were] flying from all parts into the Fort, with loads of furniture, beds, bedding" (3:227). The immense wealth of the Europeans, with their "loads of furniture," were flying in the face of the native rebellion that was set off in Agra by the hanging of a Brahmin who had proposed that the "Sepoys massacre the Europeans, and seize all the property of individuals and of the State" (213).

In the account of the Sepoy Rebellion that Jonathan Small, using almost the same words as those in Kaye's *Sepoy War*, gives to Holmes and Watson, the real wealth lies beneath the colonial presence, beneath the "garrison, women, children, stores, and everything else" (Conan Doyle 217). The real wealth lies in India itself, in the old city of Agra, which is huge and labyrinthine and frightening compared to the modern European city of Agra where the whites are holed up. It is to be found in the "old quarter, where nobody goes, and which is given over to the scorpions and the centipedes. It is all full of great deserted halls, and winding passages, and long corridors twisting in and out, so that it is easy enough for folk to get lost in it" (217). Surrounded by revolt, war, and death—the human cost of the British Empire in India—the treasure lies cold, clean, and perfect. "There were one hundred and forty-three diamonds of the first water," Small recalls, and "ninety seven very fine emeralds, and one hundred and seventy rubies.... There were forty carbuncles, two hundred and ten sapphires, sixty-one agates, and a great quantity of beryls, onyxes, cats' eyes, turquoises, and other stones" (224). India is robbed, and its wealth taken back to Britain by officers of the East India Company. A rebel pamphlet, "*Dihli Urdu Akhbar* (21 June 1857)," denounced this theft, "tell[ing] its readers the English have been depriving India of its wealth by taking it away to England" (Habib 61). That is where the Agra treasure goes: as Holmes and the police are closing in, Jonathan Small drops the treasure, jewel by jewel, into a five-mile stretch of the Thames. He sinks the wealth of India into the collective totality of England. And, for the late Victorians, that still meant middle-class domesticity.

In the *Sign of Four*, the wealth of India is literally translated into the language of domesticity through the marriage of Miss Morstan and Dr. Watson. For, as Watson reveals, "I did not know how this Agra treasure had weighed me down until now that it was finally removed. It was selfish, no doubt, disloyal, wrong, but I could realize nothing save that the golden barrier was gone from between us" (211). For with the loss of the treasure, Watson feels liberated to marry Miss Morstan. The brutal repression of the Sepoy Rebellion of 1857, the bodies piled on bodies, the extraction of billions of pounds of mineral and material wealth, and the "winding passages, and long corridors, twisting in and out" (Conan Doyle 217) of the British Empire's accumulation of India's wealth are naturalized through love and marriage. "Whoever had lost a treasure," Watson adds, "I knew that night that I had gained one" (211). Thus the violence of history is once again sanctified through marriage—all thanks to Sherlock Holmes.

The aristocrat has become the servant. Watson's narration, his waiting, worrying, and his hero worship, are all forms of surveillance. In Sherlock Holmes, the crisis of masculinity is turned into a commodity and Holmes's aristocratic rebellion serves the ideological and economic interests of the British Empire. By chasing Jonathan Small through the Docklands and the empire, Holmes, the romance masculinity, helps turn the treasures of India into domesticity for his friend. As Watson says to Holmes,

> "'The division [of the treasure] seems rather unfair.... You have done all the work in this business. I get a wife out of it, Jones gets the credit, pray what remains for you?'
> 'For me,' said Sherlock Holmes, 'there still remains the cocaine-bottle.'" [236].

The romance masculinity is allowed to consume some distance from the stale world of bourgeois domesticity. That is about all his rebellion, his journey into the totality allows him. That will not be the case for the criminal version of the Watson-Holmes relationship.

Conclusion: The Death(s) of A.J Raffles and the Ideology of Form

The first Raffles story, "The Ides of March," was published in *Cassell's Magazine* (1898) and introduced British readers to a safe-cracking gentleman cricket player, Raffles, and his dedicated, narrating sidekick, Bunny. E.W. Hornung's Raffles stories are the political unconscious of Holmes and Watson. Their author was the son of Hungarian immigrants and Sir Arthur Conan Doyle's brother-in-law. In fact, the premise for the stories was suggested by Conan Doyle and they were simply an inversion of his immensely popular Holmes stories. The first collection, the *Amateur Cracksman* (1899), was dedicated to "A.C.D. This Form of Flattery." After the publication and success of the Raffles stories, however, Conan Doyle began to question whether they were not "dangerous in their suggestion" that a thief could be a hero (*Life* 391).[5] For in the Raffles stories, the master detective (Holmes) becomes the master thief and the honest, loyal chronicler (Dr. Watson) becomes the criminal and loyal chronicler, Bunny. This inversion of the Holmes-Watson formula, whereby the romance heroes of the domestic order become total social outlaws, allows us insight into the political unconscious, to use Jameson's phrase, of late Victorian masculinity. "The ideology of form" (Jameson 98) that turns the crisis of masculinity in the 1880s into a supervised rebellion in the Holmes stories is reproduced in the Raffles Stories. Yet they are reproduced on the most basic formal level as a "discontinuous and heterogonous formal processes" (Jameson 99) because Bunny and Raffles are criminals, anarchists, and utopianists.

The first scene of the first Raffles story, "The Ides of March," is set in the heart of late Victorian privileged male consumption, The Albany, where Lord Byron had briefly lived (in apartment, or set, A2) from 1814 until his marriage in 1815. The Albany has a long literary and social history for upper-class men. From Byron's day to Hornung's, it contained apartments for young, wealthy man-about-town bachelors. Once belonging to the Duke of York, it was transformed into what might today be called a co-op. Each apartment (or "set") was owned by its tenant, and thus they were called proprietors. The Albany, from its creation by the developer Alexander Copeland in 1802 through the end of the nineteenth century, had a distinctly aristocratic and masculine personality. As Bernard Beatty writes of Lord Byron's apartment in the Albany, "Byron furnished it in a strongly masculine way. With silver urns brought from Greece, swords, a screen decorated with pugilists and an untidy assortment of books" (2). This "strongly masculine way" of the Byronic was not lost either in Hornung's description of Raffles, perhaps one of the most unabashedly Byronic characters in British fiction, or his place of lodging. Raffles lives at E4, which is on the first floor, the same floor that Lord Byron occupied.

In "The Ides of March," the ideal, upper-class, privileged male life is breaking down. The narrator, Bunny, has been playing baccarat at Raffles' swank, bachelor's rooms in The Albany all night. He loses steadily and completely and is forced to write a check that isn't "worth the paper it was written on" (12). In the morning, when the winners try to collect their gains, he will be exposed as a fraud, and there will be a scandal. While it is one thing to owe the hatter, the tailor, the butcher, and the landlord—members of the lower, working classes—it would be unthinkable to welch on a gambling debt to another gentleman. It would mean Bunny's instant exclusion from that rarified class, but he really is not a member any more. He tries to claim his right to gentleman status through one of the institutions that perpetuated privileged class difference, the English public school. Bunny asks Raffles for help because, he remind him, "I fagged for you at school, and you said you remembered me" (11).[6] When Bunny comes to Raffles, having no family, and claims the right of an old school chum and member of the same class, Raffles meets him with "as little of mercy as of sympathy in that curling nostril, that rigid jaw, that cold blue eye which never glanced [his] way" (13). So Bunny puts a gun to his head: "The barrel touched my temple, and my thumb the trigger. Mad with excitement as I was, ruined, dishonoured, and now finally determined to make an end of my misspent life" (14).

In this swank apartment, in front of a man he thinks is rich, Bunny speaks the language of despair and misery that marks the turbulent years before 1914; he speaks the language of suicide. As the anarchist philosopher, publisher of *L'Anarchie*, street fighter Albert Libertad, put it in the beginning of the *Joy of Life* (circ. 1904) "wearied by the struggle of life, how many close their eyes, fold their arms, stop short, powerless and discouraged. How many, and they among the best, abandon life as unworthy of continuance?" Suicide, for Libertad, is the culmination of political, economic, and social powerlessness: "complete suicide is nothing but the final act of total inability to react against the environment" (Libertad). It is a death for Bunny. His life as a privileged purchaser, a gentleman about town, is over. He is joining the déclassé, joining the ranks of those that belong nowhere.

Ironically, what saves Bunny from killing himself is his poverty. Raffles is happy to forgive what he is owed, but he cannot give more because, he tells his former schoolmate, "Bunny, I'm as hard up at this moment as you are yourself!" (15). Bunny is not having it; "How am I to sit here and believe that?" he shouts back.

> "Did I refuse to believe it of you?" he returned, smiling. "And with your own experience, do you think that because a fellow has rooms in this place, and belongs to a club or two, and plays a little cricket, he must necessarily have a balance at the bank? I tell you, my dear man, that at this moment I'm as hard up as you ever were. I have nothing but my wits to live on—absolutely nothing else.... We're in the same boat, Bunny; we'd better pull together [15].

What saves Bunny is the comradeship of poverty, the "absolutely nothing" of the déclassé, the brotherhood of thieves and criminals. As George Orwell wrote in "Raffles and Miss Blandish" (1944), Bunny and Raffles "think of themselves not as sinners but as renegades, or simply as outcasts" (718). They are not alone. There are real, historical outcasts around them.

The first floor of The Albany was also occupied by George Cecil Ives, whom, as Richard Lanceylyn Greene has persuasively argued, is the "model for Raffles" (xxiv). It was at Ives's set at The Albany that Oscar Wilde first met John Francis Bloxam, writer of the notorious "The Priest and the Acolyte" (1894). In addition to being a friend of Wilde and classmate of Lord Alfred Douglas, Ives was an eccentric, a practicing homosexual, and, like Raffles, a brilliant cricket player. He was also a groundbreaking historian of crime and punishment. His most important work, *A History of Penal Methods: Criminals, Witches, Lunatics* (1914), was an elegant and radical historical archeology of the structures of power, property, and crime from the Middle Ages through the Edwardian era. The Albany was a meeting place for those on the outside of domestic doxa—homosexuals, socialists, and those subscribing to the "rational anarchy" (Greene xxv) of Cecil Ives.

The anti-capitalist and anti-domestic discourses in the air in fin de siècle London are embedded in the "discontinuous and heterogonous formal processes" (Jameson 99) of the Raffles stories. The masculine crisis is schizophrenic again. George Orwell, aware of it or not, suggests just such a shared ethos in his review of Wilde's "Soul of Man" (*The Observer* 1958). According to Orwell, Wilde's socialism, "which at that date was probably shared by many people less articulate than himself, is Utopian and anarchistic" ("Soul of Man" 1281). It certainly makes sense that Raffles, "as renegade" ("Miss Blandish" 718), would share in Wilde's "Utopian and anarchistic" discourse. Raffles indeed gestures toward his own clubman's socialism in "The Ides of March." After his speech to Bunny about the joys of crime ("excitement, romance, danger") he adds, "the distribution of wealth is very wrong to begin with" (29).

All these anti-establishment discourses are always mediated through Raffles's romance masculinity. He is perhaps the most stereotypical Byronic hero we have come across other than Dickens's Steerforth. He is beautiful, a master of all the masculine arts, sneering and ironic, homoerotic and heterosexual. Bunny worships him like David worships Steerforth. Of course, the worship is always from a distance. Raffles withholds his plans from Bunny. He stays away from him for days at a time. As he admits in "Gentleman and Players," "the 'thinking' was done entirely by Raffles, who did not always trouble to communicate his thoughts to me. His reticence, however, was no longer an irritant" (53). Despite the distance, his dedication is rewarded when Bunny is given a glimpse of his romance hero swimming through the totality.

Like Byron's Conrad, Dickens's Steerforth, and Holmes's first death in combat with Moriarty at Reichenbach Falls, Raffles's dive is an absorption into a an infinite totality. It is escape into immortality. Raffles's death is a continuation of romance. That is to say, it is not a death at all. The end of the final story of the first collection, "The Gift of the Emperor," puts Raffles and Bunny on the coast of Italy, ten miles from the isle of Elba, a location associated with another great figure of romance, Napoleon. After being caught for stealing a priceless pearl, Raffles stands on the rail of the ship about to jump in the sea. At Raffles's request, Bunny takes hold of one of the mates and his hero's "lithe, spare body cut the sunset as cleanly and precisely as though he had plunged at his leisure from a diver's board."

> Suddenly the sun sank behind the Island of Elba, the lane of dancing sunlight was instantaneously quenched and swallowed in the trackless waste, and in the middle distance, already miles astern, either my sight deceived me or a black speck bobbed amid the grey ... a mere mote dancing in the dim grey distance, drifting towards a purple island, beneath a fading western sky, streaked with dead gold and cerise. And night fell before I knew whether it was a human head or not [153–54].

Raffles moves into the totality, "a mere mote dancing in the dim grey distance." Like Byron, the heroic swimmer of the Hellespont, Raffles is making his way toward the "fading western sky," where the infinite sea and the infinite sky meet, a journey rendered more sublime and beautiful by the fragile human form and the potential of a conscious death it always carries with it.

Comradeship

If Hornung had stopped there, the Raffles stories would have a classic and conservative enclosure of the dangers of romance masculinity, the dive into the infinite. Arthur Conan Doyle stepped in again and suggested to Hornung that he leave open the possibility of his hero's return. The return of the dead, which Conan Doyle would use himself in the *Return of Sherlock Holmes* (1905), finds Bunny and Raffles in the next volume of Raffles stories in a very different space than the club and the cricket green. In *The Black Mask*, they live in a bleak industrial landscape, filled with competitors and police, total disgrace, the fear of poverty, and the beauty of comradeship. Their déclassé state breakdowns the distance between domestic and romance masculinity and replaces it with the joys of masculine friendship. Bunny stops being the empty worshiper and becomes the friend.

This friendship is defined by their shared labor. As Jeremy Larance sees it, in *The Black Mask* "Raffles and Bunny each wear a mask in a distinctive way, [but] their individual masks are similar in that both have disgraced themselves in the eyes of the public" (115). As Bunny makes clear in the "Narrator's Note" to the second collection, he and Raffles are "professionals of the deadliest dye; knowing nobody, without a Club between us, doing little in broad daylight and nothing in our own name;

but peeping our last upon a law-abiding world, through the narrow eyelets of The Black Mask" (*Collected Stories* 179). Gone are the "old festival, unsuspected, club and cricket days" (*Collected Stories* 208). But in place of the privileged consumption and the crime for sport, there is shared work for mutual survival. From that work comes friendship, and genuine equality in the face of this disgrace; as Laurance argues, "Bunny essentially labels his own work as criminal and reprehensible in terms of normal social ... standards" (113). In the *Black Mask*, Bunny says again and again how immoral they are, "how we played no more for love" (*Collected Stories* 179) But the "we" gives him away. Underneath the moral asides, Raffles's and Bunny's journey into the totality of London "without a club" and "knowing nobody" is about another kind of love than the love of play. It is a journey to the love of comradeship.

Their shared workmanship, home, and lives become a brief utopian déclassé freedom. For Raffles "had cost me [Bunny] every tie I valued but the tie between us two" (164). The distance that separates Steerforth from David, Watson from Holmes, and the Byronic hero from the common man becomes a tie, a connection, as the two make their way through the violent underworld of late Victorian capitalism. When Raffles asks for Bunny's help. He instantly replies,

> "I'm on for any mortal thing! My voice rang true, I swear, but it was the way of Raffles to take the evidence of as many senses as possible. I felt the cold steel of his eyes through mine and through my brain. But what he saw seemed to satisfy him no less than what he heard for his hand found my hand, and pressed it with a fervour foreign to the man" [175].

The moments in the *Black Mask* where Hornung's "voice rang true" are moments like these when romance masculinity is reaching for the hand of domestic masculinity. They connect in a déclassé space where the distance between one masculine rhetoric and another, one way of being a man and another way of being a man, is overcome through comradeship and a shared struggle to survive: "his hand found my hand, and pressed it with a fervour foreign to the man." Raffles, weakened by his life on the run, becomes "the man" again not through marriage like Macbeth or transgression like Steerforth or distance like Holmes, but through touching the hand of another.

Romance Masculinity at War

This intense shared life lasts until the war comes. With Raffles's and Bunny's enlistment into the Boer War (1899–1902), as we will see, the distance returns. The final story in the *Black Mask*, "The Knees of the Gods," captures the fervor with which the British people entered into the longest and bloodiest colonial war of Victoria's reign. George Orwell quipped that "a practiced reader would foresee ... from that start" Raffles's death in the Boer War because "in the eyes of both Bunny and his creator this cancels his crimes" (720). But his death does more than "cancel his crimes." Raffles's participation in the conflict reconnects the commodity of romance masculinity to cultural use value. Raffles and Bunny take the déclassé space of the *Black Mask*, a brief moment of masculine utopia, and turn it into the comradeship of militarism. Though Bunny and Raffles were not "earlier victims of the fever" (282) surrounding the conflict, the first genuine defeat at Eland's Laagte (which they both have trouble pronouncing) raises their temperature and Raffles wants to join the war effort.[7] But he does not give up his anti-domestic romance masculinity: he connects it, without thought, to war itself. As he tells Bunny, after hitting on a plan to join the fight against the Boers without being recognized, "*Dulce et decorum est*, Bunny, my boy!" (284).[8] Bunny immediately stops being the partner behind the black mask and returns to being the worshipful follower. Like David looking down at Steerforth on the beach after he has been drowned, Raffles is turned into a commodity again. Bunny immediately makes him into a eulogy: "He had had his innings; there was no better way of getting out. He had scored off an African millionaire, the Players, a Queensland Legislator, the Camorra, the late Lord Ernest Belville, and again and again off Scotland Yard. What more could one man do in one lifetime? And at the worst it was the death to die: no bed, no doctor, no temperature" (284). Romance masculinity is more than the anti-domestic, anti-bourgeois way to live life, a way to stretch "one lifetime"; it is also the best way to die.[9] A romance death is a beautiful and meaningful death, especially when it is for queen and country.

It is thus the first moment of real, moral surveillance in the Raffles stories. Bunny is deeply affected by the union of the highest virtue of heroic patriotism with romance masculinity. The distance between Bunny and Raffles, domestic and romance masculinity, is mediated through the language of masculine morality, the penitence of duty. Raffles's plan to join the war effort incites in Bunny "enthusiasm, admiration, affection, and also ... a sudden regret that he had not always appealed to that part of my nature to which he was appealing now. It was a little thrill of penitence" (284). The "penitence" is sealed with Raffles's death.

The commodification of romance masculinity, where the "I" is made authentic through transgression, is transformed through the communal act of war into a image of national glory. Like the scene of Steerforth's death, Bunny "can see [Raffles] now," beyond history and time, in the forever present tense. Trading shots with a Boer commando, Raffles shoots his enemy's hat off. He asks the wounded Bunny, "I wonder if he's sportsman enough to take a hint? His hat-trick's foolish. Will he show his face if I show mine?" (301). Certainly, Raffles is "sportsman enough" (301). "Sitting upright" to fight the Boer commando while extoling the pleasures of war, Raffles "was shining" (301). Hornung preserves Raffles's heroic "shining," his aura, through a permanent dying, an ever-suspended falling. Raffles turns to Bunny and says, "I'm not half-sure—" Raffles is shot dead in mid-sentence. His death, however, echoes far beyond him. "The sentence was not finished," Bunny tells us, "and never could be in this world" (301).

The joy of comradeship in battle, which Raffles calls "the best time I ever had" (301), connects romance masculinity to national warfare, the pleasure of transgression with the pleasure of war. The half-finished sentence at the moment of death instantly battle turns the dangerous, criminal romance masculinity into a symbol of national glory. Raffles sums the code up before going off to fight in the Boer War: "At the worst it was the death to die: no bed, no doctor, no temperature." As Raffles told Bunny only a moment before, *"Dulce et decorum est,* Bunny, my boy!" (284). The brutal irony of the sweet and fitting death is not lost on the Great War poet Wilfred Owen,

> My friend, you would not tell with such high zest
> To children ardent for some desperate glory,
> The old Lie: Dulce et decorum est
> Pro patria mori [21–28].

World War I will not end the history of romance masculinity, but it will change it.

CHAPTER EIGHT

The Double Agent
Romance Masculinity
in Rudyard Kipling's *Kim*,
Baden-Powell, and the Boy Scouts

> For some absurd reason their weight on his shoulder was
> nothing to their weight on his poor mind.
> —Kipling, *Kim*

With the death of Raffles, the fiction of romance masculinity flows into the newspaper accounts of the British conquest of South Africa. Fiction and history began coming together in the Boer War (1899–1901). This interweaving of adventure fiction with geopolitical realities would only intensify in the years leading up to World War I. Romance masculinity, the genealogical heir to the Byronic hero, became an outright instrument of imperial, militaristic propaganda and at the same time maintained its identity as rebel and outsider. This contradictory, and thus alluring, symbolic commodification, where the inside of national interests meets the outside of violent fantasy structures the spy. The spy, as I will show, in one of its earliest and most influential appearances in a novel, Rudyard Kipling's *Kim* (Jan.–Nov. 1901), is both the figure of male revolt as well as a servant of the state. In this sense, the spy, like the detective, reconciles the power of the patriarchy with the pleasures of the son's revolt. But unlike the detective, the spy, as a direct agent of state power, is a political and historical actor. With the emergence of the spy novel, the treasure islands and lost civilizations of the early romance revival are replaced by the romance of history. Romance masculinity thus comes to play an open and central rhetorical role in British political and cultural discourse from the turn of the century through the years leading up to World War I. In this final chapter, we will uncover how the history of how romance masculinity provides ideological cover for threats to the imperial and economic hegemony of Britain's ruling class.

Whether it is the detective, who serves the state's domestic regime, or the spy, who serves the state's global interests, romance masculinity is joined to national discourse in an intimate and direct way. Kipling's hero Kim thus represents a genealogical bridge between Stevenson's romance masculinity and the fully formed twentieth-century romance masculinities of Sapper's Bulldog Drummond and Ian Fleming's James Bond, two iconic British spies. By looking closely at how romance masculinity is constructed as a state servant, we can begin to unravel how the Byronic hero's commodification throughout the nineteenth-century novel became one of many tools for mobilizing national violence, one of many rhetorical tools used to create the kind of young men that would turn Europe between 1918 and 1914 into a mass grave for the ruling classes. We will use the history of the spy to tell this story.

Although Michael Denning is interested in the post–World War I spy thriller, his concept of the cover story is helpful in locating the roots of the spy genre in Kipling's late romance revival *Kim*. As he puts it, "spy thrillers have been 'cover stories' for our culture, collective fantasies in the imagination of the English-speaking world, paralleling reality, expressing what they wish to conceal ... translating the political and cultural transformations of the twentieth century into the intrigues of a shadow world of secret agents" (1–2). It specifically elucidates how hegemonic masculinity shifts from the domestic middle-class male ideal of the mid–Victorian period to the violent competitor of the late nineteenth and early twentieth century. The figure of the spy and the narrative of spying work to cover how cripplingly outmoded the myth of romance masculinity already was. It was outmoded because by the turn of century the fantasy at the heart of romance masculinity, the fantasy of masculine wholeness actualized through independent and personal violence, is annihilated by mass artillery, high explosives, and the machine gun. Even after experiencing modern warfare in the Second Boer War (1899–1902) (I will refer to this simply as the Boer War throughout this chapter), writers and right wing activists like Kipling and Col. Baden-Powell continued to push the fantasy of masculine wholeness through a violence that was both transgressive and state sanctioned. As we will see, both the character of Kim and the representation of Boer War Hero and Boy Scout founder Baden-Powell were mediated through the rhetorical legacy of romance masculinity derived from the Byronic hero. The fantasy began to create reality.

That fantasy is part of the cover story that works hand in hand with the developing trope of the spy. For as Denning goes on to point out, the spy novel attempted to solve the problem at the heart of democratic capitalism in the industrial age: the total powerlessness of the individual in the face of inhuman and impenetrable forces such as global markets and imperial conflict. It did so through a generic inversion. The spy novel maintained, Denning writes, "a fairly traditional plot by making the spy the link between the actions of an individual—often an 'ordinary person'—and the world historical fate of nations and empires" (14). This "traditional plot" is nothing less than the plot of Stevenson's *Treasure Island*, the founding work of the romance revival: it is the potential for the common, average man to access the fantasy of a romance masculinity through the mediation of violence. That is the hard kernel of *Treasure Island*, which would grow into the spy subgenre. Despite all of spy fiction's immediate connections to geopolitical power, the form maintains the same fantasy kernel of violent self-realization over and against faceless, inhuman forces such as international capitalism and the industrialized international conflicts it fosters. At the same time, it is these very same inhuman forces that create and reinforce the growth and continued popularity of adventure fiction.[1]

Cover Stories: Paranoia and Sportsmanship

The obvious topological connection between adventure fiction of the romance revival and twentieth-century spy fiction speaks to the deep genealogical relationship between romance masculinity and fantasies of controlling state power central to spy fiction. Critics, however, have often separated them. According to Thomas Hitchner, "the advent of British spy literature at the turn of the twentieth century is often thought to have reflected a shift in the tone of British popular literature, and British culture generally, from optimism to pessimism" (413). The setbacks of the Boer War and the increasing economic and military growth of the newly united German Empire, led to the transformation of adventure fiction into an "increasingly insular, even paranoid, genre stressing vigilance and protection against invasion" (Denning 41). Though paranoia and pessimism no doubt defined early twentieth century adventure fiction, this sense of impending decline and its subsequent pressure was not, in fact, new at all. As I pointed out in my reading of *Treasure Island*, the Long Depression (1873–96) and the intense international competition of the 1880s deeply informed the repackaging of the Byronic hero into romance masculinity.

What we will find in *Kim*, and much of the spy fiction that follows, is not a break from the golden days of adventure fantasy, but instead a roiling up of the tensions and fears that created the romance revival in the first place.

There is another essential ingredient to the fantasy of early twentieth-century romance masculinity: the ethic of sporting adventure. It was fueled in part by two cultural phenomena of the second half of the nineteenth century: the prevailing sportsman's culture in public schools and Charles Kingsley's Muscular Christianity, both of which were popularized in books like Thomas Hughes's *Tom Brown's School Days* (1857) and *Tom Brown at Oxford* (1861). Though there was a sense from the beginning that there was little balance between masculine prowess and Christian virtue (as J.A. Mangan and James Walvin put it, "Muscular Christianity ... tended to exaggerate commitment to muscles at the expense of Christianity" [3]), as we will see in *Kim*, by the turn of the century, the Victorian Christian ideal personified in Dickens's heroes had been replaced in large part by the ethic of romance masculinity. That is to say, the point of hyper masculinity (muscular) was no longer to serve, even superficially, moral reformation, but hyper-masculinity itself (romance masculinity). As we will see in *Kim*, the cult of sporting adventure coalesced with the paranoid obsession surrounding international competitors as a way to manufacture a new kind of male subject—romance masculinity as state servants. Kim's ability to adventure, to play the Great Game, is driven by invasion paranoia: the fear of the Russian Empire would cross the Afghan frontier and supplant the British in India. The cult of game playing and the cult of adventure create a romance masculine ethos ideal for the seemingly endless list of enemies to the British Empire. But it is just this long list of enemies that makes *Kim* a departure from both the romance revival and the ethic of the sportsman born, at least anecdotally, on the playing fields of Eton and Rugby.

This paranoia created the possibility for romance masculinity as a British ideal, but more importantly it negated an entire host of long established class and social barriers to participation by working class men in the sport of spying and war, or I should say, participation as something more than cannon fodder. That is a distinct social change that can be seen in Kipling's novel *Kim*. For Kipling is far from ambivalent about Kim's background. His father was an Irish-Catholic, a solider, and a railroad worker who fell into alcoholism and addiction, the plague of the working class. And his mother was a servant. Kim's ascent into the civil service class, his education at Saint Xavier's, his relationship to Colonel Creighton, and the opportunity to serve the Empire as a romance masculinity all work to cover, if not wholly erase, the Irish working-class stain on his background. Difficult to imagine just twenty years before, this new inclusion of an Irish working-class orphan (romance masculinities are almost always orphans) into the ranks of romance masculinity was made possible by two important forces in late Victorian colonial life. One of these I have ready mentioned: British paranoia of being supplanted by a rival nation. This was the economic and political impetus for recruiting working-class boys. As we will see, the rationale for their sudden inclusion into the potential ranks of romance masculinity, of spies and adventurers, was their whiteness. If the growing threat of Russia consolidating power in Afghanistan in order to threaten British India and the industrial and military power of the newly unified Germany tilting the balance of power in Europe was driving the requirement of working-class young men, the doctrine of white supremacy was the road that allowed an Irish-Catholic working-class orphan to become a hero and, in Baden-Powell's *Scouting for Boys* (1908), a role model for the ideal British boy.[2] At once *Kim* is a democratization of the gentlemanly sport of the Great Game of imperial politics and power, while at the same time it is based on the brutal logic of white supremacy.

The contradiction of a democratization of working-class opportunity based on white supremacy is only deepened in the novel *Kim*. For at the heart of Kim is the fantasy of freedom from both racial and class constraint, a fantasy central to the most Byronic modes of romance masculinity. *Kim* is a novel in which the brutal racist history of colonialism meets a fantasy of non-white passing that becomes at times almost a racial disappearing. Of course, the fantasy of non-white passing as means to sensual freedom is merely another racialist narrative. But it is, as Teresa Hubel argues, an escape for Kipling and his class as well. Kipling "projects his own desire to be free of British middle-class cultural restrictions onto his working-class protagonist[,] being free of middle-class restrictions, they are, he assumes, free from all restrictions" (247). This genuine desire for escape from middle class white constriction, however, is mediated through Kipling's own hardened Orientalist organization of reality. Edward Said argues in *Imperialism and Culture* (1993) that a stark and absolute biological binary plays itself out in the organization of every aspect of colonial life: a binary where whites are rational, analytical and superior to emotional, spiritual, and ultimately inferior non-whites. This worldview might allow for the humanity, value, and even beauty of non-whites and non-white culture, but never its equality.

When Kim enters the camp of his dead father's old regiment, the Mavericks, the Anglican priest Bennett makes the white supremacy clear, "We cannot allow an English Boy" to go native, and "the sooner he goes to the Masonic Orphanage the better" (136). But Kim, as usual, sees into the very depths of Bennett's certainty and tells the Lama "he [Bennett] thinks once a Sahib is always a Sahib" (136). It is this theme that we will see repeated in changing contexts throughout the novel. For "in the end," as Said writes in *Orientalism* (1978), "being a White Man, for Kipling and for those perceptions and rhetoric he influenced, was a self-confirming business."

> One became a White Man because one was a White Man; more important, "drinking that cup," living that unalterable design in "the White Man's day" left one little time for idle speculation on origins, causes, historical logic. Being a White Man was therefore an idea and a reality. It involved a reasoned position towards both the white and non-white worlds. It meant—in the colonies—speaking a certain way, behaving according to a code of regulations, and even feeling certain things and not others [228].

Being ethnically white is not identical with being the master, but it is the biological foundation for being the genuine Raj Sahib. It is a mode of being, "a code of regulations"; it is an emotional structure, a way of "feeling certain things and not others." On the other hand, what we learn from *Kim* is that to be the master means a certain education, an "idea" that creates "a reality," and for Kim that means a romance education. Yet Kim's distaste for whiteness and middle-class life never changes, to the end of the novel, he genuinely maintains his role as chela to the Lama. Denning's concept of the cover story is helpful here. For each fantasy (native religious seeker and white spy) functions to mystify, to cover for the other: to be a good servant to the crown is to transgress all the rules of middle class whiteness, and to be a rebel means to transgress all the rules of middle class whiteness. The servant becomes the rebel and the rebel becomes the servant in mutually reaffirming cover stories

What follows is a text that is on every level a fantasy of escape from the strictures, including racial division, of middle class colonial life and also, on every level, absolutely dedicated to maintaining the privileges of whiteness. These utterly contradictory impulses are, once again, resolved through the mediation of the commodity of romance masculinity. We have seen it over and over in our study of this figure: to be truly good one must be deeply bad like Raffles, to serve justice one must kill like Jim Hawkins, and in the case of Kim to be truly white he must take on the tint of the Other. The spy that Kim will be trained to be thus incorporates two rival fantasy structures: one is to escape from middle class whiteness and the other is to serve that whiteness's right to rule at the risk of death.

Once we place Kim within the genealogy of nineteenth century Byronic heroes, as a romance masculinity, then the complex relationship between his fantasy of escaping the bonds of middle class whiteness and his desire to serve its ends, even at the constant risk of death, makes more sense. It is, in fact, this internal tension between servant and rebel, a tension only released through violence that made *Kim* such an important tool for military minded reformers like Baden-Powell. *Kim* presents a model of trespass that promises respectability: it is a novel about how to transform the figure of romance masculinity into a state servant. As such, it is a novel deeply concerned with men and masculinity. As Said argues in his introduction to *Kim*, whether we focus on Kipling's racialist views or his love of India and its diversity, as revealed in "his affectionate description of Indian life on the Grand Trunk Road" (12), there is "one thing about *Kim* [that] will strike every reader[:] it is an overwhelmingly male novel" (12). It is more, as Said clearly sees, than a novel about men. It is concerned with a certain kind of man: "So not only are we in a masculine world dominated by travel, trade, adventure and intrigue, we are in a celibate world, in which the common romance of fiction and the enduring institution of marriage have been circumvented, avoided, all but ignored" (12).

At this point in our study of romance masculinity, Said's insight into Kim's masculine value system is familiar to us. The intense anti-domesticity, which defines Kim's Great Game world, has its roots in the Byronic hero's journey through the nineteenth century. Kim's status as an orphan and an outsider is a definitive trait of the Byronic hero's evolution into romance masculinity, like Byron's Conrad and Manfred, Brontë's Heathcliff, and Stevenson's Jim Hawkins with his dead father and fainting mother. Also like Conrad, Manfred, Steerforth, Sherlock Holmes, and Raffles, Kim is exceptional in almost every way. That all is obvious, but what concerns us is how this ideal of British masculinity is connected first to biological whiteness and then to classed whiteness.

The class integration that marks Kim's rise from orphaned street boy to educated sahib in the secret service of the Crown is made possible by his whiteness. His Irish heritage, his very nominal Catholicism, all of these can be forgiven because, in the sea of Otherness that marks Kipling's novel, Kim is white. This is the foundation on which all other possibilities are built. It is on this racial division that colonialism itself was established. The immense mechanics of military, judicial, and educational occupation served the economic exploitation of vast swaths of the earth's surface by the French and British most significantly, but also by Germans, Dutch, and Belgians as well. In various guises, Europeans controlled coastal Africa, the Indonesian archipelago, Indochina, and the subcontinent of India at the time of *Kim*'s publication. Central to *Kim* the novel is the colonial system, which, despite all its ambiguities, contradictions, potential technological benefits and unimaginable injustices, was based on the foundational fantasy of white supremacy. For Kim, that means the difficulties of class, religion, and nationality can be washed away by adherence to the code of romance masculinity—because he is *white*.

The Creditor and Debtor

It should come as no surprise that Kipling's *Kim* echoes a mode of masculine education outlined in earlier chapters, first in Dickens's *David Copperfield* and then reimagined and refined in Stevenson's *Treasure Island*. That is to say, first Kim will be beaten and then will give the beatings. This structure is at the center of male gendering and at the core of romance masculinity. Like David Copperfield before him, Kim's white education is one of physical violence and loneliness. As soon as he enters into the world of white men, he meets with its essential atmosphere: that of loneliness. For "the indifference of native crowds he was used to; but this strong loneliness among white men preyed upon him" (149). Like David Copperfield's fall from the female wholeness of his mother and Peggoty into the cold cruelty of Mr. Murdstone, where "firmness ... was the grand quality" (49), Kim's entrance into white male life was a fall from the flowing humanity of Lahore street life and the gentle benevolence of the lame.

But for both Kim and David, loneliness is only the first lesson. The second is inscribed on the body. David gets his lesson from Murdstone; Kim gets his from the army:

> When he wished to sleep he was instructed how to fold up his clothes and set out his boots; the other boys deriding. Bugles waked him in the dawn; the schoolmaster caught him after breakfast, thrust a page of meaningless characters under his nose, gave them senseless names, and whacked him without reason.... Three days of torment passed in the big, echoing white room. He walked out of afternoons under escort of the drummer-boy, and all he heard from his companions were the few useless words which seemed to make two-thirds of the white man's abuse. Kim knew and escaped them all long ago. The boys resented his silence and lack of interest by beating him, as was only natural [152].

Like David Copperfield, Kim is the victim of white male violence. David connects himself to another marginalized and abused group, women. Like David, Kim connects himself, again and again, to an abused group; in this case, the victims of colonial rule, native Indians. That is where the similarity between Kim and David Copperfield ends.

Like Jim Hawkins, the romancer hero of *Treasure Island*, Kim's ultimate trajectory is toward masculine wholeness through command and violence. He begins to understand more than the limitations of white masculinity, its beatings and loneliness, when he is at the Catholic School, St. Xavier's. He begins to see its power. As we will see during his time at the colonial Catholic school, Kim transforms himself into a Sahib, into a master. He does this through repression and for a clear purpose: to access the power of whiteness, even if he continues to hold it in disdain. For Kim "remembered to hold himself lowly. When tales were told of hot nights, Kim did not sweep the board with his reminiscences; for St. Xavier's looks down on boys who 'go native all-together'" (169). Kim learns that white masculine wholeness is achieved through the lonely internalization of his genuine subjectivity.

Kim's willingness to repress his native life, the only one he knew, in order to stay "lowly" and keep his "reminiscences" to himself, to internalize the loneliness that is central to white masculinity, where one feels "certain things and not others" (Said 228), is his real initiation into white masculinity. And he does it because "one must never forget that one is a Sahib, and that some day when examinations are passed, one will command natives" (169). At the heart of Kim's acceptance and nurturing of his whiteness is the opportunity to "command natives," and even more the chance held out to him by Colonel Creighton, of playing the Great Game against the Russians on the Raj's frontiers.

That is to say, Kim takes on the loneliness and structural violence of whiteness in order to become a figure of romance masculinity. Said locates Kim's transformation into full Sahib after he has defeated the Russian and French spies, taken their maps and correspondence, and suffered and recovered from a fever. This is the moment, according to Said, when Kim genuinely experiences a "newly sharpened apprehension of mastery, of 'locking-up,' of solidarity, of moving from liminality to dominion [which] is to a very great extent a function of being a Sahib in colonial India: what Kipling has Kim go through is a ceremony of re-appropriation, Britain (through a loyal Irish subject) taking hold once again of India" (*Culture and Imperialism* 144). But there is another much earlier and just as essential moment of "solidary, of moving from liminality to dominion"; Kim's ability to pass the mesmerism test given to him by Lurgan Sahib. This scene is the key to Baden-Powell's conception of Kim as the ideal Boy Scout. But the test is even more. It is the culmination of Kim's first real use of his newfound power as a Sahib and Kipling's foundation for white rule in India.

Language, Logic and Whiteness

After Kim's first term at Saint Xavier, he is sent to study the art of spying at Lurgan Sahib's curiosities shop. It is during his first stay with the master of oriental arts and antiquities (who by the logic of Orientalism must be white) that Kim discovers the true powers of his whiteness. In his first long and frightening night at the curiosities shop, Lurgan Sahib's "boy" refuses to answer Kim's questions. Kim, in turn, shows how quickly he has learned the power of the Sahib's whiteness since going to the colonial public school. After asking him a question and getting no response, Kim "crawled across the floor and cuffed into the darkness [at the boy], crying: 'Give answer, devil! Is this the way to lie to a Sahib?'" (193). Even after finding out that the boy had kept silent by order of Lurgan Sahib, Kim promises himself, "*How* I will beat that Hindu in the morning!" (193). Suddenly the Lahore street boy, Kim, is the white and the Other is "that Hindu."

Kim's promise to himself that he will beat "that Hindu" comes from a long and reasoned internal monologue on his own newfound power as a Sahib and his own place inside the white colonial order. For he is a "Sahib and the son of a Sahib," but even more he is a "a boy of St. Xavier's" and Lurgan Sahib "is only a trader ... but Creighton Sahib is a Colonel— and I think Creighton Sahib gave order that it [training] should be done" (193). This journey through the logic of class power positions, which finds Kim at the mercy of Lurgan Sahib, ends with his reaffirmation of his power through the promise to beat the Hindu boy in the morning.

Kim's new status of master, however, is challenged by Lurgan Sahib the next morning. He tries to mesmerize Kim. This attempt to mesmerize Kim, and his ability to hold up under it will help us untie the two knots, class and race, with which we have been struggling. For this mesmerism test is really a test of whiteness inside the logic of Orientalism, of the demonstrable difference between white skin and brown skin. Lurgan Sahib first employs some slight of hand to make a water pitcher travel unaided fifteen feet to Kim's elbow. After Kim exclaims that it was "magic" (196), the real test begins. Lurgan Sahib is going to try and mesmerize him. If Kim is mesmerized, he fails. If he is not, he passes.

Lurgan Sahib tells him to throw the pitcher on the ground. Kim says it will break. Lurgan Sahib says to throw it down anyway. Kim drops the pitcher and as he does, Lurgan Sahib "laid one hand gently on the nape of his neck, stroked it twice or thrice and whispered":

> "Look! It shall come to life again, piece by piece. First the big piece shall join itself to two others on the right and the left—on the right and left. Look!"
> To save his life, Kim could not have turned his head. The light touch held him as in a vice, and his blood tingled pleasantly through him. There was one large piece of the jar where there had been three, and above them the shadowy outline of the entire vessel. He could see the veranda through it, but it was thickening and darkening with each beat of his pulse [196].

Kim is on the verge of failing the test, of falling prey to the magic of the room, but Kipling makes it clear that this mystifying magic is deep inside of Kim. It is the mystical, superstitious thinking of India, the Orientalist's India, that is magically repairing the broken jar. He must free himself from the Other's deepest structure: language.

The entire time he is on the verge of being mesmerized, "Kim had been thinking Hindi" and "how slowly the thoughts came" (196), but in his effort to free himself from the grip of mesmerism, Kim truly becomes the Sahib and the master. For "with the effort of the swimmer like that of a swimmer before sharks, who hurls himself half out of the water, his mind leaped up from a darkness that was swallowing it and took refuge in—the multiplication tables in English!" (196).

It is English language and English logic that saves him: "he clung desperately to the repetition" and "the shadow-outline of the jar cleared like a mist after rubbing eyes" (196). It should be no surprise that what saves Kim from the "darkness" of his mind is the twin sources of Orientalism's power: European language and European logic. At the bottom of the biological power structure of whiteness what manifests itself as Eurocentric symbolic knowledge is actually power. To Kipling's credit, he does not rely on the mere arbitrary manifestations of biology, he outlines the logic of Orientalism in its clearest formulation: the power of the white Westerner is a symbolic system which makes reality through knowledge, and therefore to have true knowledge of the world through Western symbolic systems is to have access to a more genuine reality. That Western language and logic is merely one (indeed more than one) symbolic system amongst many is anathema to an Orientalist mind like Kipling's. Kipling, on purpose or not, exposes the fact that this organizing system is outside of biological determiners and is just as easily adopted by a darker skinned Indian as by a white skinned Indian, Kim. This is to say, whiteness as language and logic is only a cover story, and a pretty shabby one, at that.

If his biological whiteness translates into a white way of seeing reality, a European way of using symbolic power, Kim can become a genuine romance masculinity, the servant of the Empire, and enjoy all the pleasure of violent gamesmanship heretofore reserved for middle and upper class young men in the colonial services. Kim, orphan, Irish-Catholic, working-class, more Indian than white in his tastes and attitudes, at least in Kipling's mind, can still be a romance masculinity, if at the very deepest core of his seeing he is defined by symbols of white language (English) and white logic (multiplication tables in English). This moment shows that, according to Said's formulation of whiteness, Kim is capable of "speaking a certain way, behaving according to a code of regulations, and even feeling certain things and not others" (*Orientalism* 228). Kim has been recruited. By proving he is "white" at heart, his class (working), national (Irish/Indian), and religious differences (Catholic/Buddhist) can be put aside. These vague and easily acquired symbols, this rudimentary "whiteness," reveal the very meaninglessness of whiteness and instead speak to Kim's real value: violent servant of the ruling class.

On one level, *Kim* is simply a story about the recruitment, training, and activation of an imperial asset. That story, as we have seen, reimagines the possibilities for someone born and raised outside of the ruling middle and upper class order, but of course it is only as a servant to that order. When Kim asks Lurgan Sahib why he was tested, he gets an honest (if opaque) answer: "It was only," Lurgan Sahib says, "a way to see if there was—a flaw in a jewel. Sometimes very fine jewels will fly all to pieces if a man holds them in his hands" (197). In less metaphoric language, Kim is a commodity, and he has passed inspection.

Kim, however, stays close to his native roots and joins the Mahbub Ali and Hurree Babu as a native operative in the service of the empire in India. And while the Pashtun horse trader and the Bengali doctor are dashing (Mahbub anyway) and brave, it is clear they cannot be heroes: neither one can be a romance masculinity. In Kipling's India, that role is reserved for whites only. So while there is an element of class mobility in *Kim*, it means betraying real class understanding and unity with non-whites in order to serve upper class white masters and their economic empire. The story of Kim's whiteness as a foundation for his recruitment into the ranks of romance masculinity is merely a cover story for his use as tool for the global competition between imperial and industrial nations and those powers, industrial and imperial, that both create and control them.

The Cult of Romance Masculinity

Kim's publication *in Cassell's Magazine* (Dec. 1900–Oct. 1901) coincided with Britain's longest and bloodiest colonial war—the Boer War. In fact, the first instalment of the serial story very much suggests that *Kim* is a novel about war in India, since it includes Kim's initial message to Colonel Creighton and his discovery of the deployment of troops. But *Kim* is published along side more overt pieces about the war against the Dutch colonies, such as "Christmas at the Front" by W.B. Wollen, R.I., which purports to explain what is "uppermost in peoples' minds during the last few days of 1899—those who had husbands, sons, or other relatives engaged wondering what they were doing in the plains and hills of South Africa" (189). Gossip about MPs who were ruined by uttering pro–Boer sentiment, or accounts of speeches at the Thames Rowing Club, where W.H. Eyre calls to mind the members fighting in South Africa and hopes the younger members of the Thames Rowing Club "will do all the better in the future for remembering the example of their comrades' pluck" (193) gives a sense of the atmosphere of *Kim's* serial publication. It was an atmosphere deeply immersed in colonial war fever.

In fact, the serialization of *Kim* and Boer War hero Baden-Powell's subsequent use of certain elements of the novel in his *Scouting for Boys* (1908), hint at how deeply the text is connected not to only India, but to the larger imperial struggle as it was playing out on the global chessboard. Though *Kim* is a novel about India and the colonial life of India with all its dizzying diversity, the character Kim as an imperial ideal of romance masculinity is connected to South Africa and the Boer War. For Kim is the ideal servant of the state.

For one thing, Kipling was deeply implicated in South African affairs. In fact, as much as any British public figure, Kipling was invested in the British struggle to control the Dutch colony and its exploited indigenous population. Typical of the man, he did not participate from afar. From 1898 until 1908 Kipling traveled to South Africa every year (except 1899). During his stays, he became an intimate of the leading lights of the British contingent in South Africa, including the founders of De Beers, Cecil Rhodes and Sir Alfred Milner, and became a quick and deep admirer of the British action and pluck these men embodied. As was the case

Eight. The Double Agent

throughout his career, his championing of the working class, common soldiers, or native populations stopped short of criticizing men such as Rhodes. Kipling mostly ignored their avarice and their role in manufacturing a conflict that would take the lives of 58,000 people (23,000 of them civilians), as well as 21,000 of his beloved Tommies.

Though Kipling, as usual, was critical of the war effort or the officer class that led it, as well as the government in Whitehall that oversaw it, he never doubted the ideological mission of the war. As David Gilmore points out, he "embraced Salisbury's argument that it was a war for political freedom of white men, even going so far as to equate it with the English Civil War and the American Revolution" (144). The thin veil of white suffrage was a cover story for a greedy play for gold and diamond mines by Rhodes and Beit's De Beers mining company who had tried to force a war by using their company troops to attack Paul Kruger's Transvaal Republic after Christmas in 1896, the so-called Jameson Raid. But even under the sway of his own imperial rhetoric, Kipling still saw the larger shadow of the global power struggle looming in the South Africa, writing that "the war was not 'so much against the Transvaal as a struggle against the doings of German influence. It is the Germans that have forced the issue'" (qtd. in Gilmore 144). The paranoia brought on by global competition drove ideological construction of masculinity at the end of the nineteenth century.

But Kipling was not the only heir to the romance revival who was transforming the fantasy of domestic transgression and escape encapsulated in the genealogical derivative of the Byronic hero, British romance masculinity, into an ideological tool of British imperial interests. As we have seen, E.W. Hornung redeemed his hero, Raffles, on the battlefields of the Transvaal, and Sir Arthur Conan Doyle, Kipling's friend and golf instructor, would turn romance masculinity into history with his account of the hero of the Mafeking siege, Colonel Baden-Powell. In fact, the fantasy of violence and transgression, the fantasy at the heart of romance masculinity, became a way of justifying the conflict itself. Once the conflict got under way, the real war for mineral rights in South Africa, the phony war for white suffrage, nor the proxy war with Germany that Kipling imagined the British were fighting were enough to ideologically justify it. The failure of the British to crush the Boers in a matter of weeks as promised drove a new rationale for the war. It became the place where the real sportsmen tested their skill. It was an adventure story made real. And Sir Arthur Conan Doyle would write the history of this new British pastime.

Mafeking: "A spontaneous public celebration"

Baden-Powell's place inside this developing narrative of romance masculinity as an ideal for British men is the product of the popular press's need for a hero. The war became a trial for British men, and therefore its own justification. Thus rhetoric of romance masculinity comes to the rescue of the British cause in the face of withering defeat after defeat. For the first year of the Boer War was an unqualified disaster for the British. As Denis Judd and Keith Surridge write: "It proved to be a far larger undertaking, and far costlier, than many had anticipated at the outset. It also provided a series of embarrassments and traumas deriving mainly from unexpected and decisive Boer victories in the early stages of the conflict" (8). This "series of embarrassments and traumas," as Judd and Surridge explain, was aggravated by technical developments in the British media. The popular *Daily Mail* and Churchill's war correspondence, including his daring escape from a Boer prison camp in Pretoria, recounted for readers of the *Morning Post*, made an insurgent war fought at the southernmost tip of Africa omnipresent in British life. By the beginning of the twentieth century, "the popular press was now a new estate" that used war correspondence, as well as criticism of the British execution of the war, as a means to "command the steady attention of a reading public that ... could also be easily distracted from issues of national or international importance" (Judd and Surridge 10).

It was not only the impact of expansive press coverage or books like Conan Doyle's *The Great Boer War*, which was written and revised throughout the conflict, but the advent of film that made this conflict so very different from previous British colonial wars. In the newly constructed movie palaces, rapt audiences watched actual footage of the shifting front and experienced, for the first time, the power of modern propaganda so central to the European conflicts that marked and scarred the twentieth century.[3] In this sense, the Boer War was a dress rehearsal for the barrage of propaganda that would become a powerful tool for all sides in World War I. Still more, the impact of media coverage of the Boer War worked to create amongst many in the British public a deep anxiety about Great Britain's readiness to face a more capable enemy, the newly unified Germany— something already very much on the mind of Rudyard Kipling. Due to the constant setbacks and mistakes of the British Army against their first European enemy since the Crimean War (1854–56), "the fighting seemed to be a more genuine test of the nation and the Empire's character" (Judd and Surridge 10). Most were not pleased with the results. It was a war with few definable victories and even fewer heroes. Thus, the rhetoric of romance masculinity came to the rescue of the British cause in the face of withering defeat after defeat.

It was the dearth of victories that made the successful defense against the Boer's siege of the British garrison at Mafeking a cause for national celebration and the garrison's commander, Col. Baden-Powell, the most celebrated military hero in a war where heroes were hard to come by. With 754 volunteers, 450 townspeople, and the famed Cadet Corp (the model for the Boy Scouts), Baden-Powell defended Mafeking against 9,000 Boer commandos. Heavily outgunned by the Boers, with their impressive 94-pounder Creusot capable of hitting the center of the town at will, Baden-Powell had three advantages: dynamite to construct mines, African combatants that the Boers would not use, and a highly effective communication tool between outposts that stretched over five miles, thanks to his boy soldiers. As with most sieges, it was as much a battle against starvation and disease as it was against the enemy. The prosaic nature of the siege did not stop the British public, and even its sovereign, from romanticizing Baden-Powell and turning him into a hero even before the siege had been lifted. Queen Victoria summed up the sentiment of many of her subjects in a private letter to Baden-Powell, "I continue watching with confidence and admiration in the patient and resolute defense which is so gallantly maintained under your ever resourceful command. VRI" (qtd. in Judd and Surridge 158). The legend had already outpaced history.

The siege was lifted on May 11, 1900, after 217 days. The celebrations in London, and indeed across Great Britain, were immense, intense, and lasted two days. Crowds moving through the streets, the singing of patriotic songs, dancing, and evening bonfires turned the end of the siege into a national celebration. The impromptu celebration became a verb: to maffick—to rejoice spontaneously and publicly. Judd and Surridge are correct that "the pandemonium was pathetic, the relieved reaction of a nation fed on grandiose notions of imperial might, but, underneath all the glitter, pomp and circumstance, insecure" (182). The importance of Baden-Powell was symbolic, and however "pathetic" mafficking might have been, Baden-Powell's military success was not his most lasting legacy, but merely its beginning.

The reason that Baden-Powell is more than an interesting historical footnote is due to the migration of the tropes and fantasies of the romance revival from fiction to history. There had always been a close relationship between romance and history, patriotic myths and military history were expounded in the great canvases of history paintings like Benjamin West's *Death of General Wolfe* (1770) or George Joy's ubiquitous *General Gordon's*

Last Stand (1893), enshrined in popular biographies for boys, in which men like Admiral Nelson were held up as ideal images of virtue and manliness. But what made works like Hornung's final story of Raffles, Kipling's *Kim*, and Conan Doyle's representation of Col. Robert Baden-Powell in *The Great Boer War* (1900–02) different is how they overtly connected the fantasy of romance masculine transgression against Victorian domestic values into a form of imperial service. The generic language developed in the romance revival became the language of celebrate correspondence like the young Winston Churchill narration of his escape from a Boer prison camp in the *Morning Post*, updating histories and, in *Scouting for Boys*, a language with which to instill gentlemanly reflexes in young working-class men. The illicit and hidden fantasy at the heart of the romance revival had become a new ethic during the Boer War. And that ethic was that transgressive violence is pleasurable.

Col. Baden-Powell became the living, flesh-and-blood embodiment of romance masculinity, a real-life *Kim*. In his memoires, *My Life as a Spy* (1915), as well as *Scouting for Boys*, he would make explicit and implicit connections between himself and the romance masculinities of late Victorian adventure fiction. The fact of the matter is he was a character of adventure first. That is to say, his later reputation was created in large part by the generic language that created characters like Jim Hawkins and Kim O'Hara. By first looking at how the popular press, and Conan Doyle in particular, painted Col. Baden-Powell as the embodiment of the fictional virtues of romance masculinity, and then seeing how Baden-Powell took his new fame, and with the help of friends like Kipling, parlayed it into the Scouting Movement, we can see how the journey to romance masculinity, the journey we outlined in *Kim*, became, for some, an answer to Britain's mounting global threats.

What defined Baden-Powell was the pleasure he took in danger and warfare. All other success, his capacity as a leader and an administrator, flowed from the unadulterated pleasure he took in cheating and beating death. It was for those reasons that, according to Sir Arthur Conan Doyle, "Colonel Baden-Powell is a soldier of a type which is exceedingly popular with the British public. A skilled hunter and an expert at many games, there was always something of the sportsman in his keen appreciation of war" (*Great Boer War* 405). It is no surprise that the relationship between sport and war, so clear in Hornung's final Raffles story, is repeated as history in Conan Doyle's representation of Baden-Powell: "there was always something of the sportsman in his keen appreciation of war." Conan Doyle goes on to write the romance hero as historical figure, using a trope that mixes the aesthetic "appreciation of war" with sporting "spirit." In the Matabele War (1896–97), fought against the indigenous people of Zimbabwe, the Ndebele Baden Powell found "his pleasure" in getting ahead of his own "savage scouts" and letting them try to track him "among their native mountains" while using his "rubber-soled shoes" to jump from rock to rock (405–06). In Conan Doyle's description of Baden-Powell we can see Kim dodging his enemies or Sherlock Holmes among the docks, leading the search for a murder through the bowels of London.

Pleasure and love of the sport drive Baden-Powell, just as they drive Holmes and Kim. "An impish humor," Conan Doyle writes of Baden-Powell, often "broke out in him, and the mischievous school boy alternated with the warrior and the administrator" (405). Central to writers like Conan Doyle's vaunting of Baden-Powell and his later self-promotion lies this connection between pleasure and warfare. The theme that war is "pleasure" (405) runs throughout Conan Doyle's narrative of the Siege of Mafeking as well. The "mischievous school boy" and the "sportsman [with] ... his keen appreciation of war," could be a description of Kim, spying on the borders of India. That is not to say that Conan Doyle's description of Baden-Powell is directly related to *Kim*. It is the opposite. Both the character of Kim and the representation of Baden-Powell were mediated by the rhetorical legacy of romance masculinity derived from the Byronic hero. It was the fantasy that created reality. In fact, Conan Doyle was so blind to his own rhetoric that he was apt to fall into outright contradiction. For example, he finds it in keeping with the spirit of sportsmanship that Baden-Powell ordered a hundred of his men to execute a night raid on the Boers's trenches, using only their bayonets; a raid where "many of the Boers [were] bayoneted before they could disengage themselves from the tarpaulins which covered them" (409). Killing defenseless men in their sleep when they could not unwrap themselves from their blankets does not seem all that sporting.

The Boy Scouts and Romance Masculinity

As in *Kim*, the playfulness and exuberance that marks the cult of sportsmanship are never challenged when the game turns serious and deadly, whether in India, South Africa, or, in less than twenty years, on the fields of France. The point of playful exuberance in sportsmanship is in fact that it *does* turn into a deadly reality. The genuine pleasure in sporting, or more specifically, the paramilitary training in *Scouting for Boys*, is anticipation for its one day becoming a life or death sport. The journey of Stevenson's Jim Hawkins and Kipling's Kim, the journey to romance masculinity, became the ideal for the Boy Scouts' founder, Baden-Powell. And at the same time, the legend that surrounded Baden-Powell materialized the ideological fantasies of late Victorian adventure fiction. As Robert Macdonald, in his history of the Scouts Movement in Great Britain and North America, explains, "the [abstract] hero is a hero because he expresses a particular social truth; his myth is a dramatization of collective belief, a story which both vitalizes and justifies an ideology" (112). Part of Baden-Powell's mythological status as hero rested on the preformed fantasy of romance masculinity. As Macdonald points out, his pedigree and his position as an officer played to class prejudices. It was this capacity for romance violence personified in the works of the romance revival that, more than anything else "could be represented as belonging, in the interests of the nation, to the working class" (MacDonald 112). *Kim* and Baden-Powell's use of *Kim* demonstrates just that capacity for working-class boys to ultimately embody imperial British values, the newly commodified romance masculinity.

Kim is lifted out of the sordid, though useful (to the Empire) reality of a working-class orphan life on the streets of Lahore, and given the opportunity to become a figure of romance masculinity in the service of the state. By becoming a romance masculinity, Kim shares in the martial and class glow of his aristocratic recruiter, Colonel Creighton. This became a model for the Boy Scouts.

Kipling was all for using *Kim* as a means of correcting Great Britain's lack of compulsory military service. Nor was he alone. As Macdonald notes,

> Kipling, [historian C.R.L.] Fletcher, and other martially-oriented Conservatives—most notably Lord Roberts and Robert Baden-Powell—ultimately concluded that the chief problem with Britain was the deplorable state of its men that this prolonged period of quiescence [post-Crimea peace] had engendered, and that a reinstituting of British greatness, therefore, depended on a replenishing of the nation's manhood [442].

Paranoia driven by international competition blended with the developing ideal of romance masculinity to "replenish" British manhood and therefore buoy her flagging fortunes. Thus the Boy Scouts were born. Kipling exclaimed it was "the best thing for boys outside boarding schools that [had] ever been invented" (qtd. in Gilmore 238). And it is in this mélange of paranoia and fantasies of masculine rejuvenation through violent transgression that the Byronic hero's long journey through the nineteenth century ultimately became a model for British boys.

Eight. The Double Agent

This indoctrination of young British men into a state sponsored romance masculinity is clear in the very first chapter of Baden-Powell's *Scouting for Boys*, "Campfire Yarns." After a long day of scouting and after setting up the military inspired camp, Baden-Powell's imagined troop leader settles into telling a few stories for the boys. One is the history of the first boy scouts during the Siege at Mafeking and the other is *Kim*. Because, according to Baden-Powell, "a good example of what a Boy Scout can do is to be found in Rudyard Kipling's story of 'Kim'" (18) Not surprisingly, the themes of class and ethnic mixing, religious identity, and sexual potential are not part of Baden-Powell's "reading" of *Kim*. Kim is simply a servant of King and Country, and that service allows Kim to enact the fantasy of adventure, violence, and ultimately, like so many male heroes, allows for the working class orphan's rise in masculine value.

Along with indoctrinating and educating working-class boys on the pleasures of war and the potential threat of imperial enemies, Baden-Powell's reading of *Kim* suggests a new ideology of male ambition at the beginning of the twentieth century. Baden-Powell's reading of *Kim* was also a means of teaching working-class boys about the Empire and their duty to protect it. So when Baden-Powell writes about the "Government Intelligence Department" (15) it is followed by a note to the Troop Leader to "[explain this]" (15), and when Baden-Powell narrates Kim's "capturing of two Russian officers" (15) there is a note for the Troop Leader to "[point out on map respective positions of British and Russians]" (18). Like David Copperfield and Pip Kim is an orphan, but Kim makes a space for his social advancement through his ability *not* to be the respectable domesticated male, but a romancer for the Empire: "These and other adventures of Kim are well worth reading, because they show what valuable work a boy scout could do for his country if he were sufficiently trained and sufficiently intelligent" (18). Baden-Powell's version of Kim represents a new form of respectability, a new kind of David Copperfield, inside a new kind of romance enclosure of masculine potential.

The driving force for cohesion in the imaginary world of *Scouting for Boys* is paranoia of invasion. This paranoia is also what gives scouting its sense of urgency and potential for real life violence. Baden-Powell's *Scouting for Boys* exemplifies how the fantasy of patriotic romancing worked openly to create boys who were trained, prepared, and ideologically certain of the cause of imperial defense (however widely defined) and thus turned boys into inchoate soldiers for the state. Indeed, Baden-Powell is quite honest about the purpose of *Scouting for Boys* and the Scouting Movement. Just as boy "scouts" were used during the Siege of

Mafeking for communication and logistic support, boys "must be prepared" (10) to do the same at home "in Britain" (10):

> It just shows you how you must be prepared for what is *possible*, not only what is *probable* in war; and so, too, we ought to be prepared in Britain against being attacked by enemies; for though it may not be probable, it is quite as possible as it was at Mafeking; and every boy in Britain should be just as ready as those boys were in Mafeking to take their share in its defense [10].

Beyond adding a menacing tone to the Boy Scout motto, "always be prepared," Baden-Powell's first "Camp Fire Yarn," along with his version of *Kim*, illustrates how the method of indoctrination migrates from fantasy ("possible") to reality ("probable"). The confused interplay between possible and probable in Baden-Powell's call to "share in [Britain's] defense" is not only due to his sloppy prose. There is a reversal of meaning which illustrates the decisive move from fantasy space to historical reality. Scouts, as Baden-Powell points out, not only must be prepared for what is possible, but what is probable. But he reverses the meaning of probable and possible in the same sentence, rendering them identical: "though it may not be probable, it is quite as possible as it was at Mafeking." There is little difference between what "may not be probable" and "quite as possible," particularly when the historical reality, "at Mafeking," was more than "probable"—it already happened.

Baden-Powell not only confuses the possible fantasy with the probable reality, he narrates the pleasure of the possible fantasy made real. The boy scouts at Mafeking were "a jolly smart and useful lot" (12), who used bicycles to deliver messages between lines of defense. As Baden-Powell reminisces over the "campfire": "I said to one of these boys on one occasion, when he came in through rather heavy fire: 'You will get hit one of these days riding about like that when shells are flying.' And he replied: 'I pedal so quick, sir, they'd never catch me.' Those boys didn't seem to mind the bullets one bit" (12). The boys that "didn't seem to mind the bullets one bit" became the romance ideal for the boys being called on to defend Britain in the future. They are the fantasy, which "is quite as possible" in the future. "Those boys" do not fear death or maiming "when shells are flying" because it is sport: "I pedal so quick, sir, they'd never catch me," one boy glibly replies, as if bullets and shells are merely competitors in a bicycle race. Baden-Powell goes further in fusing the fantasy of war as sport with its reality by using not only historical anecdotes to create martial commodities out of boys, but in the first "Camp Fire Yarns," by connecting a brutal historical siege with the adventure novel *Kim*.

For Baden-Powell is not the only public man who imagines war is the place for men to become romance masculinities, and fulfill the wholeness of their manhood. This conception of masculine renewal through violence and warfare would darken even the brightest Edwardian minds while war fervor swept through every level of British life in the summer and autumn of 1914. As Samuel Hynes so persuasively argues in *A War Imagined,* his cultural history of World War I, the war would be a "disinfectant" or even a "purge." For critics and academics like Edward Gosse and Selwyn Image, the war was a way to purify the ideological health of the British state, particularly that of its male members (the fear of an emasculating homosexuality being upmost on the minds of even two practiced homosexuals like Gosse and Image). "England," Hynes writes, "like some Edwardian glutton, must take the cure, and would be the better of it. It is a medical metaphor that would turn up again and again as men … strove to justify the war as a social activity" (16).

We are in a position to see this rejuvenation through violence by the light of the longer history of the nineteenth century. We can see the germ of this late-Edwardian cultural fantasy in the heart of the domestic novel tradition, in David Copperfield's continued adoration of Steerforth even though the latter breaks every rule of respectable Victorian domestic life. David cannot get over Steerforth because he represents a model of masculine wholeness through violence and rebellion that goes to the very core of masculine fantasy, one Dickens places in the pain (often bodily) of male gendering. The mass commodification of romance masculinity from the publication of *Treasure Island* to the Boer War and up to World War I, through the popularity of works like *Kim* and the phenomenon that was the Scouting Movement, sales masculine wholeness through state sanctioned violence.

By the time World War I came around, culturally sanctioned masculine freedom lay in its anti-domesticity and its dedication to masculine fulfillment through group violence and/or individual glory. The language of masculine resistance to the domestic modes of masculinity and the domestic doxa of the Victorian novel that marked the earliest works of the romance revival, from *Treasure Island* to Haggard's *She,* became a political tool for the creation of this romance enclosure. As Elleke Boehmer points out the anti-domestic indoctrination of *Scouting for Boys* in which "many of the skills of camping … involve finding a farcical substitutes for domestic chores and utensils, to replace mothers and sisters at every possible level. The ideal scouting life of the frontiersman and the tracker meant enjoying the company of men only … it was this woman-free condition, too, which added to the appeal" (xxxi). The fantasy space that marks all of the works of the romance revival found, in the Scouting Movement, its historical function in the larger history of the British Empire. Boy Scouts get to enter all of those male fantasy spaces beyond female control—the pirate ship and the open range are transformed into the military barracks.

Two Kims: Cover Story as Representational Schizophrenia

Whiteness is the cover story, to combine Denning's and Said's insights, for the recruitment of working class boys into the ranks of this new, nationally sanctioned romance masculinity. After the fiasco of the Boer War, it became clear to Tory intellectuals like Kipling and Baden-Powell that "reinstituting of British greatness ... depended on a replenishing of the nation's manhood" (MacDonald 442), and that replenishment had to reach the working-class young men that would fill the ranks of common soldiers. Class, of course, still mediated every aspect of British life at the end of the century, particularly the army, but the fantasy of transcending class through biological whiteness and the successful journey to romance masculinity, was a powerful recruitment tool. It allowed oppressed and marginalized working-class young men to feel they could occupy positions of upper- and middle-class masters by reenacting the violence central to their own subject creation—to be the one to give the beatings.

We have certainly seen that in *Kim*. But his new status as the Sahib, as opposed to being just another white working-class derelict, does not liberate Kim. Far from it: his new status transforms him from the roving, openhearted "friend of the world," in the opening chapters of the novel into the paranoid and anxiety-riddled bureaucratic mind, that is the real gift of middle-class subjectivity. We see this after Kim steals the documents and, at the insistence of the Lama, travels back into the hill country, burdened more and more by fever. Teetering on the edge of death, his thoughts remain with the stolen documents, kept in a locked box. The heavy weight of the box is nothing to the mental pain it caused him. Once the documents are safely locked away, right next to him of course, "he groans with relief. For some absurd reason their weight on his shoulder was nothing to their weight on his poor mind" (308).

In this, we see the two Kims speaking to each other. The Kim before his recruitment thinks mental worry is absurd compared to the real world of physical pain, but the new officious, bureaucratic Kim cannot help but feel the anxiety of "weight on his poor mind. His neck ached under it [the mental weight] of nights" (308). The great irony of *Kim* is that its hero trades the real possibility of being a Byronic romance masculinity at its most radical, one where he exists beyond national, racial, and gender boundaries in a wandering freedom, for the mental "weight" of middle-class whiteness. And yet what makes *Kim* so compelling today is that the Kim of the beginning of the novel, the wanderer beyond boundaries, the Kim that the Lama loves, never wholly disappears. How these two Kims continue to exist together remains the great quandary of the novel.

It is tempting to try and consolidate or prioritize these two Kims: the spy and the servant of the state and the wandering follower (chela) of the Tibetan Buddhist monk. That is to say, it is tempting to see one as a cover story for the other. That is how Kinkead-Weekes and Said ultimately read the novel. For Kinkead-Weekes, the artistry of the novel—and this is unique to *Kim* in Kipling's oeuvre—transcends the imperial ideology Kipling is always pushing. For Said, this artistic transcendence is a moment of total reification—a complete locking up of Kim's place into the flow of colonial rule. Their arguments center around the beautiful and ambivalent ending of the novel.

After Kim has recovered from the fever, the Lama tells him he has found the river sprung from the arrow of the Buddha, the river which washes away the sin of desire and the pain of illusion. As the Lama tells this to him, in the moving final moments of the novel, his "soul went free, and, wheeling like an eagle."

> "There was no Tashoo Lama nor any other soul. As a drop draws to water, so my soul drew near to the Great soul which is beyond all things.... I saw every camp and village, to the least, where we have ever rested. I saw them at one time and in one place; for they were within the Soul. By this I knew the soul had passed beyond the illusion of Time and Space and of Things" [320].

The Lama creates infinite complications for a historical reading of *Kim*. And Said agrees, the Lama is "a kind of anti-self" (*Culture and Imperialism* 145), making ridiculous Kim's journey to romance masculinity by the implicit and constant connection of the Great Game, to "the Wheel of Things": the endless cycle of birth, unfulfilled desire, death, and rebirth that marks one of the key Buddhist philosophical concepts. Said, with good reason, privileges the colonial reading as opposed to the inherent critique of colonial power in the person of the Lama. There is, as Said notes, a tendency to excuse Kipling, *Kim*, and, by extension, elements of the colonial experience through the spiritualized rhetoric of art.

Point taken. And yet, the tension in Kim between being a dedicated searcher for escape from the nothingness of illusion and a dedicated player of the Great Game still remains tantalizingly tense through the last word of the novel. For us, and our study, this clearly schizoid relationship between two totally contradictory worldviews, state servant and spiritual rebel, defines one of the core elements of romance masculinity at its most Byronic. For Kim's search with the Lama, his "anti-self," speaks to that Byronic rebel's desire to transgress against its own power so that it can finally move beyond the limiting and mutilating illusion of gender and history. Kim sees that potential liberation in himself: these two selves, the Indian and the white, the government servant and the religious seeker, the confined and the escape artist, equally erase and maintain each other. The masterful player of the Great Game (the ultimate illusion) and the rebel against the illusions of all systems is a perfect balance of the Byronic hero's two sides: the dread pirate or master sorcerer and the self-destructive rebel against the political, sexual, and ethnic systems that created the power to begin with. This alluring and allusive contradiction at the heart of the Byronic hero and its genealogical heir, romance masculinity, is still being commodified today.

Of course, it is the very privilege of the subject position of white masculinity (for most of our study, middle or upper class class subject positions to boot) that creates the fantasy of escaping it. And yet the growth of capitalism through the twentieth and into the twenty-first centuries, along with the dizzying pace of accessible media that defines our world, should give us pause. The growing purchasing power of historically subjugated groups from the Indian subcontinent, the Chinese mainland, and western Africa and beyond has not erased the fantasy of romance masculinity derived from the Byronic hero. In fact, with the growth of the global middle class it is only more successful than ever. The old Byronic commodity repackaged as romance masculinity is alive and well in James Bond or Batman.

The wheel of things keeps moving.

Conclusion
Romance Masculinity and Contemporary Masculinity

Issues surrounding masculinity have become pressing.[1] In a recent article in *The New York Times*, for example, popular columnist David Brooks outlined the possibilities for Westernized men in the twenty-first century. On one hand, he writes, there is a "new masculine ideal" and it is "an unalloyed improvement on all the earlier masculine ideals." That is because "today's ideal man honors the women in his life in whatever they want to do. He treats them with respect in the workplace and romance in the bedroom. He is successful in the competitive world of the marketplace but enthusiastic in the kitchen and gentle during kids' bath time" (Brooks). That is to say, he is the product of sentimental, domestic Victorian literature. Though the new ideal man is improved by the waves of feminist descent that encourage him to support the woman in "whatever [she] want to do," he still looks a great deal like Austen's Captain Frederick Wentworth, Emily Brontë's Hareton Earnshaw, or Dickens's David Copperfield. Again, he is the domesticated male of Victorian domestic literature, and one imagines that his virtues grace homosexual and transsexual men with this "unalloyed improvement" in masculinity as well. But to give David Brooks credit: he does not sugarcoat a key element to this new and improved man's list of virtues. Because for all his sensitivities, "he is successful in the competitive world of the marketplace" (Brooks).

The centrality of marketplace aggression in this meditation on the new and improved middle-class domestic masculinity gives a sense of how blind even a thoughtful observer, like Brooks, is to the real forces that construct masculinity. In fact, that blindness is on full display in the very same article where Brooks bemoans new forces in American politics whose "central arena of life is male completion." Women, other men, friends or enemies, moral right and wrong, all of these are viewed through the lens of male competition, Brooks complains. That is to say, they are behaving how they have been gendered to behave. Because this violent competition is at the heart of male gendering in any ideological system that grows out of capitalism, what Nietzsche calls the creditor and debtor structure of subject creation. Perhaps the real story is how cultural initiations like patriarchal nationalism, Christianity, and the fantasy of middle-class love for so long focused and contained masculinity's inherited violence, its chaotic center. Either way, those days are over. The center of hegemonic masculinity is marketplace aggression and that aggression is breaking out in politics, mass shootings, rape culture, and the cult of the CEO.

The breakdown to which Brooks is blindly pointing is between the outside of aggressive capitalism and the inside of domestic passivity: "He is [supposed to be] successful in the competitive world of the marketplace but enthusiastic in the kitchen and gentle during kids' bath time." This breakdown, however, as we have seen, has a long history in the British literature of the nineteenth and early twentieth century. The desire to square the circle of compassion and competition in the manufacture of masculinity, like our Victorian forbearers, has meet with some success, as Brooks points out, but it tends to fade back into the hyper-masculinity inherited from the romance tradition.

In the heady days of 1970s gender revolutions, as sociologist Michael Kimmel tells the story in *Masculine Mystique*, the ideological demystification of patriarchy led by the Women's Rights Movement engendered a moment of clarity where men asked the admirable question: "If men were supposed to be so powerful and oppressive, how come so many men were still living lives of quite desperation—working in boring and unfulfilling jobs, trapped in unhappy marriages with little or no relationship to their children, with few, if any, close friends, isolated, lonely, and unaware of their feelings" (22). There were a plethora of books that followed this, Kimmel goes on to tell, with now forgotten titles like the *Men Liberation* (1975), *Male Machine* (1975) *The Hazards of Being Male* (1975) and *The New Male* (1979). This reimagining of masculinity, as we all know, failed. As Kimmel concludes, "the main theme of men's liberation—that changing men's *roles* would somehow magically transform the enormous economic and social structure—revealed a theoretical naiveté that would easily sour into the whine of a new voice of victimhood" (28). And he is right.

This study has been an attempt, at least in small part, to reverse the "theoretical naiveté" that has created the mix of hyper masculine violence and defensive victimhood that defines a great deal of male discourse, particularly in the world of social media. As I argued in the introduction, the evolving rhetoric of masculinity and its consequences and rebellions are interrelated to the ever more aggressive global marketplace into which more men are thrust each year. Though out study helps outline the bipolar structure of masculine, domestic and romance, representation that still informs men's subject potential, there is much more to be said.

The trauma of World War I starts the process of eroding the great myths of progress and civilization, and the fantasy of bourgeois love will turn into a stark cynicism in postwar adventure fiction, the hard-boiled detective novels of World War I veterans like Dashiell Hammett and Raymond Chandler. Through the twentieth century the pressures of success in the marketplace will start whittling away the remaining virtues of the classical masculinity of Roman and Greek literature drilled into generations of Victorian school boys—virtues such as honesty, integrity, loyalty, piety, and friendship—will be replaced by a single, supreme virtue: winning in the marketplace. In the twentieth century and the twenty-first century the story of romance masculinity has only been reborn in books, movies, television, and now video games. We have not left the Byronic hero behind. He lives on in men's fantasies.

Chapter Notes

Introduction

1. Both Ricoeur and Althusser use the term, but with a different emphasis. For Ricoeur, the always already of subjectivity is connected to emplotment, life as narrative construction. For Althusser, the always already of subjectivity is the ideological creation of the subject inside the ruling class's articulation of power. In this study, the always already of the Byronic commodity is both a narrative construction and a product of historical ideology.

2. The subscript is Ricoeur's method of differentiating the different levels of mimesis.

Chapter One

1. Lord Byron, *The Corsair* [1814], from *Lord Byron: The Complete Poetical Works*, ed. Jerome J. McGann, 7 vols. (Oxford: Oxford University Press, 1981), III.148–214.

2. It is this popularity of Byron's early work that has to be understood. Though the first installment of *Childe Harold* and the *Bride of Abydos* sold well, the immense popularity of *The Corsair* had no previous measure. As John Murray wrote to Byron, "I believe I have now sold 13,000 Copies a thing perfectly unprecedented & the more grateful to me too as every buyer returns with looks of satisfaction & expressions of delight. You cannot meet a man in the Street who has not read or heard read the Corsair" (72).

3. See Rachel M. Bronstein, "Romanticism, A Romance: Jane Austen and Lord Byron, 1813–1815," *Persuasions* 16 (1994), 177. Bronstein argues that Benwick is constructed ironically, which "implies and urges mutual understanding between writer and reader based on a shared suspiciousness of verbal and other inadequate, because inflexible, forms and constructs" (177). Benwick is no doubt a "romantic-ironic ... social and literary construction" (177), but he is not the romance hero of *Persuasion*, merely the "social and literary" foil for Wentworth.

4. By "gender potential," I am suggesting that male and female representations are products of historical frames (in this case, the Regency), and that both texts push the limits of the historically inscribed potential of gender representation. As Judith Butler observes in *Gender Trouble: Feminism and the Subversion of Identity*, "words, acts and gestures, articulated and enacted desires create the illusion of an interior and organizing gender core, an illusion discursively maintained for the purposes of the regulation of sexuality within the obligatory frame of reproductive heterosexuality" (185–86). In *The Corsair* and *Persuasion*, I am arguing that the articulation of "words, acts and gestures" used to maintain the "illusion of an interior and organizing gender core" is challenged in regard to both masculine and feminine representations. In the context of both texts' violent interruptions, this means a "challenge" to the bipolarity between violent, assertive masculine power based on prowess and the passive, domestic female onlooker.

5. Critics such as Peter Shaw-Knox, Susan Allen Ford, and Anna W. Astell have noted the explicit and complex relationship

concerning generic discourse between Anne and Benwick on the danger of Second Generation poets, Scott and particularly Byron. In Sarah Wootton's "The Byronic in Jane Austen's *Persuasion* and *Pride and Prejudice*," she is correct that "despite Austen's engagement with his work, references to Byron are invariably cited as evidence of her distain for Byronic despair" (30). As Wootton goes on to point out, however, the "disdain for Byronic despair" cannot wholly mediate Austen's allusions to Byron: "Austen may be suspicious of Romanticism, particularly if it encourages an unhealthy self-absorption or thoughtless behavior, but it is not rejected" (31). The ambivalence between Austen's "disdain" and her "preoccupation" (31) with Byron, as I have argued, deserves close textual scrutiny.

6. Diego Saglia's "Touching Byron: Masculinity and Celebrity Body in the Romantic Period" gives an excellent account of the historical sea-change that Byron and the Byronic would have on how celebrity, literature, and masculinity are changed by representations of the Byronic body during the Regency.

7. See Wootton's "The Byronic in Jane Austen's *Persuasion* and *Pride and Prejudice*." As Wootton points out, while critics have often cited the Byronic in Austen, it has been "a misreading" to see Wentworth as Byronic; however, Wootton makes a compelling argument that there are "notable characteristics that mark him as Byronic" (33), particularly that Wentworth is "mostly silent during the episode in Lyme, remaining 'mute' like Conrad at crucial moments in *The Corsair*" (33). Though Wootton's focus is more on "an indirect connection though shared sources" (27) in Austen and Byron, the insight she brings to the Byronic construction of Wentworth is compelling enough to demand delving deeper into the textual relationship between *The Corsair* and *Persuasion*.

8. While Ford's "Learning Romance from Scott and Byron" connects Anne to Gulnare, it is as "damsels in distress" (86). Though Anne is able to reverse "Wentworth's chivalric perspective" (86) that "like Conrad's rescue of Gulnare, casts her [Anne] as a damsel in distress" (86), Ford glosses Gulnare's killing of Syed as "motivated by her love for Conrad" (84) though in the poem, he repeatedly begs her not to kill him (3.358–69). Indeed, as with Shaw Knox, it is Louisa, to use Ford's term, that is "Byronized ... she never speaks or appears in the novel again" (85). It is my contention that what makes *Persuasion* and *The Corsair* uniquely connected, beyond allusion and representational tropes (romance heroines and "chivalric perspectives"), is the way that masculine power is pirated from not just men, but violent men, and how that pirating effects both texts' gender representations, and their "possibilities and limitations" (Morgan, "Captain Wentworth, British Imperialism and Personal Romance," *Persuasions* 18 [1996], 87).

9. As Susan Morgan persuasively argues in "Captain Wentworth, British Imperialism and Personal Romance," the interconnection between gender potential and the Napoleonic Wars cannot be overlooked in Austen's *Persuasion*. Though a "story of heterosexual love" (89), *Persuasion* is framed by "the possibilities and limitations of men and women of Austen's social class at the beginning of the nineteenth century" (89). Both the "possibilities and limitations" are created by the upheaval of the Napoleonic Wars (ending in 1815) and the subsequent class and social changes concomitant with its conclusion. Though Morgan is ultimately interested in the domestication of British sailors and the Royal Navy (96), her reading of Wentworth's demonstrable change throughout the novel, from "self-satisfied aggressiveness" (96) to a domesticated openness "to outside influences and possibilities" (96), suggests the extent of his gender reversal in the context of a military, hierarchal, male-dominated institution such as was the Royal Navy during the Regency.

10. See *ukpublicspending.co.uk*, "Debt in 1816" and "Debt to GDP in 1816" for raw data.

11. See Michael Lewis, *A Social History of the Navy, 1783–1814*.

12. For both Conrad and Wentworth the reversal of roles, their feminization, is predicated on the loss of male mastery as

it relates to violence and their ability to control that violence. Though the contours of the texts are very different, the loss of mastery, either in the fall of Louisa or Conrad's imprisonment, highlights how the tenuous fantasy of patriarchal control is undercut. What cannot be stressed enough is how both Byron and Austen use this failure of male mastery to recreate male value and representation.

13. Corsairs were privateers authorized to raid ships from nations at war with France in the name of the French nation. The etymology of the word is French, and in the history of the Regency, the point should not be missed that it is French law that is protecting Napoleon's legal pirates, *les corsairs*. Though neither *The Corsair* nor *Persuasion* is directly concerned with Napoleonic naval politics, both works are engaging potential gender possibilities such a historical upheaval might promise. That being said, their respective trajectories are oppositional. In this regard, *Persuasion* works as an answer to Byron's "sensational" *Corsair*.

14. This female piracy is what Ann W. Astell calls "revolutionary impulses" in *Persuasion* (2). Both Astell and Ford are correct that "in *Persuasion*, the elements of romance ... are naturalized by the novel's realistic texture" (Ford 87). I, however, see the text as a realist reconstruction of the fantasy space made so popular by Byron's Eastern Tales. Either way, for both Astell and Ford the object of this educational process, "the learning of romance," is Anne. But if Astell is correct that "in the end Anne's happiness depends less on Wentworth's loving her than on her loving him, freely" (2), then it is not she who must be educated, but Wentworth. Where Astell sees "a mature romance which derives its spiritual splendor from selfless intentionality" (2), I see Anne Elliot as pirating Wentworth's masculine command. Anne is the pirate, the captain, the figure of masculine control. It is Anne that transforms him into a male object that she can love "freely, unconditionally, and eternally" (2). Yet this recreation of Wentworth means that he must recognize Anne as essential to his own ability to romance. And that comes through her piracy of power in a moment of violent interruption.

15. As Slavoj Žižek argues in the *Parallax View*, by taking "a step further from this external opposition (or mutual reliance) into direct, internalized overlapping," my reading seeks the "internalized overlapping" as opposed to the "external opposition" of genre and gender that both texts superficially perform (36). As Žižek goes on to argue, when these external oppositions are "brought to the extreme they coincide with the opposite" (36). When Wentworth and Conrad, for example, are "brought to the extreme" of masculinity (powerlessness in this case), they "coincide with its opposite," femininity. Perhaps even more important is the way *The Corsair* and *Persuasion* perform the illusion, as Žižek points out, of the "polar opposition of two principles (male and female)," and give instead a glimpse of "the minimal gap between an element and itself" (36). That is to say, the parallax view of women and men is erased for a moment through violent or traumatic interruptions, leaving a passing visage of "the Void of its [the subject created by language] own place of inscription" (36).

16. In *Byron and His Fictions*, Peter Manning concludes that "throughout the poem Conrad tries to define himself by superiority to women: it is consistent that he should both hold himself above Medora's pleas and as the guardian of damsels in distress. For Conrad to owe his life to a woman is equivalent to his having lost it: it is evidence that he is not yet a man" (49). There is no doubt that the one element of the Byronic romance is a search for the elusive "evidence" of manhood. But what Manning sees as "a loss of autonomy," making Conrad once more "his mother's satellite" (49), or what Giuliano sees as a "stigmatization" created by the castrating act of having a woman wield the "phallic dagger" (789), is the final desire of *The Corsair*. Conrad escapes the need to "evidence" manhood because a woman usurps it.

17. See Knox-Shaw, "*Persuasion*, Byron and the Turkish Tale," for a discussion of "firmness" (55) in Anne Elliot. Though Knox-Shaw notes the importance of "firmness" in Anne's evolution into a romance heroine, he does not connect it to Gulnare's

"'firmness' of the female hand" (3.381) in her own moment of pirating male power, nor to the fact that Conrad's hand "lost its firmness" (3.540).

Chapter Two

1. See Nancy F. Anderson's "The 'Marriage with a Deceased Wife's Sister Bill' Controversy: Incest Anxiety and the Defense of Family Purity in Victorian England," *The Journal of British Studies* 21.02 (1982): 67–86.

2. It is important to reaffirm the critical and theoretical argument for close reading as a way to uncover deeper historical implications of ideological development. As I have said, Armstrong's contention "that novels think like individuals about the difficulty of fulfilling oneself as an individual under specific cultural historical conditions" (*How* 10) is true of poetry as well. But more importantly, close reading, "under specific historical conditions," the construction of limitation and resistance to limitations of a particular form of representation, romance masculinity, elucidates British masculinity's oscillations across the long nineteenth century. The subtle shifts that occured in writing reflected deeper fissures and connections for both literary genealogy and its relation to and impact on historical conditions—or to be more frank, on historical conditioning.

3. I use the term Byronic gothic because it is Heathcliff's Wuthering Heights, and he is definitively Byronic.

4. It is interesting to see the continuity and contrast between the second Catherine's education of Hareton and that of Wentworth. Though both texts work to create a masculinity reformed by female supervision, the extent of that supervision and the real aggression with which the second Catherine teaches Hareton gives us an idea of how much of the doxa of domesticity has made women the *de facto* monitors of the new ideological power structure. It is also telling how Hareton in particular, and masculinity in general, is represented as animal-like and beastly, making him more important to control and supervise.

5. In many ways Lockwood's image of Catherine the second and Hareton completes the rewriting of *Manfred* in *Wuthering Heights*. As Manfred fights "Satan and his legions," ultimately to be free of Astarte, "*They*" are joined in battle against these figurative foes. The point is perhaps too obvious to stress. But what is telling is how Brontë, after creating a domestic enclosure for the Victorian incarnations of the Byronic Catherine the first and Heathcliff, again uses figurative language, stressing the transgeneric mode of her fictional language as well as the figurative foundation of their union, "*They.*" In this sense, Brontë is undercutting her own realist construction of the domestic enclosure by giving a final glimpse of the two soon-to-be married lovers through the lens of figurative allusion, or one might argue, simply illusion.

6. In some ways *Wuthering Heights* and its relation to the romance revival of the 1880s deserves more than a footnote. But it is worth pointing out, even if it does not do the subject justice, how important the novel is to works that seem quite different. The best example, in my mind, is Stevenson's *The Master of Ballantrae: A Winter's Tale* (1889). The "tale," like most of *Wuthering Heights*, is narrated by a family servant, Ephraim Mackellar, whom like Nelly is often torn in loyalty between the Master, one of the most blatantly Byronic representations in the romance revival, and his kind, domesticated younger brother, Henry Durie. It is Heathcliff and Linton as brothers, but after a duel Henry wins against the Master; it is the domesticated Henry (now married to the Master's former fiancée and, no surprise, cousin) who becomes a fat, loutish, greedy, paranoid Tory. While the main narrator Ephraim struggles to remain loyal to his Laird, Henry, it is clear as the Master reemerges in Colonial New York State that domestication breeds in him a hateful, jealously aggressive masculinity that is constantly associated with protection of his wife and child, while the Byronic romance masculinity remains alluring, dangerous, and, for the narrator, irresistible. Not only does Stevenson employ narrative strategies drawn from *Wuthering Heights*—seamless multiple narrations and multiple histories—he rewrites Brontë's

collusion between romance and domestic masculinity as brothers interconnected in opposition.

Chapter Three

1. The trope of the lonely boy only touched on here is one that is implicitly connected to the denial of reality's incarnation in language or vice versa. By privileging "dreaming" and separation from domestic education, male and female characters develop a romance mind that, depending on the author and the work's place in this genealogical history, either ends in correction (as with Waverley), catastrophe (for Lydgate), or in the aesthetic movement and the romance revival, celebration (Kipling's Kim, for instance).

2. The same can be said for Dorothea, but she is saved by Casaubon's death and her own wherewithal, which is essential not only for the plot of *Middlemarch*, but for the larger Victorial social implications of wealth, success, work, marriage, and marriage. Wealth, in short, allows for romancing.

3. The quotation is taken from "About Fiction" published on New Year's Day, 1887. Haggard employs all the chest-pounding Tory rhetoric to discount anything domestic and, by association, "female." "Immodest and provocative" (xix) as Norman Etherington calls the essay, it is in many ways a call, to again quote Etherington, "for all previous schools of literature to be displaced by Haggard's genre of 'romance'" (xix). It was not, as one might expect, received by critics and authors with applause on all sides, and Haggard was attacked. Yet for all of the self-congratulation and genuine naïveté that marks "About Fiction," what is important about the essay is how clearly Haggard sees the development of British romance, born out of the success of Stevenson's *Treasure Island* and his own *King Solomon's Mines*, as a departure from domestic realism and the domestic control of masculinity. His call for a new kind of fiction is connected with a new form of British masculine representation, and it is one that is implicitly connected with British militarism and imperial expansion.

Chapter Four

1. It is no surprise that Nietzsche, like Dickens, places the creditor-debtor transaction at the heart of family life. According to Nietzsche, "parents still punish their children, from anger at some harm or injury, vented on the one who caused it—but this anger is held in check and modified by the idea that every injury has its equivalent and can actually be paid back, even if only through the pain of the culprit" (63).

2. One of the best expositions of Steerforth's Byronic genealogy is William Harvey's "Charles Dickens and the Byronic Hero." Harvey argues Steerforth is "a symbol of the Byronic poet in disguise—Byron in particular—[and] most critics have either failed to see the type in Dickens's work or have ignored it" (305). Though Harvey explicates the Byronic in Steerforth, he is more concerned with Byronic elements in novels as diverse as *Hard Times* (1854) and *Little Dorrit* (1857) and gives a particularly strong reading of Eugene Wrayburn from *Our Mutual Friend* (1864–65) as a redeemed Byronic hero. My focus is on Steerforth alone, which Harvey points out is most the Byronic figure in Dickens, because he remains unredeemed and still worshiped.

3. In one of the shortest chapters in *David Copperfield* (LVI), "The New Wound, and the Old," there is a remarkable exchange between David, Steerforth's mother, and the woman Steerforth disfigured, Rosa Dartle. David goes to Steerforth's family estate with the news of Steerforth's drowning, only to find Mrs. Steerforth in a near coma in her son's room. Indeed, she is already in a state of mournful remembrance: "his old sport and accomplishments, by which she was surrounded, remained there, just as he had left them" (671). Odder still is the exchange that follows. Rosa Dartle begins to upbraid Steerforth's mother for the anti-social and dangerous son she raised. It is a battle between David and Rosa (for his mother only moans over his memory) about who loved him more:

"Who feels for me?" she [Rosa] sharply retorted. "She [Mrs. Steerforth] has sown this. Let her moan for the harvest that she reaps to-day!"

"And if his faults—" I began.

"Faults!" she cried, bursting into passionate tears. "Who dares malign him? He has a soul worth millions of the friends to whom he stooped!"

"No one can have loved him better, no one can hold him in dearer remembrance, than I" [674].

It is a remarkable moment considering all Steerforth had done to David and Rosa Dartle. No matter the crime, Steerforth still has a "soul worth millions of his friends" and "no one can have loved him better," in life and in "remembrance." In death, romance masculinity moves beyond social structure and is almost canonized.

Chapter Five

1. At the outset of the Romance revival, the romance character was only capable of existing as a boy and his romance could only occur in the romantic past, the days of pirates and treasure, on a wild island that has no moral dilemmas: a world of buccaneers, mad marooned sailors, and wealth to be gained through violence. Stevenson's half-hearted attempt to justify the theft by Jim Hawkins and his pirate band of what has already been stolen—the "gold"—is by the most obvious means: drunkenness. For, as Hawkins reminds the reader before he kills one of the pirates, "Certainly, since the mutiny began, not a man of them could have been sober" (133). That is to say, he relies on the bourgeois conception of self-discipline and sobriety to ideologically mystify the underlying desire *to be the pirate*, as Dickens in *Great Expectations* hides Pip's convict's guilt in boyish fear. At the heart of *Treasure Island* in the 1880s is that it overcomes the great Dickensian limit for the male romance hero: a necessary trajectory toward domesticity and the respectable accruing of wealth, which eliminates the pleasure of transgression. Hawkins and his pirates are a mystification of the kernel of resistance central to romance masculinity: individual desire over social structure. What is absent in Jim—domestic responsibility and the check on impulsiveness brought on by social guilt—is filled by the guiltless desire to romance. Though the entire text of *Treasure Island* is mystified by a Victorian fantasy of romance masculinity without transgression, there cannot be romance masculinity without transgression. At the earliest stage of the romance revival, this can only be accomplished by exclusion, by creating, as Haggard says in *King Solomon's Mines*, a history in which "there is not a *petticoat*" (6). In fact, the only female character in the novel, Jim's mother, faints at the first sign of violence.

2. This is a return to the generic theme that, as we have seen in Chapter One, occupied both Austen's last novel and one of Byron's earliest narrative poems—the Regency theme of piracy. The difficulty of reading *Treasure Island* either as artistic juvenile literature or juvenile art is removed once Stevenson's novel is seen in light of a tropological return. The desire to escape the economy of accumulation and exchange is central to the fantasy of piracy. Of course, Jim Hawkins and his companions are as much pirates as Long John Silver and his. Neither vying party plans to return the heaps and heaps of gold to the Spanish, French or English from whom it was stolen. This transgression against the rigors of lawful earning already places *Treasure Island* outside the economy of the domestic enclosure where outside, accumulative aggression must be used for maintaining the pacific domestic enclosure. In *Treasure Island*, there is only aggression, competition, and violence. Nor, as I will show, is Stevenson able to contain or focus this desire for violent transgression through ideological mystification. Stevenson's *Treasure Island* provokes the same transgressive desire that marks piracy in both Austen's *Persuasion* (a being gone from the confines of the country house) and Byron's *The Corsair* (a being gone from gendered existence itself). Yet, the complex matrix of gender liberation and limitation that defines both *The Corsair* and *Persuasion* is "buried" in *Treasure Island*.

3. Chesterton's insight into the popularity of Stevenson's *Treasure Island*, though little more than a phrase, is one of the most revealing and suggestive of critical remarks concerning *Treasure Island* and the Romance revival in general. For the "sort of

sanguinary innocence against a sort of silent and secretive perversion" (83), to which "he [Stevenson] was appealing" in some ways encapsulates the entity of my argument in regard not only to *Treasure Island*, but to the repression and reemergence of romance masculinity in the closing decades of the nineteenth century. Bloodthirsty innocence against social and sexual repression, "a sort of silent and secretive perversion," when taken as a genealogical concealment, can only be explored, at least in the beginning of the romance revival, by being removed from the Victorian domestic economy. Jim's innocence, like David Copperfield's before him, is merely a mystification of the critique of patriarchal power structures that create, in representation, the valuation of masculinity. This internecine function of "sanguinary innocence" and "silent and secretive perversion" highlights a conflict of masculine valuation, domestic and romance, which is unleashed by the romance revival and remains in many ways the continuum through which the ideological superstructures of patriarchy are maintained. The representational products of patriarchal control, whether domestic or romance, are merely mirrors of the omnipresent competition that defines masculine gendering and value, that "silent and secret perversion."

4. Dorothy Van Ghent, R.G. Strange, and Julian Moynahan "have stressed guilt as the dominant theme" (Moynahan 60) in *Great Expectations*.

Chapter Six

1. The *homme de fatal*, to use Peter Graham's term, speaks to the decadence remittance of the Byronic hero, the product of Childe Harold's cosmic malaise, returned to English culture via Swinburne's reading of French poetry, particularly Baudelaire. Like Baudelaire's Samuel Cramer, the decedent is "complications bizarres de ce caractère ... pur et noble, les yeux brillant comme des gouttes de café, le nez taquin et railleur, les lèvres impudentes et sensuelles, le menton carré et despote" (39). Likewise, Dracula and Dorian Gray are the "dieu[x] modern[s] and hermaphrodite[s]" (39) to use Baudelaire's formulation.

2. It is the same masculine crisis that Gilbert and Gubar see as concomitant with the raise of the Modern Woman.

3. As Eric Hobsbawn puts it "the increasingly vast accumulation of capital for profitable investment ... is best illustrated in railroad construction" (88). Hobsbawn goes on to argue railroad construction itself, not the distribution and transportation it served, grew this "vast accumulation of capital." See his chapter "Industrialization: The Second Phase 1840–95" from *Industry and Empire*, 87–111.

4. Money drives Utterson's investigation as well. The first connections of the unity of Jekyll and Hyde are financial: the check that Jekyll pays to get Hyde (himself) out of trouble and the schizo will, that which leaves all of Jekyll's significant fortune to Hyde (himself) if he disappears.

5. Michael Patrick Gillespie calls Dorian's relationship to his picture the "privileged position of multiplicity" (392) and it then goes beyond "the class stratification of late-nineteenth century life" (389) into the realm of metaphysics.

6. In Sheldon W. Liebman's "Character Design in *The Picture of Dorian Gray*," the dense and oscillating history of the critical tradition of Wilde's novel is succinctly and methodically traced. From early critical receptions that tended to read the novel as a "picture" of *fin-de-siècle* Aestheticism to twentieth century approaches where "recent critics have seen Dorian Gray as in some sense a running debate between two of its major characters, Henry Wotton and Basil Hallward" (297), Liebman goes on to argue that "Dorian's failure to integrate his opposing 'selves' is not a consequence of his own psychological inadequacy, but a condition of modern life" (297).

7. As Norbert Kohl and Matthew Beaumont point out, Wilde's "Soul of Man" (and I would add Raffles as well) is in part the product of middle-class doubt following the Long Recession, which lasted in Great Britain from 1873 to 1896. Written after attending a Fabian lecture where George Bernard Shaw spoke as well as his reading of the anarchist philosopher, Peter Kropotkin,

Wilde's "Soul of Man" enters into the debates surrounding militarized socialism advanced by George Bellamy's *Looking Backward* (1888). Dismissing out of hand Bellamy's grey overall school of socialism, Wilde utilizes Fabian concepts, as well as William Morris's aesthetic critique of capitalism, to argue for a socialist economy that will usher in an age of personal freedom, what he calls "Individualism." In Wilde's map to this utopian future, the abolition of private property along with the addition of steampunk technology will inevitably create a kind of Oxfordian Hellenism for all. Dated as its particulars might be, Wilde's future society is ultimately geared to create authentic individuals, which he calls personalities. See Norbert Kohl, *Oscar Wilde: The Works of a Conformist Rebel*, trans. David Henry Wilson (Cambridge: Cambridge University Press, 1989) and Matthew Beaumont, "Reinterpreting Oscar Wilde's Concept of Utopia: 'The Soul of Man under Socialism'" *Utopian Studies: Journal of the Society for Utopian Studies* 15. 1 (2004), 13–29.

Chapter Seven

1. The "real life" model for Conan Doyle's famous detective was Dr. Joseph Bell, a professor of medicine at Edinburgh University. As Julian Symons and other critics have pointed out, Dr. Bell's science of deduction and his "piercing grey eyes and a narrow aquiline nose" (19) resembled Holmes. Dr. Bell, it is important to point out, was not the only model for Holmes; Poe's Dupin, for example, informs Holmes's character. There is no doubt that both historical and literary imitation went into the representational structure of Holmes. I would argue, however, that there is in Holmes, when seen in the light of the larger history of the romance revival, another antecedent representational model, namely Byronic romance masculinity as it evolved in late Victorian adventure fiction.

2. Sometimes called heroin chic.

3. See Chapter 5, "Romance Masculinity" for a reading of this pivotal moment in the romance revival.

4. As I pointed out in chapter 3 J. Hills Miller sees totality as one of the central semiotic effect of *Middlemarch*'s narration, particularly in Lydgate's courtship and marriage to Rosamond. As Miller sees it, "the metaphor of a web ... is also used repeatedly in [the novel] to describe the texture of the smaller scale entities within the larger social fabric. The lovemaking of Rosamond and Lydgate, for example, is described as the collective weaving of an intersubjective tissue" (130). In Conan Doyle, the totality is London's infinite possibilities, one that Holmes, unlike the failed romancer Lydgate, enters and exits while maintaining his mastery. This is another central fantasy of romance masculinity.

5. Conan Doyle saw the literary merit of the Raffles stories immediately, which placed him in a rather rarified class, but he did not like the heroic construction of Raffles. As he wrote to his wife:

H[ornung's] famous character Raffles was a kind of inversion of Sherlock Holmes ... [Hornung] admits as much in his kindly dedication. I think there are few finer examples of short-story writing in our language than these, though I confess I think they are rather dangerous in their suggestion. I told him so before he put pen to paper, and the result, I fear, has borne me out. You must not make the criminal a hero [391].

6. Their school relationship is quite similar to that of David and Steerforth. In fact, as their relative positions at the old school are clarified, Raffles and Bunny become a romance revival parody of Dickens's David and Steerforth. Bunny was a "little literary cuss" (12) and Raffles was captain of the cricket eleven, which (in the English public school ethos Hornung draws from), like the American football quarterback, makes him a figure of awful worship.

7. For the purpose of the larger trajectory of the Byronic across the long nineteenth century, it is important to remember that the Napoleonic Wars expanded British naval and colonial powers into uncharted territory in ways that would have unforeseeable consequences. There is no better example than the Boer War (1899–1902). As Judd and Surridge make clear in their

Boer War, British interest in the Dutch Colony of South Africa, like so much of their tactical policy, was focused on securing trade routes to the Crown's most valuable asset: India. The annexation of Cape Town in 1814 was meant to control the Cape of Good Hope and secure shipping routes to India. Indeed, the British had little interest in the interior disputes between Dutch Afrikaners and indigenous tribes. Before, however, the opening of the Suez Canal in 1869, Cape Town and Simonstown were important tactical bases for the Royal Navy. Ironically, in the same year that the Cape of Good Hope lost much of its tactical importance, 1869, enormous fields of diamonds were found in Kimberley. With the leadership of Cape ministers, such as the ubiquitous Cecil Rhodes, the little-contested interior of South Africa became worth contesting.

8. Raffles "dye for his country" (284) is because he is dying his hair to hide his identity.

9. This connection between romance masculinity and death is key to Bryon's "Pirate Song" in *The Corsair*. "Let him who crawls enamour'd of decay /" the pirates sing, "Cling to his couch, and sicken years away (1.27–28).... Ours [death]—the fresh turf, and not the feverish bed" (*The Corsair* 1.30). "It was the death to die" according to Bunny.

Chapter Eight

1. In fact, in Erskine Childers's *Riddles in the Sand* (1903), which critics point to as the first modern spy novel, the villains use the plot of *Treasure Island* as a literal cover story. The German spymaster, Von Brunning, and his agents search for a treasure on an island in the Baltic Sea as a cover for their scheme to invade Great Britain.

2. Teresa Hubel makes a compelling argument that *Kim* is also a novel of class and that we need read *Kim* through the lens of "not only the men who staffed the imperial railways and telegraphs, who served in the British army ... but the women who married these men and themselves became servants, hairdressers, shop-assistants, [or] prostitutes" (230). This is undoubtedly the class from which Kim hails and her argument about Kim's liberation from his class status and the price of that liberation is helpful to keep in mind as we look more closely at how working class subjects are hailed by the elite patriarchy to colonial service

3. "A typical example of such fare," Judd and Surridge write, "is a short film showing a British nurse tending a wounded Afrikaner who is shamming ... [he] assaults her, necessitating her rescue by some of the 'brave boys in khaki'" (10).

Conclusion

1. See for example, Jessica Bennett's "A Masters Degree in ... Masculinity," *New York Times*, August 8, 2015, Michael S. Rosenwald's "Damaged Masculinity Help Explain Mass Shootings," *Washington Post*, and David Brooks's "Teaching Men to be Emotionally Honest," *New York Times*, April 21, 2016.

Works Cited

Accardo, Pasquale. *Diagnosis and Detection: The Medical Iconography of Sherlock Holmes.* Rutherford: Fairleigh Dickenson University Press, 1987. Print.

Althusser, Louis. *Lenin and Philosophy and Other Essays.* Trans. Ben Brewster. London: BLB, 1971. Print.

Anderson, Nancy F. "The 'Marriage with a Deceased Wife's Sister Bill' Controversy: Incest Anxiety and the Defense of Family Purity in Victorian England." *The Journal of British Studies* 21.02 (1982): 67–86. Print.

Arata, Stephen. *Fictions of Loss in the Victorian Fin-De Siècle.* New York: Cambridge University Press, 1996. Print.

Aristotle. *Treatise on Rhetoric.* Trans. Theodore Buckley. New York: Prometheus Books, 1995.

Armstrong, Nancy. *Desire and Domestic Fiction: A Political History of the Novel.* New York: Oxford University Press, 1987. Print.

———. *How Novels Think: The Limits of Individualism from 1719-1900.* New York: Columbia University Press, 2005. Print.

———. "Some Call It Fiction: On the Politics of Domesticity." *The Critical Tradition: Classic Texts and Contemporary Trends.* Ed. David H. Richter. 3rd ed. New York: Bedford/St. Martin's, 2007. 1418-31. Print.

Arnold, Matthew. *The Works of Matthew Arnold.* London: Macmillan, 1903. Print.

Astell, Ann W. "Anne Elliot's Education: The Learning of Romance in *Persuasion*." *Renaissance* 40 (1987): 2–14. Print.

Austen, Jane. *Jane Austen's Letters: To her Sister Cassandra and Others.* Ed. R.W. Chapman. 2 vols. Oxford: Clarendon, 1932. Print.

———. *Persuasion.* Ed. Patricia Meyer Spacks. New York: Norton, 1995. Print.

Baden-Powell, Robert. *Scouting for Boys.* Ed. Elleke Boehmer. New York: Oxford University Press, 2004. Print.

Baer, Cynthia M. "'Lofty hopes of divine liberty': The Myth of the Androgyne in *Alastor, Endymion,* and *Manfred*." *Nineteenth Century Contexts* 9.2 (1985): 25–49.

Beatty, Bernard. "A2 at Albany: Byron in 1814." *The Byron Journal* 36.2 (2008): 1–10. Print.

Beaumont, Matthew. "Reinterpreting Oscar Wilde's Concept of Utopia: 'The Soul of Man under Socialism.'" *Utopian Studies: Journal of the Society for Utopian Studies* 15.1 (2004): 13–29. *Jstor.* Web. 1 July 2014.

Benjamin, Walter. *Illuminations: Essays and Reflections.* New York: Penguin, 1969. Print.

Boehmer, Elleke. "Introduction." *Scouting for Boys.* By Robert Baden-Powell. Ed. Elleke Boehmer. New York: Oxford University Press, 2004. xi-xl. Print.

Booth, Martin. *The Doctor and the Detective: A Biography of Sir Arthur Conan Doyle.* New York: St. Martin's, 2000. Print.

Bourdieu, Pierre. *Outline of a Theory of Practice.* Trans. Richard Nice. Cambridge: Cambridge University Press, 1977. Print.

Bronstein, Rachel M. "Romanticism, A Romance: Jane Austen and Lord Byron, 1813–1815." *Persuasions* 16 (1994): 177–86. Print.

Brontë, Emily. *Wuthering Heights*. New York: Modern Library, 2000. Print.

Butler, Judith. *Gender Trouble: Feminism and the Subversion of Identity*. New York: Routledge, 2006. Print.

Byron, George Gordon. *Byron's Letters and Journals: The Complete and Unexpunged Texts of All Letters Available in Manuscript and the Full Printed Versions of All Others*. Ed. Leslie A. Marchand. 5 vols. Cambridge: Harvard University Press, 1973–82. Print.

———. *The Complete Poetical Works*. Ed. Jerome J. McGann. 5 vols. New York: Oxford University Press, 1983–93. Print.

Chesterton, G.K. *Robert Louis Stevenson*. New York: Dodd, 1928. Print.

Chrisman, Laura. *Reading the Imperial Romance: British Imperialism and South African Resistance in Haggard, Schreiner, and Plaatje*. New York: Clarendon, 2000. Print.

Conan Doyle, Arthur. *The Great Boer War*. New York: McClure, 1902. Print.

———. *A Life in Letters*. Ed. Jon Lellenberg, Daniel Stashower, and Charles Foley. New York: Penguin, 2007. Print.

———. *Memories and Adventures*. London: Doubleday, 1930.

———. *Sherlock Holmes: The Complete Novels and Stories*. 2 vols. New York: Bantam, 2003. Print.

Cookle, Mary. *Lines Addressed to Lady Byron*. Newcastle: Hodgson, 1817.

Cordery, Gareth. "Foucault, Dickens, and David Copperfield." *Victorian Literature and Culture* 26. 1 (1998): 71–85.

Coleridge, Samuel Taylor. *Coleridge's Poetry and Prose*. Ed. Nicholas Halmi, Paul Magnuson, and Raimonda Modiano. New York: Norton, 2004. Print.

Davidoff, Leonore, and Catherine Hall. *Family Fortunes: Men and Women of the English Middle Class, 1780-1850*. Chicago: University of Chicago Press, 1987. Print.

Deane, Bradley. "Piracy and the Play Ethic." *Victorian Studies: An Interdisciplinary Journal of Social, Political, and Cultural Studies* 53 (2011): 689–714. Print.

Deleuze, Giles, and Félix Guattari. *Anti-Oedipus: Capitalism and Schizophrenia*. Trans. Robert Hurly, Mark Seem, and Helen R. Lane. New York: Viking Press, 1977.

De Man, Paul. *Allegories of Reading: Figural Language in Rousseau, Nietzsche, Rilke, and Proust*. New Haven: Yale University Press, 1982. Print.

———. *Blindness and Insight: Essays in the Rhetoric of Contemporary Criticism*. New York: Oxford University Press, 1975. Print.

Denning, Michael. *Cover Stories: Narrative and Ideology in the British Spy Thriller*. 2nd ed. New York: Routledge, 2014.

Dickens, Charles. *David Copperfield*. Ed. Jerome H. Buckley. New York: Norton, 1990. Print.

———. *Great Expectations*. Ed. Edgar Rosenberg. New York: Norton, 1999. Print.

Elfenbein, Andrew. *Byron and the Victorians*. New York: Cambridge University Press, 1995. Print.

———. "Byron: Gender and Sexuality." *The Cambridge Companion to Byron*. Ed. Drummond Bone. Cambridge: Cambridge University Press, 2004. 56–73. Print.

Eliot, George. *Essays*. Ed. Thomas Pinney. London: Routledge, 1963. Print.

———. *Middlemarch*. Ed. Bert G. Hornback. 2nd ed. New York: Norton, 1994. Print.

———. "The Natural History of German Life." *Middlemarch*. By George Eliot. Ed. Bert Hornback. 2nd ed. New York: Norton, 1994. 520–521. Print.

Etherington, Norman. "A Critical Introduction." *The Annotated She: A Critical Edition of H. Rider Haggard's Victorian Romance with Introduction and Notes*. Ed. Norman Etherington. Bloomington: Indiana University Press, 1991. xi-xliii. Print.

———. *H. Rider Haggard*. Boston: Twayne, 1984. Print.

Foldy, Michael S. *The Trials of Oscar Wilde: Deviance, Morality, and Late-Victorian Society*. New York: Yale University Press, 1997. Print.

Ford, Susan Allen. "Learning Romance from Scott to Byron: Jane Austen's Natural Sequel." *Persuasions* 26 (2004): 72–88. Print.

Gager, Valerie L. *Shakespeare and Dickens: The Dynamics of Influence*. New York: Cambridge University Press, 1996. Print.

Gallarotti, Guilio M. *The Anatomy of an In-*

ternational Monetary Regime: The Classical Gold Standard, 1880-1914. OUP Catalogue, 1995.

Garret, Peter K. "Cries and Voices: Reading Jekyll and Hyde." Dr. Jekyll and Mr. Hyde After One Hundred Years. Ed. Gordon Hirsh and William Veeder. Chicago: University of Chicago Press, 1988. 59–72. Print.

Gérin, Winfred. Emily Brontë: A Biography. New York: Oxford University Press, 1971. Print.

Gilbert, Sandra M., and Susan Gubar. No Man's Land: Sexchanges. Vol 2. New Haven: Yale University Press, 1989. Print.

Gillespie, Michael Patrick. "Picturing Dorian Gray: Resisting Reading in Wilde's Novel." The Picture of Dorian Gray. Ed. Michael Patrick Gillespie. 2nd ed. New York: Norton, 2007. Print.

Gilmore, David. The Long Recessional: The Imperial Life of Rudyard Kipling. New York: Farrar, Straus, and Giroux, 2002.

Ginsburg, Michal Peled. "Dickens and the Uncanny: Repression and Displacement in Great Expectations." Dickens Study Annual 13 (1984): 115-124. Print.

Girard, René. The Girard Reader. Ed. James G. Williams. New York: Crossroad, 1996. Print.

Giuliano, Cheryl Fallon. "Gulnare/Kaled's 'Untold' Feminization in Byron's Oriental Tales." Studies in English Literature, 1500-1900 33.4 (1993): 785-807. Print.

Green, Richard Lancelyn. "Introduction." The Amateur Cracksman. By E.W. Hornung. New York: Penguin, 2003. xvii-xlvii. Print.

Greg, W.R. "Why Are Women Redundant?" National Review. April 1862. Print.

Gross, Jonathan David. Byron: The Erotic Liberal. New York: Rowman and Littlefield, 2001. Print.

Gwynn, Stephen. Robert Louis Stevenson. London: Folcoft, 1939. Print.

Habib, Irfan. "Understanding 1857." Rethinking 1857. Ed. Sabyasachi Bhattacharya. Delhi: Orient Longman, 2007, 58-69. Print.

Haggard, H. Rider. "About Fiction." She. Ed. Andrew M. Stauffer. Orchard Park, NY: Broadview, 2006: 290-299. Print.

———. King Solomon's Mines. Ed. Gerald Monsman. Orchard Park, NY: Broadview, 2002. Print.

———. She: A History of Adventure. New York: Modern Library, 2002. Print.

Harvey, William. "Charles Dickens and the Byronic Hero." Nineteenth-Century Fiction 24 (1969): 305-316. Print.

Haynes, Samuel. A War Imagined: World War I and English Culture. New York: Macmillan, 1990.

Hazlitt, William. The Spirit of the Age; or, Contemporary Portraits. London: George Bell, 1886. Online.

Hitchner, Thomas. "Edwardian Spy Literature and the Ethos of Sportsmanship: The Sport of Spying." English Literature in Transition, 1880-1920. 53:4 (2010), 413-430.

Hoagwood, Terence Allen. Byron's Dialectics: Skepticism and the Critique of Culture. Lewisburg: Bucknell University Press, 1993. Print.

Hobsbawn, Eric. Industry and Empire: The Birth of the Industrial Revolution: From 1750 to Present Day. New York: New York Press, 1999. Print.

Hogle, Jerrold E. "The Struggle for a Dichotomy: Abjection in Jekyll and His Interpreters." Dr. Jekyll and Mr. Hyde After One Hundred Years. Ed. Gordon Hirsh and William Veeder. Chicago: University of Chicago Press, 1988. 161–207. Print.

Holland, Merlin. The Real Trial of Oscar Wilde. New York: Harper, 2012. Print.

Hopkins, Gerard Manley. Gerard Manley Hopkins: Selected Letters. Ed. Catherine Phillips. Oxford: Clarendon, 1990. Print.

Hornung, E.W. The Complete Raffles. 2 vols. New York: Leonaur, 2008. Print.

———. Raffles: The Amateur Cracksman. New York: Penguin, 2003. Print.

Huble, Teresa. "In Search of the British Indian in British India: White Orphans, Kipling's Kim, and Class in Colonial India." Modern Asian Studies 38.1 (2004), 227-251.

Hurber, Werner. "Byronic Bioplays." Byromania. Ed. Frances Wilson. New York: St. Martin's, 1999. 93-109. Print.

Ives, George Cecil. A History of Penal Methods: Criminals, Witches, Lunatics. Montclair, NJ: Patterson Smith, 1970. Print.

James, Henry. "The Art of Presentation."

Century Magazine Apr. 1888: 887–888. Print.

———. *Partial Portraits*. Westport, CT: Greenwood Press, 1970. Print.

Jameson, Fredric. *The Political Unconscious: Narrative as a Symbolic Act*. Ithaca: Cornell University Press. 1981.

Johnson, Claudia L. *Jane Austen: Women, Politics, and the Novel*. Chicago: University of Chicago Press, 1988. Print.

Joyce, Simon. "Sexual Politics and the Aesthetics of Crime: Oscar Wilde in the Nineties." *English Literary History* 69.2 (2002): 501–523. Print.

Judd, Denis, and Keith Surridge. *The Boer War*. New York: Palgrave, 2003. Print.

Katz, Wendy R. *Rider Haggard and the Fiction of Empire: A Critical Study of British Imperial Fiction*. New York: Cambridge University Press, 1987. Print.

Kaye, John William. F.R.S. *The Sepoy War in India: A History*. 3 vols. W.H. Allen: London, 1880. Print.

Kenwood, A.G., and A.L. Lougheed. *The Growth of International Economy, 1820–1990: An Introductory Text*. 3rd ed. London: Routledge, 1992. Print.

Kinkead-Weekes, Mark. "Vision in Kipling's Novels" in *Kipling's Mind and Art*. Ed Andrew Rutherford. London: Oliver and Boyd, 1964. 197–234. Print.

Kipling, Rudyard. *Kim*. Ed. Máire ní Fhlatúin. Toronto: Broadview, 2005.

Knight, Roger. *Britain Against Napoleon: The Organization of Victory, 1793–1815*. Allen Lane: London, 2015. Print.

Knox-Shaw, Roger. "Persuasion, Byron and the Turkish Tale." *Review of English Studies* 173 (1993): 47–69. Print.

Kohl, Norbert. *Oscar Wilde: The Works of a Conformist Rebel*. Trans. David Henry Wilson. Cambridge: Cambridge University Press, 1989. Print.

"Ladies Sculling Club: Off for a Spin." *Cassell's*. Dec, 1900–1901.

Lang, Andrew. *The Strange Case of Dr. Jekyll and Mr. Hyde*. By Robert Louis Stevenson. Ed. Katherine Linehan. New York: Norton, 2003. 93–94. Print.

Larance, Jeremy. "The A. J. Raffles Stories Reconsidered: Fall of the Gentleman Ideal." *English Literature in Transition, 1880–1920*. 57:1 (2014), 99–125.

Lewis, Michael. *A Social History of the Navy 1783–1814*. London: Chatham, 1960. Print.

Libertad, Albert. "The Joy of Life." *Anarchist Library* (2012): n. pag. Web. 26 July 2015.

Liebman, Sheldon W. "Character Design in *The Picture of Dorian Gray*." *Studies in the Novel*. 31.3 (1999): 296–316. Print.

Linehan, Katherine. Preface. *The Strange Case of Dr. Jekyll and Mr. Hyde*. By Robert Louis Stevenson. Ed. Katherine Linehan. New York: Norton, 2003. xi-xv. Print.

———. "Sex, Secrecy, and Self-Alienation in *Strange Case of Dr. Jekyll and Mr. Hyde*." *The Strange Case of Dr. Jekyll and Mr. Hyde*. Ed. Katherine Linehan. New York: Norton, 2003. 204–213. Print.

———, ed. *The Strange Case of Dr. Jekyll and Mr. Hyde*. New York: Norton, 2003. Print.

MacCarthy, Fiona. *Byron: Life and Legend*. New York: Farrar, 2002. Print.

MacDonald, Robert H. *Sons of Empire: The Frontier and the Boy Scout Movement, 1890–1918*. Toronto: Toronto University Press, 1993.

Mangan, J.A., and James Walvin. "Introduction." *Manliness and Morality: Middle-class Masculinity in Britain and America, 1800–1840*. Manchester: Manchester University Press, 1987.

Manning, Peter. *Byron and his Fictions*. Detroit: Wayne State University Press, 1978. Print.

———. *Reading Romantics: Texts and Contexts*. New York: Oxford University Press, 1990. Print.

McClintock, Anne. *Imperial Leather: Race, Gender, and Sexuality in the Colonial Contest*. Routledge, 2013.

McGann, Jerome. *Byron and Romanticism*. New York: Cambridge University Press, 2002. Print.

Marchand, Leslie. *Byron: A Portrait*. Random House, 1970.

Matin, A. Michael. ""The Hun is at the gate!'" Historicizing Kipling's Militaristic Rhetoric, from the Imperial Periphery to the National Center: Part Two: The French, Russian and German Threats to Great Britain." *Studies in the Novel* 31.4 (1999): 432–470. Print.

Marx, Karl, and Friedrich Engels. *The Marx-Engels Reader*. Ed. Robert C. Tucker. 2nd ed. New York: Norton, 1978. Print.

Michalson, Karen. *Victorian Fantasy Literature: Literary Battles with Church and Empire*. Lewiston, NY: Mellon, 1990. Print.

Middleton, Richard. "*Treasure Island* as a Book for Boys." *Treasure Island*. New York: Modern Library, 2001. 219–224. Print.

Miller, D.A. *The Novel and the Police*. Berkeley: U of California P, 1988.

Miller, J. Hillis. "Optic and Semiotic in Middlemarch." *The Worlds of Victorian Fiction*, 1975: 125–45.

Monsman, Gerald. "Introduction: Of Diamonds and Deities in *King Solomon's Mines*." *King Solomon's Mines*. By H. Rider Haggard. Ed. Gerald Monsman. Orchard Park: Broadview, 2002.

Mole, Tom. *Byron's Romantic Celebrity: Industrial Culture and the Hermeneutic of Intimacy*. New York: Palgrave, 2007. Print.

Moore, Thomas. *Life, Letters and Journals of Lord Byron*. London: John Murray, 1838.

———. *The Works of Lord Byron: With his Letters and Journals, and his Life*. 14 vols. New York: Bigelow, Brown, and Company, 1900.

Morgan, Susan. "Captain Wentworth, British Imperialism and Personal Romance." *Persuasions* 18 (1996): 88–97. Print.

Morris, David. "The Gothic Sublime." Eds. Fred Botting and Dale Townshend. *Gothic: Eighteenth-century Gothic: Radcliffe, Reader, Writer, Romancer*. Routledge, 2004, 50–68. Print.

Moynahan, Julian. "The Hero's Guilt: The Case of *Great Expectations*." *Essays in Criticism* 10 (1960): 60–79. Print.

Murray, John. *The Letters of John Murray to Lord Byron*. Ed. Andrew Nicholson. Liverpool: Liverpool University Press, 2007. Print.

Nabokov, Vladimir. "A Phenomenon of Style." *The Strange Case of Dr. Jekyll and Mr. Hyde*. Ed. Catherine Linehan. New York: Norton, 2003. 184–188. Print.

Newman, Cardinal. *The Idea of a University Defined and Illustrated: In Nine Discourses Delivered to the Catholics of Dublin*. Project Gutenberg. 2008. Web.

Nietzsche, Friedrich. *On The Genealogy of Morals*. Trans. Walter Kaufmann. New York: Vintage, 1989, 15–163. Print.

"The New African Gold Rush Fever." *Dundee Courier*. 9 April 1887. British Newspaper Archives. 1 July 2004. Web.

Newton, K.M. *George Eliot: Romantic Humanist*. Totowa, NJ: Barnes and Noble, 1981. Print.

Orwell, George. *Selected Essays*. Ed John Carey. 2nd ed. New York: Everyman, 2002. Print.

Owen, Wilfred. *The Collected Poems of Wilfred Owen*. Ed. C. Day Lewis. New York: New Direction, 1963. Print.

Pinion, F.B. *A Brontë Companion: Literary Assessment, Background and Reference*. New York: Barnes and Noble, 1975. Print.

Pollock, Frederick, and Frederic William Maitland. *The History of English Law Before the Time of Edward I*. 2 vols. Cambridge, 1895. Print.

Poovey, Mary. *Uneven Development: The Ideological Work of Gender in Mid-Victorian England*. Chicago: University of Chicago Press, 1988. Print.

Poplawski, Paul. *A Jane Austen Encyclopedia*. Westport: Greenwood, 1998. Print.

Pykett, Lyn. *Emily Brontë*. New York: Barnes and Noble, 1989. Print.

Ragland-Sullivan, Ellie. "The Phenomenon of Aging in Oscar Wilde's *Picture of Dorian Gray*: A Lacanian View." *Memory and Desire: Aging—Literature—Psychoanalysis*. Ed. Kathleen M. Woodward and Murray M. Schwartz. Bloomington: Indiana University Press, 1986. 114–33. Print.

Raina, Badri. *Dickens and the Dialectic of Growth*. Madison: Wisconsin University Press, 1986. Print.

Ricoeur, Paul. *Time and Narrative*. Trans. Kathleen McLaughlin and David Pellauer. 3 vols. Chicago: University of Chicago Press, 1983. Print.

Rogers, Nicholas. *The Press Gang: Naval Impressment and its Opponents in Georgian Britain*. London: Continuum, 2007. Print.

Rogers, Samuel. *Recollections of the Table-Talk of Samuel Rogers*. New York: Appleton, 1856. Print.

Russell, Bertrand. *The History of Western Philosophy*. New York: Simon, 1967. Print.

Saglia, Diego. "Touching Byron: Masculinity and Celebrity Body in the Romantic Period." *Performing Masculinity*. Ed. Rainer Emig and Anthony Rowland. New York: Palgrave Macmillan, 2010. 13-28. Print.

Said, Edward W. *Culture and Imperialism*. New York: Vintage, 1994.

———. "Introduction." *Kim* by Rudyard Kipling. New York: Penguin, 1987.

———. *Orientalism*. New York: Penguin, 1977.

Sartre, Jean-Paul. *The Reprieve*. Trans. Eric Sutton. New York: Vintage, 1973.

The Saturday Review 9 Jan. "Review." 1886. 55-56. Print.

Scott, George Ryley. *A History of Corporal Punishment: A Survey of Flagellation in its Historical, Anthropological, and Sociological Aspects*. 25 Aug. 2015. Web.

Sedgwick, Eve. *Between Men: English Literature and Male Homosocial Desire*. New York: Colombia University Press, 1985.

Seelye, John. Introduction. *Treasure Island*. By Robert Louis Stevenson. New York: Penguin, 2009. vii-xxvi. Print.

Shakespeare, William. *The Riverside Shakespeare: The Complete Works*. Ed. G. Blackemore Evans. 2nd ed. Boston: Houghton, 1997. Print.

Showalter, Elaine. *Sexual Anarchy: Gender and Culture at the Fin de Siècle*. New York: Viking, 1990. Print.

Smiles, Samuel. *A Publisher and his Friends: Memoir and Correspondence of the Late John Murray, with an Account of the Origin and Progress of the House, 1768-1843*. New York: AMS, 1973. Print.

Stauffer, Andrew. "Introduction." *She*. By H. Rider Haggard. Ed. Andrew M. Stauffer. Orchard Park: Broadview, 2006. 290-299. Print.

Stevenson, Robert Louis. *The Essays of Robert Louis Stevenson*. London: Macdonald, 1950. Print.

———. *The Master of Ballantrae: A Winter's Tale*. New York: Penguin, 1997. Print.

———. *The Strange Case of Dr. Jekyll and Mr. Hyde*. Ed. Catherine Linehan. New York: Norton, 2003. Print.

———. *Treasure Island*. New York: Modern Library, 2001. Print.

Symons, Julian. *Conan Doyle: Portrait of an Artist*. New York: Mysterious, 1979. Print.

Thorslev, Peter L. *The Byronic Hero*. Minneapolis: Minnesota University Press, 1962. Print.

Truzzi, Marcello. "Sherlock Holmes: Applied Social Psychologist." *The Sign of Three: Dupin, Holmes, Peirce*. Ed. Umberto Eco and Thomas A. Sebeok. Bloomington: Indiana University Press, 1983. 55-80. Print.

Veeder, William. "Children of the Night: Stevenson and Patriarchy." *Dr. Jekyll and Mr. Hyde After One Hundred Years*. Ed. Gordon Hirsh and William Veeder. Chicago: University of Chicago Press, 1988. 107-160. Print.

Wilde, Oscar. *De Profundis*. London: Methuen, 1915. Print.

———. "Pen, Pencil, Poison." *The Complete Works of Oscar Wilde*. New York: Harper, 2003. 1093-1107. Print.

———. "Phrases and Philosophies for the Use of the Young." *The Complete Works of Oscar Wilde*. New York: Harper, 2003. 1244-47. Print.

———. *The Picture of Dorian Gray*. Ed. Michael Patrick Gillespie. 2nd ed. New York: Norton, 2007. Print.

———. "The Soul of Man Under Socialism." *The Complete Works of Oscar Wilde*. New York: Harper, 2003. 1174-97. Print.

Wolfson, Susan. *Formal Charges: The Shaping of British Romanticism*. Stanford: Stanford University Press, 1997. Print.

Wollen, W.B. "Christmas at the Front." *Cassell's* Dec. 1899. Print.

Wootton, Sarah. "The Byronic in Jane Austen's *Persuasion* and *Pride and Prejudice*." *Modern Language Review* 102 (2007): 26-39. Print.

Wordsworth, William. *The Major Works*. New York: Oxford, 2008. Print.

Žižek, Slavoj. *Parallax View*. Boston: MIT Press, 2006. Print.

———. *The Sublime Object of Ideology*. New York: Verso, 1989. Print.

Index

"About Fiction" (Haggard) 53, 67; romance revival as anti-domestic in 68, 155
The Albany 127
Alcibiades 12
Althusser, Louis 7, 13; father's name 96–97; hailing 94–97, 110
American Revolution 2
Anti-Oedipus (Deleuze and Guattari) 103–5; schizophrenia and capitalism 105, 111
Armstrong, Nancy: *Desire and Domestic Fiction* 14, 38, 40, 41; *How Novels Think* 13, 47, 50, 102; "Some Call It Fiction: On the Politics of Domesticity" 14
Arnold, Mathew: *Grande Chartreuse* 35; "Haworth Churchyard" 32
Austen, Jane 2, 17–20, 22, 23, 28–31, 159, 163n3, 163–64n5, 164n7, 164n9, 164–65n12, 168n2; Elizabeth Bennet 60; see also *Persuasion*

Baden-Powell, Robert 3, 61, 134, 135, 147–49, 152, 156; *Scouting for Boys* 3, 138, 143, 146, 150–155; see also *Kim*
Bank Charter Act of 1844 2, 99
Beit, Alfred 89, 100
Benjamin, Walter 3, 8, 85
Berlin Conference of 1884–85 90
Berlin West Africa Conference *see* Berlin Conference of 1884–85
Bildungsroman 89, 91
Boer War 3, 100, 131–36, 170–71n7; influence on Scouting Movement 150, 155–56; see also Kipling, Rudyard
Bourdieu, Pierre 43, 44, 59; "Return of Azal" 57–58
British East India Company *see* East India Company
British imperialism 131, 135, 137, 150, 152, 155
Brontë, Charlotte: *Jane Eyre* 31
Brontë, Emily 2, 12, 31–32, 93, 159, 166n5; influence of Byron 37–39, 41; themes of incest and blood 43, 45, 47, 51; see also *Wuthering Heights*
Brooks, David 159
Bulwer-Lytton, Edward 106
Burke, Edmond 37, 40
Butler, Judith *see Gender Trouble*
Byron, George Gordon 5, 6, 7, 8, 11; at the Albany 127; contemporary criticism of 35; and homoeroticism 106, 113–114; House of Lords speech 21; influence on Emily Brontë 51; marriage and exile 34–35; in Moore's biography 36; popularity 19; swimmer of Hellespont 130; Victorian reputation 59, 78, 101; see also *Childe Harold*; *The Corsair*; *Manfred*
Byronic hero 2, 3, 5–6, 8, 19, 169n1; afterlife 161; description 9–14; and the gothic 48, 50, 54; influence on contemporary female characters: *Alias* 15; *Buffy the Vampire Slayer* 15; *Hunger Games* 15; *Kill Bill I and II* 15; and the rhetoric of romance 56–58; and the romance revival 134–36; and Victorian domesticity 33–35

Capital 6
capitalism 6–8, 13–15, 95–96, 169–70n7; crime 131, 136; and The Great Game 158; hailing of men 95–96; and male gendering 13–15, 77; and masculinity 160; in the nineteenth century 8, 57–58; as totality 118–120, 123–24; see also *Anti-Oedipus*; Bourdieu, Pierre
Carson, Edward 106
Cassell's Magazine 126, 146
Chandler, Raymond 118, 161
Chesterton, G.K. 89
Childe Harold (Byron) 5, 9, 10, 12, 117, 163ch1n2, 169n1; and *The Strange Case of Dr. Jekyll and Mr. Hyde* 108–9

179

180 Index

Cobain, Kurt 119
commodity 1; commodification of Byron 36; defining literary/Byronic 3–9, 11; domestic 52; masculine 13–15; rhetoric as 58–59; romance literature 76; schizophrenia and consumption 102, 107, 111–13; *see also* romance masculinity
commodity fetish 6
Conan Doyle, Sir Arthur 3, 9, 124–126, 130, 147, 148, 150–151, 170n1, 170n4, 170n5; dinner with Wilde 115; *Hound of the Baskervilles* 116; *Memories and Adventures* 115; *see also The Sign of Four*
Congo Conference *see* Berlin Conference of 1884–85
Connell, R.W. (Raewyn) 11, 14
Corn Laws 21
corporal punishment 77
The Corsair (Byron) 2, 12, 163ch1n1, 163ch1n2, 163n4, 164n7, 164n8, 165n16, 168n2, 171n9; Byronic hero in 18, 19, 20, 22, 24–3; and *David Copperfield* 85; and Raffles stories 121; and *She* 65, 66; and *Treasure Island* 93, 97, 98; and *Wuthering Heights* 33, 37, 43

The Daily Mail 148
Dante Alighieri 53
David Copperfield (Dickens) 3, 69, 71, 78, 80–88, 90, 167ch4n2, 167–68ch4n3, 168–69n3; Byronic hero in 71–73, 78–79, 80–81, 85; domestic enclosure 76, 79, 83–84, 86; homosocial masculinity 75, 79, 83, 85; as model for *Kim* 141–42, 153; and Sherlock Holmes stories 11; and *Treasure Island* 90, 96; and Victorian domesticity 68, 75, 78, 82, 86; violence of 155
De Beers Mining Company 100
Defoe, Daniel 61
Deleuze, Gilles *see Anti-Oedipus*
Desire and Domestic Fiction (Armstrong) 14, 38, 40–41
Dickens, Charles 60, 74, 76–77, 79, 87–88, 90, 91–95, 129, 137, 159, 167ch4n1, 167ch4n2, 168n1, 170n6; *see also David Copperfield*; *Great Expectations*
Disraeli, Benjamin 106
domestic doxa 2; and Bourdieu 59; in *Middlemarch* 60, 64–65; romance revival against 102, 109, 129, 155; in *She* 62–63, 67–68
domestic education 24, 46–48, 50–52
domestic enclosure 166, 168; and Byronic rhetoric 45, 47–51, 57; creation of 24, 32; as romance enclosure 119; as schizophrenia in 101, 109–10, 116; *see also*

David Copperfield; *Middlemarch*; *She*; *Treasure Island*
domestic masculinity 69, 72, 74–75, 84, 88, 91, 95, 118, 131, 159, 166–67n6
domestic orthodoxy 57, 66, 71
Douglas, Lord Alfred 129
"Dulce et Decorum Est" 133

East India Company 125
Elementary 116
Elfenbein, Andrew 5–8, 19, 31, 106, 118
Eliot, George *see Middlemarch*
Evans, Mary Anne *see* Eliot, George

female gaze 26, 85
fin de siècle 33, 169n6
First Reform Bill *see* Reform Act 1832
Fletcher, C.R.L. (Charles Robert Leslie) 152
Franco-German War *see* Franco-Prussian War
Franco-Prussian War 99

Gender Trouble (Butler) 26, 43, 66, 84–85, 163n4
Genealogy of Morals 77, 95, 120, 160
George IV 33–34, 59
German Ideology 52
Germany 90, 99, 138, 147, 148
Gilbert, Sandra *see The Madwoman in the Attic*
Girard, René 79–80, 85; triangular desire 80
Gladstone, William 89
Goethe, Johann Wolfgang von 36
gold standard 99, 102
Gosse, Edward 155
Gramsci, Antonio 13–14
Grande Chartreuse 35
Great Expectations (Dickens) 168–69; and *Treasure Island* 89, 90, 92, 94
The Great Game 137–138, 140, 142, 157–158
Grundrisse 1
Guattari, Félix *see Anti-Oedipus*
Gubar, Susan *see The Madwoman in the Attic*

Haggard, H. Rider 2, 53, 54, 57, 61–63, 67, 155, 167ch3n2, 168n2; *King Solomon's Mines* 88, 167ch3n2, 168n2; *see also* "About Fiction"; *She*
Hammett, Dashiell 161
"Haworth Churchyard" 32
Hazlitt, William 117–18
hegemonic masculinity 3, 14, 135, 160
heretical rhetoric 59, 62
Homer 53
homosocial masculinity 61–63, 73, 75, 79, 83, 85; *see also David Copperfield*; *She*

Index

Hornung, E.W. (Ernest William) 3, 115, 126–127, 147, 150, 170n5, 170n6; Boer War 130–131, 133; *see also* Raffles stories
Hound of the Baskervilles 116
How Novels Think (Armstrong) 13, 47, 50, 102
Hughes, Thomas: *Tom Brown at Oxford* 137; *Tom Brown's School Days* 137

"The Idea of the University" 122
Image, Selwyn 155
Imperialism and Culture (Said) 138, 142, 157
incest 34–39, 40, 117; gothic 37
Indian Mutiny 124
Indian Rebellion of 1857 *see* Indian Mutiny
Ives, George Cecil 89, 100, 128

James, Henry 54–57, 59–60
James Bond (fictional character) 1, 2, 15, 81, 118, 135, 158
Jameson Raid 100, 147
Jane Eyre 31
Jay Cooke and Company 89
Joy, George 149

Kant, Emmanuel 37, 40
Kim 3, 12, 60, 96, 99, 134–35, 137–146, 150–58, 167ch3n1, 171n2; and Byronic hero 140, 147, 151–52, 158; and *Scouting for Boys* 134–35, 140, 143; *see also Scouting for Boys*; Stevenson, Robert Louis
Kimmel, Michael 160
King of England *see* George IV
King Solomon's Mines 88, 167ch3n2, 168n2
Kipling, Rudyard 3, 12, 96, 134–48, 150, 152, 156, 157, 167ch3n1; and the Boer War 146–148; *see also Kim*; *Scouting for Boys*

Leigh, Augusta 34–35
Letters and Journals of Lord Byron with Notices of His Life (Moore) 5, 36
Libertad, Albert 128
Lippincott's Monthly Magazine 115
London Docklands 123–24, 126
Long Depression 3, 89–90, 96, 99, 106, 116, 122, 136
Longman's Magazine 54

Macbeth (Shakespeare) 27, 83–85, 131; and capitalism 83; Lady Macbeth, 27, 83–84
The Madwoman in the Attic (Gilbert and Gubar) 68
Manfred (Byron), 10, 12; and *David Copperfield* 73, 81, 82, 85; influence on Sherlock Holmes character 117; and *Middlemarch* 60, 64; and *She* 68; and *The Strange Case of Dr. Jekyll and Mr. Hyde* 104, 108; and *Wuthering Heights* 32, 37, 38–39, 40–45, 48
marriage 44, 63–64
Marx, Karl 7–8, 45, 52, 81; *Capital* 6; *German Ideology* 52; *Grundrisse* 1
masculinity: commodification 2; guilt 95, 156; loneliness 76, 141; *see also* domestic masculinity; hegemonic masculinity; romance masculinity
Memories and Adventures 115
Middlemarch (Eliot) 2, 53–54, 57–59, 61, 119–120, 167ch3n3, 170n4; domestic enclosure in 60–68; Rosamond and Lydgate 63
Milbanke, Annabella 34
Mill, John Stuart 89
Mimesis 7–8, 81
Mr. Holmes (film) 116
Moore, Thomas *see Letters and Journals of Lord Byron with Notices of His Life*
The Morning Post 148, 150
Murray, John 18, 36, 163ch1n2
Muscular Christianity 61, 137

Napoleonic Wars 18, 20, 22, 98; and capitalism 22; national mobilization 21
Newman, Cardinal John Henry: "The Idea of the University" 122
Nietzsche, Friedrich: *Genealogy of Morals* 77, 95, 120, 160, 167ch4n1

Orientalism (Said) 139, 145
Orwell, George 128–29, 132
Owen, Wilfred: "Dulce et Decorum Est" 133

Pater, Walter 61
Persuasion (Austen) 2, 17, 23, 28, 29, 159, 163n3, 163n4, 163–64n5, 164n7, 164n8, 164n9, 164–65n12, 165n13, 165n14, 165n15, 165–66n17, 168n2; Byronic hero in 18–20, 22, 24–31; and Byronic language 30–33; Louisa's fall 18, 23, 26; Napoleonic Wars 20–22; Wentworth's letter 28–29
Phillips, Thomas: "Portrait of a Nobleman in the Dress of an Albanian" 19
The Picture of Dorian Gray (Wilde) 101–3, 106–117, 169n1, 169n6
"Portrait of a Nobleman in the Dress of an Albanian" 19
prize money 22

The Queen Caroline Affair 33–34
Queen of England *see* Victoria

Index

The Race for Africa *see* The Scramble for Africa
Raffles stories (Hornung) 126–27; and Byronic hero 129, 131
Reform Act 1832 21, 57, 58, 102
Regency era 2, 19, 21–22, 26, 33, 59, 78, 163*n*4, 165*n*6, 165*n*13
"Return of Azal" 57–58
Rhodes, Cecil 89, 100
Ricoeur, Paul 7–8, 163*intro.1*
Roberts, Frederick (First Earl Roberts) 152
romance masculinity 3, 77, 98, 109, 135, 138, 148, 150; birth 88; in Byron 33, 37; as commodity 69, 81, 85–86, 88, 97; connection to Dickens 74; and imperialism 134–37, 147–149; racism 156; in Raffles stories 126, 132; rhetoric 15, 7, 76, 79, 80–81, 85–86, 51–52, 54, 61, 69; in romance revival 2, 9, 15, 54, 69, 166*n*6, 167*ch3n*1, 168*n*1, 168–69*n*3, 170*n*1, 170*n*6; in scouting movement 150, 152, 155; whiteness 139, 158
romance revival 2, 9, 15, 54, 69, 166*n*6, 167*ch3n*1, 168*n*1, 168–69*n*3, 170*n*1, 170*n*6; birth 54, 61, 74; Byronic influence on 33, 37, 51–52; Dickens' influence on 88; in pre-WWI British militarism 135–137, 149, 150, 152, 155–156; and rejection of Victorian domesticity 88–89, 91–93, 96
Royal Navy 20–21

Said, Edward "Introduction" to *Kim* 140; *see also* Imperialism and Culture; Orientalism
Saint Augustine 120
Salem House 73, 78
Scipio Africanus 12
Scotland Yard 132
Scott, Sir Walter 18–19, 77, 93, 163–64*n*5; *Waverly*, 59, 60
Scouting for Boys (Baden-Powell) 3, 138, 146, 150–53, 155; and bicycles 154; and *Kim* 134–135, 140, 143, 150–151, 153, 155; *see also* Baden-Powell, Robert
scouting movement 3, 61, 150–51, 154–55
The Scramble for Africa 96
Sepoy Mutiny *see* Indian Mutiny
Shakespeare, William 27, 76, 105; Sonnet 144 76; Sonnets 105; *see also Macbeth*
She (Haggard) 2, 53–54, 57, 61–66; Byronic hero in 62, 68; domestic enclosure in 60–68; homosocial masculinity 61–63; University of Cambridge 61–63, 68
Sherlock (TV show) 116

Sherlock Holmes (literary character) 15, 102, 115–18, 121–22, 124, 126, 140, 151; as Byronic hero 117–18; and capitalism 116
Sherlock Holmes (2009 film) 116
Sherlock Holmes: Game of Shadows (film) 116
Siege of Mafeking 147–49, 151, 153–54
The Sign of Four (Conan Doyle) 116, 118, 124–126, 130, 147, 148, 150–51; and *The Picture of Dorian Gray* 123–24
"Some Call It Fiction: On the Politics of Domesticity" 14
"Soul of Man Under Socialism" 114, 129, 169–70*n*7
Stevenson, Robert Louis 3, 9, 166–67*n*6, 167*ch3n*2, 168*n*1, 168*n*2, 168–69*n*3; argument with Henry James 52–59, 61; creation of romance masculinity 90–95, 98, 99; influence on Conan Doyle 115, 120; influence on *Kim* 135–36, 140–41; 152; and pre-WWI paranoia 136; product of Long Depression 90–92; relationship to Dickens's bildungsroman 88–89; in *Sign of Four* 122; *see also The Strange Case of Dr. Jekyll and Mr. Hyde*; *Treasure Island*
Stoddart, J.M. 115
The Strange Case of Dr. Jekyll and Mr. Hyde (Stevenson) 3, 101–3, 106–7, 109, 111, 116, 169; Byronic hero in 104, 108–109
Swinburne, Algernon 61, 169*n*1

Tom Brown at Oxford 137
Tom Brown's School Days 137
transgeneric writing 30, 33, 45, 47, 51, 166*n*5
Treasure Island (Stevenson) 3, 88–89, 167*ch3n*2, 168*n*1, 168*n*2, 168–69*n*3, 171*ch8n*1; Byronic hero in 88–89, 98; domestic enclosure in 88
triangular desire *see* Girard, René

University of Cambridge 61–63, 68; *see also She*

Vicious, Sid 119
Victoria (Queen of England) 149
Victorian domestic fiction 9
Victorian domesticity 33; and marriage 44, 63–64; rhetoric 54, 56–57; *see also* romance revival
Victorian era 2–3, 12–13, 166*n*5, 168*n*1, 168–69*n*3, 170*n*1; masculine schizophrenia 106, 108, 110, 113; racism 144–45; relationship to contemporary culture 160–61

Victorian masculinity *see* domestic masculinity
Victorian middle class   3, 9, 10, 14, 33–40, 41–45, 59, 62, 67, 101, 102, 109, 116, 117, 123
Victorian womanhood   75
Victorian working class   138–140, 158

Walpole, Horace   37
West, Benjamin   149
Whig history   57–58, 121
Wilde, Oscar   3, 101, 102, 115–116, 123, 128; legal trial 106–107, 113; "Soul of Man Under Socialism" 114, 129, 169n6, 169–70n7; *see also The Picture of Dorian Gray*
World War I   2–3, 112, 133–35, 148, 155, 161; and British pre-WWI paranoia 138
Wuthering Heights (E. Brontë) 37–52; Gothic and domestic framework 48; Heathcliff as Byronic hero 36–39, 41–42, 44, 46; and *Manfred* 82; and transgeneric writing 33, 42, 44

www.ingramcontent.com/pod-product-compliance
Lightning Source LLC
Chambersburg PA
CBHW032103300426
44116CB00007B/868